A PERFECT LAWN
The Easy Way

A

PERFECT

LAWN

The Easy Way

Revised Edition
Originally titled *The Lawn Book*

ROBERT W. SCHERY

Macmillan Publishing Co., Inc.
NEW YORK
Collier Macmillan Publishers
LONDON

Macmillan Publishing Co., Inc.
Collier-Macmillan Canada Ltd., Toronto, Ontario

Library of Congress Catalog Card Number: 72-88150

First Printing 1973

Printed in the United States of America

contents

Good turf is needed in the shade, too. Fine fescues are notable shade grasses for northern lawns.

introduction

A Perfect Lawn is intended particularly for the homeowner contending with the establishment and sensible maintenance of a lawn. As far as possible, the text is written in everyday language, avoiding technical terms understood only by the specialist. Conclusions are generally advanced without detailed documentation of the often abstruse research which underlies them.

But I feel that the serious reader will want more than just a "what-to-do" recitation of lawn-keeping steps. Therefore an effort has been made to explain the reasons behind recommended procedures. If one understands why a particular action is advisable, good decisions can be made more intelligently for untypical or altered circumstances. I hope that, having read *A Perfect Lawn*, the reader will not only have learned something about how to care for the lawn, but also have some insight into how the lawn functions and reacts. All too often, lawn-keeping is made to seem mysterious and rather terrifying because it is "so complicated." This need not be the case if the relatively few important principles governing grass growth are understood.

My hope, thus, is to present simply (but without over-simplification) information about lawn building and lawn keeping that will stand anyone in good stead, in any part of the country. This requires that the reader be asked to make certain judgments of his own, since not all individual lawn situations can be covered or even envisioned.

My apologies to those who want cut-and-dried instructions, but I feel it would be a disservice to suggest that only a single mode of action is required. For example, there are many ways to help control weeds—high mowing, proper fertilization, altered watering, etc.—and recommendation of an appropriate herbicide is really less important than properly accommodating the grass! There is also the matter of individual preference; what may be a weed to one person, may be ground cover to another (e.g., clover). Thus, while *A Perfect Lawn* should provide information, it is not dictatorial, and I do beg the reader to be willing to apply principles to his particular circumstance, rather than expect to be told exactly what to do. Only to the extent that this proves possible is *A Perfect Lawn* a worthwhile educational effort.

In this revised edition, a new chapter has been added on lawn ecology and one on lawn renovation—made relatively easy these days because of new, specialized equipment. There has had to be considerable updating of grass varieties (a torrent of new releases marks the 1970's), although the basic turfgrass species remain the same. New, more efficient chemicals have also come on the market, but their use has become uncertain and complicated because of concern for the environment that has restricted many uses while, in some cases, products have been discontinued. In fact, it appears the pendulum may have swung too far, from a lack of concern about the environment to over-reaction as far as many pesticides are concerned! I hope that *A Perfect Lawn* will aid you in making sound value judgments regarding the use of lawn products.

The original organization of *A Perfect Lawn* has proven sound, the expression readable; so we have tampered little with these, except to improve the format, expand the illustrations, and enlarge various discussions. A glossary of technical terms has been added, and the index made more comprehensive.

The publishers and I feel you will be pleased with the greater convenience, the enhanced attractiveness, and the comprehensive updating that this revision represents.

A PERFECT LAWN
The Easy Way

Grass is perhaps most highly appreciated and most carefully tended in its modern use for home lawns. Its effectiveness and beauty as a ground cover are uncontested.

1

the lawn

GRASS HAS BEEN man's companion through the ages. From a start more than fifty million years ago, grass and mammals have evolved together. With grasslands came grazing animals, the forerunners of livestock. From ancestral grasses were developed the important foodstuffs of the modern day: grains, such as wheat, corn, oats, rye, and sorghum, plus the pasture and soil-building species of range and farm. Without the grass family, there would be no flour, no beefsteak, and no attractive settings such as those enjoyed by modern, suburban homes.

Grasses are conspicuously successful in adapting to their environment. They can be found from mountaintop to seashore, from arctic tundra to equatorial savannah. Before mankind, the shade of forest trees forced grasses out of most humid lands; today, man has reversed the trend and made grassland of original forest. On the suburban lot he blends trees with grass in an environment controlled by planting and mowing, to make a pleasant setting for his home and family activities. This mowed turf (or sward, in England) is called a lawn. The grasses growing there, adaptable to mowing, are formally called turfgrasses, or, in popular usage, lawngrasses. A good lawn adds to the attractiveness and value of a house, and is the backdrop for its landscaping.

Lawngrass

The grass family embraces several thousand species, with innumerable varieties and races. Of the many kinds, relatively few have the requisites of good lawngrass: beauty, resistance to disease, adaptability to mowing, compatibility, tight growth, persistence, lengthy season, availability at reasonable price, and wide regional and soil adaptation.

It is interesting to note that almost all of the major lawngrasses in America are immigrants. North America has spawned few species that are green in winter as well as summer. When one sees green blades during the weeks following killing frost, whether in lawn or field, one is almost certain to be observing species introduced from Europe. Even in the South, the ubiquitous bermudas, zoysias, st. augustines, and centipede grasses are gifts from foreign shores.

Having arisen in climates long accustomed to the scorch of seasonal drought, most lawngrasses retire to the soil for protection during intemperate times. Though appearing sere to casual examination, tenacious life resides in crown and rhizome. At more favorable seasons, or at the onset of rains, this life infiltrates the faded brown tangle of old leaves with new shoots of green.

By observing the seasonal behavior of grass, one senses the grand rhythm of natural events. With a grassy lawn at our dooryard there is not only respite from the tension and press of the city, but instruction in biological cause and effect. For city people, watching grass respond to soil and season may be a last link to the solace and understanding once provided by our now vanishing wilderness.

We might cite civilizations built on grass, and those that declined as their grasslands were wasted. Instead, let the story of one grass— Kentucky blue, the most famous lawngrass of all—illustrate how man and grass have moved together into the new age of the suburban lawn.

The Saga of Kentucky Bluegrass

Like the Pilgrims, Kentucky bluegrass was a pioneer in America long before it was named for the Caintuck wilderness of Virginia, made a state in 1792. Early records show that bluegrass was known in ancient Greece. Indeed, the Greeks had a word for it, the source of its later scientific name, *Poa.* (Kentucky bluegrass is *Poa pratensis,* or "poa of the meadow.") Before New World exploration began, *Poa pratensis* was the familiar meadow grass of northern Europe and England.

Probably English grass, as bluegrass was known to the colonists, was just a chance passenger in hay and stock bedding on the early ships bringing supplies to newly discovered lands. In reports of these first landings in eastern America there is little mention of pasture grass. Who would send Sir Walter Raleigh a prosaic account of stock feed,

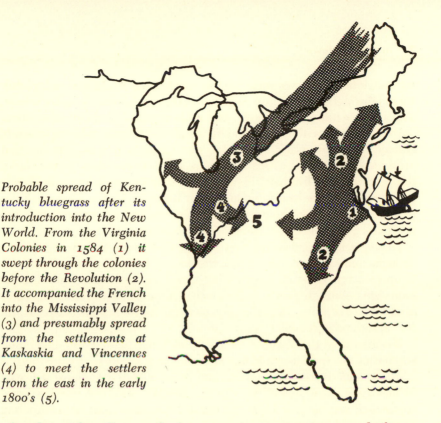

Probable spread of Kentucky bluegrass after its introduction into the New World. From the Virginia Colonies in 1584 (1) it swept through the colonies before the Revolution (2). It accompanied the French into the Mississippi Valley (3) and presumably spread from the settlements at Kaskaskia and Vincennes (4) to meet the settlers from the east in the early 1800's (5).

when he might tell instead of a romantic new continent, and of savages and treasure?

As early as 1584, however, Captain Arthur Barlowe, reporting on Virginia, mentions trial plantings to test the soil. Even then, Kentucky bluegrass may have begun its New World conquest. In 1586, the governor of Grenville's colony reported to Raleigh: "We had sown enough grain fields to give us food for a year." Was bluegrass, volunteer in cropland, already working westward to its destiny in Kentucky?

Migration of this pioneer grass could progress only as colonization felled the forest and the land was turned. Grass does not flourish in wooded areas and, except for infrequent Indian clearings, eastern North America was mostly forest at the time of Raleigh.

But by 1620 the inexorable nibblings at the seemingly limitless woodlands were well under way. John Smith reports: "James Towne is yet their chiefe seat, most of the wood destroyed, little corne there planted, but all converted into pasture and gardens; wherein doth grow all manner of herbs and roots we have in England in abundance and as good grasse as can be."

William Penn, Thomas Jefferson, Benjamin Franklin, and the few New World botanists of the day all noted in their writings the ready invasion of cleared lands by bluegrass and fellow pasture migrants.

By Revolutionary times there was no doubt that bluegrass was widely spread through all of settled America.

The latter half of the eighteenth century was marked by adventurous backwoodsmen crossing the mountains for trade and exploration. Daniel Boone and other explorers reported parts of Kentucky a sea of grass. And strangely, at least in the Ohio Valley, open land was already dominated by this Old World partner of the white man. Bluegrass seems to have beaten Boone to the West!

It is unlikely that bluegrass worked its own way westward through the forests, or that the very early explorers dispersed bluegrass seed. Yet here was bluegrass, reliably reported, in the wilderness of Ohio, Indiana, and Kentucky ahead of settlement.

The most reasonable surmise is that bluegrass slipped around the mountains through the St. Lawrence Valley with the French. Marquette and La Salle, from 1672 to 1682, had explored the Illinois country. Forts and settlements were established at Kaskaskia, Illinois, and at Vincennes on the Wabash by 1700 and 1702. These were flourishing when Charlevoix visited the area in 1721.

The French were noted for mission work with the Indians, and part of their program included distribution of seeds. The botanist Per Kalm commented in 1749 on the luxuriant bluegrass pastures of French Canada.

It seems reasonable that bluegrass was introduced to the Ohio Valley by missionaries a good half-century before Boone ever saw Kentucky. Birkbeck, in *Letters from Illinois*, 1818, writes: "Where the little caravans have encamped as they crossed the prairies, and have given their cattle hay made of these perennial grasses, there remains ever after a spot of green turf for the instruction and encouragement of future improvers."

Perhaps colonists from Virginia encountered bluegrass migrating southward in Kentucky. As early as the autumn of 1752, John Findley, an Irish immigrant to Pennsylvania turned Indian trader, and four servants are reported to have paddled in canoes down the Ohio and up the Kentucky rivers to a Shawnee village. The goods for exchange were packed in "English hay," which was scattered about an improvised stockade. Did seed from this hay make the first bluegrass planting in Kentucky? Julia H. Levering, writing on Indiana history, states: "Soldiers who fought under Harrison in the battle of Tippecanoe in 1811 discovered the superior qualities of bluegrass . . . on return home they carried seed and sowed this grass which has made Kentucky famous!" Other reports show interchange of bluegrass seed between southern Ohio and Kentucky at a slightly later date.

A natural bluegrass field in Kentucky where seed was long gathered in this fashion each June. Most bluegrass seed, now from elite cultivars, is today agriculturally cropped rather than taken from natural stands such as this one.

There is no exact date for the association of bluegrass with Kentucky. Early plant collectors writing from 1813 to 1833 list *Poa pratensis,* but do not mention Kentucky bluegrass among its twenty-seven common names. Yet David Wells' *Yearbook of Agriculture* for 1855–56 states: "In Kentucky it is called Kentucky bluegrass . . . succeeds far better . . . than in any part of Europe where it is native." Sometime shortly before mid-century it must have become popularly named for the state. In any event, flourishing on the phosphatic soils of the Lexington area, bluegrass, with the wealth and leisure it created, sponsored the first culture center west of the mountains.

Today Kentucky bluegrass is very much at home in most of America. Starting as a pasture grass, it has risen to even greater glory as America's number one lawn species, a chief ingredient of quality seed mixtures used throughout the northern two-thirds of the land (and sometimes employed for annual winterseeding in the South). Considering lawns along with the millions of acres of bluegrass pasture, perhaps no other plant is numerically so prevalent. Bluegrass is still excellent pasturage, but especially, nowadays, it is the adornment of a suburbanizing nation.

Lawn Data

Approximate acreage in mowed turf	15+ million
Total annual expenditures for its maintenance	
residential lawns	$4,325,794,086
other (highways, cemeteries, golf courses,	$3,002,101,097
parks, etc.)	$1,323,692,989
Approximate total sales of lawn-related products	
(equipment, horticultural products and services, garden	
chemicals, furniture and accessories, for "outdoor living")	$7 billion

Estimated acreage of and maintenance expenditures for turfgrass in the United States (expenditure figures as of 1965 from **Turfgrass Science**, American Society of Agronomy, Madison, Wisconsin).

Lawn Establishment and Maintenance

The mere presence of a book devoted solely to lawns and their care may seem discouraging if one is facing the prospect of making a new lawn for the first time. Must one be a turf expert to have a carpet of grass about his house? Of course not! A good lawn is possible for every homeowner in almost any climate. Here are the basic rules: begin with a little forethought; use common sense about soils and seedbed preparation; plant quality species for the climate; match care to the kind of grass and its needs.

The following chart is intended as a handy guide to planning timely lawn establishment and maintenance; the "how-to" is discussed in the chapters that follow. At the end of some chapters you will find information of a regional nature, followed by clarification of common fallacies that often confuse lawnmakers.

A Calendar for Lawn Care
North and South

Spring

North

Seed and feed—early in spring.
First "chemical trimming" of the year, edgings and around woody plants.
Use a fungicide where disease threatens.
Where mole and skunk diggings are a problem, use soil insecticides to reduce grubs and similar food.
Mow frequently, twice a week if necessary.

One scalping, very early, to remove foliage scorched in winter, encourages early lawn greening.

Pre-emergence weed controls should be applied well ahead of weed season.

Avoid tilling soggy soils.

Be careful with weed controls on new seedings.

Be cautious with herbicides for broadleaf weeds; shrubbery is very susceptible to drift when budding.

Remove thatch if it is troublesome; a good occasion to overseed with new varieties.

South

Seed, or plant sprigs and plugs; make sod patchings.

Use weed sprays and dusts on established turf.

Provide first of a series of feedings.

Clip wintergrass closely.

Rake up shading debris that may slow bermuda comeback; remove thatch.

Apply insecticides for mole crickets and other pests.

Aerify compact soils, especially in climates where there is no loosening by winter freezing.

Consider installation of automatic irrigation systems.

Summer

North

Spread insecticide if webworm, chinch bug, etc. become troublesome.

Feed (but only lightly where summer is hot or prolonged, unless ureaform nitrogen is used).

Water is needed to keep grass from wilting; except with bentgrass let the lawn dry almost to wilting point between soakings.

Mow bluegrass-fescue lawns high, especially with older varieties and in shade.

Spray and dust for weeds; arsonates for growing crabgrass; phenoxys and dicamba for clover, knotweed, and other dicots.

Feed more frequently under trees, to provide both for grass and tree roots.

Sterilize seedbed soils in anticipation of autumn planting; check that supplies are on hand (fertilizer, seed, etc.).

Watch out for summer diseases: many can be checked by reducing water and fertilization temporarily. Systemic fungicides are helpful.

South

Feed regularly.

Water as needed to keep grass green, more frequently on sandy soils.

Thin matting grasses.

Use insecticides, herbicides, and nematicides as needed.

Apply fungicides if disease threatens.

Mow regularly (heavy-duty mower for zoysia).

Autumn

North

Prepare new seedbeds; best seeding season for new lawns.

Check on quality of seed to be planted.

Renovate and upgrade "tired lawns."

Fertilize generously; less risky than in spring.

Weed control now reduces spring problems; pre-emergence controls for *Poa annua* and chickweed. A great time for weed-and-feed products.

Heavily thatched grasses should be thinned.

Repair bare spots; move sod.

Where lime is needed, spread now and through winter while soil is firm.

Rake leaves that are thick enough to shade or smother grass.

Mow lawn as long as the grass keeps growing.

Repair and service all equipment, readying it for next year.

A good time to install underground irrigation systems while the soil is workable.

South

Thin out matted grass.

Sow wintergrass.

Apply weed control for winter weeds where wintergrass plantings are not contemplated; pre-emergence *Poa annua* control possible now.

Taper off fertilization (except where wintergrass is planted) but lime if needed.

Fertilizers rich in potassium often aid with winter hardiness.

Water desiccated lawns.

Dye brown lawns with a green colorant as desired.

Treat for disease if lawngrass is a susceptible variety (e.g., Pythium on wintergrass seedings).

Winter

North

Apply snowmold preventives, especially to bentgrass, before lawn is "snowed in" or during mid-winter exposure.

Avoid concentrated traffic, as in pathways across dormant lawns.

Keep ice-removal salt away from turfed areas; use soluble fertilizer to melt ice on walks near the lawn.

Prune woody plants for convenience of lawn tending next growing season.

Don't use weedy seed in bird feeders; weed seeds are bound to be scattered onto the lawn.

It is possible to fertilize and seed even on top of the snow, for spring response, if these operations were missed in autumn.

Encourage pets to attend their functions away from the residence, in order to avoid a concentration of urine burns near the doorways.

South

Fertilize wintergrass regularly.

Mow wintergrass frequently.

Reapply lawn colorants if needed.

Check out equipment and supplies, making ready for spring.

To avoid marking the lawn limit traffic on frosted turf until the sun is up and frost is gone.

COMMON MISCONCEPTIONS

NATIVE GRASSES MAKE GOOD LAWNS. In America, most lawngrasses are immigrants from the Old World. Only within the last century have they become tended and mowed regularly. Even today, in much of the Old World, lawns are not planted; at best, they are given only incidental attention.

ARTIFICIAL TURF WILL SOLVE LAWN PROBLEMS. This is perhaps true in areas where heavy use is unavoidable, as on athletic fields. But synthetic turf is a poor substitute esthetically, and it lacks biological functions which lessen pollution, which help to cool the environment, and which generate a fresh look each growing season. Artificial turf is also far more expensive than living grass, and not as easy to maintain as might be supposed.

lawns and ecology

THE WORD "ecology" was unfamiliar to most people only a few years ago. Although it is very much in vogue today, it has always been at the heart of human affairs, one way or another, for ecology simply means the relationship of living things to their environment.

Primitive people necessarily became "ecologists" in order to survive, learning by trial and error what their environment would permit. Pioneering man, with the advantage of firearms, axe, and plow, attempted to "conquer" the environment, but was still very much at its mercy in the wilderness. Today, modern man overwhelms his environment with sheer numbers and the side effects of civilization. He is becoming aware that the massive changes he has introduced can have catastrophic consequences, and that he must achieve a greater harmony with the natural environment if life as we know it is to continue to exist.

In its small way the lawn is an ecological microcosm, behaving according to principles that make it something of an ecological laboratory for its custodian. Like all living things, grass, too, must achieve harmony with its particular environment. The lawn and garden may be the only direct link that today's city dweller has with that fundamental process which supports all life—photosynthesis, the absorption of energy from sunlight by green plants. The garden makes clear what inputs lead to growth and harvest. Complex interrelationships show clearly in the lawn; grass reacts with soil, weather, weeds, and such like, and the interplay determines the lawn's success. The homeowner is master of this ecological microcosm, and can take measures which are very influential on the lawn population. It is within his power to seed, fertilize, mow, de-thatch, spray, water, weed, and whatnot, all for the benefit of his favorite grasses. If he permits an environment hazardous to the grass, he risks weeds and scanty ground cover.

The Role of Grass in the Total Environment

In his classic eulogy to Kentucky bluegrass, Senator John J. Ingalls wrote nearly a century ago: "Next in importance to the divine profusion of water, light, and air—may be reckoned the universal beneficence of grass. Grass is the forgiveness of nature—her constant benediction."

Senator Ingalls may have been more prophetic than he knew. From the beginning of time our planet's atmosphere has slowly changed from one starved for, to one reasonably rich in, oxygen. Grass and other green plants have "consumed" the carbon compounds, and donate in their stead the oxygen we breathe. For most of time the oxygen issuing from green plants has been balanced by that consumed in decay. Recently, however, with industrialization and the burning of much fuel, the balance has tipped towards increasing concentrations of carbon dioxide. Although there is no danger of an insufficiency of oxygen for breathing, it is nonetheless reassuring that the grasses planted in our cities and suburbs are helping to maintain a healthy oxygen balance. Too much carbon dioxide worldwide could, in fact, be upsetting. It could entrap radiation as might a greenhouse. Were carbon dioxide to double within a few centuries, as some predict, the average temperature of the earth might rise 4° F., melting the polar ice cap and flooding the world's seaside cities!

What causes warm and cold cycles is not perfectly understood. But it is known that the earth's temperature is influenced by the amount of sunlight absorbed or reflected by the earth, which changes, for example, as forest is turned into cultivated land. In the same way, in cities and suburbs, the water that grass transpires, or "breathes," has a markedly cooling effect. One study showed the temperature over a paved area at 4 P.M. in early August to be 27° F. higher than over a nearby grassed area. Even at 9 P.M., the temperature was still 13 degrees cooler over the grass. Certainly, the "air conditioning" that grass provides is of real service in urban areas; all yards, parks, and medians in cities should be planted to turf and other vegetation.

Grass, and other green plantings, are also important for dust control. Dust haze over a city can reduce sunlight as much as 15 per cent, and ultraviolet radiation, 30 per cent or more in winter. These dust particles in the air over cities act as nuclei for fog, increase rainfall, and make for darker days. But, if disturbed land is planted to grass, atmospheric dust is lowered appreciably. The importance of controlling dust can be surmised should the prediction be true that a 1.6 per cent reduction of the radiation that the earth receives from the sun could initiate another glacial epoch.

Finally, evidence suggests that city vegetation is even more important as an air purifier than had been suspected. Not only do growing plants help maintain the oxygen balance, but they also absorb sulfur dioxide, one of the critical elements in air pollution. Sulfur is a secondary fertilizer element that vegetation needs; an acre of flourishing growth will probably absorb hundreds of pounds of sulfur dioxide during a year. Even using low-sulfur coal, it is difficult for urban areas to meet air quality standards, so that parks and urban landscaping play a definite role in helping to control this aspect of pollution. Studies show that vegetation is also a good air filter for ozone, one of the major smog pollutants.

For all these reasons, then, grass and other green vegetation should be recognized for their importance in the environmental balance that makes our life on earth possible. In cities and in suburbs, the importance of grass and other green plantings for pollution control in general should be recognized for the necessity they are, and not dismissed as frivolous amenities.

Ecological Guidelines

What are the opportunities and limitations in those parts of the world where we try to grow lawns? Several broad ecological principles are involved.

First of all, where the climate permits, nature tends towards diversity rather than monoculture (the growth of a single kind of plant). If warmth and moisture are adequate, forests generally result, with many different species occupying every conceivable habitat. This is true also of the most efficient gardening, in terms of yield for the input of energy, close to the primitive "farming" still practiced in such remote areas as central New Guinea. There, relatively few plants of many crop types are intermixed, taking advantage of sunlight at high, intermediate, and low levels; stem crops occupy the surface area, varying root crops successively deeper soil levels; little or no ground is bare

Ordinarily, the fine-grass monoculture is somewhat harder to maintain indefinitely than a more natural assemblage of mixed species. Here clover and coarse grass is shown to the left of the pen, and fine grass to the right. Choice of seeding mixture, level of fertilization, use of weed killers—all contribute to such distinctions.

for long. It is obvious that a modern lawn, devoted almost entirely to a single "crop" (perhaps even to a single variety), goes against nature's grain, and will require some astute management in order to survive as a monoculture.

In nature, the mature forest amasses a huge accumulation of plant tissue (biomass), and with this comes increased community stability (though less productivity per unit of biomass). A forest can absorb considerable insult, natural or man-made, yet show little damage and recover its natural balance quickly. Not so a lawn, which is a biologically immature and fast-changing plant community (left on its own it would change to forest in most environments). In fact, man does not even allow lawngrass to reach individual plant maturity, for grass looks poorly unmowed and without constant rejuvenation of fresh young leaf. Here too, man opposes nature's bent by insisting upon more or less constantly juvenile, fast-growing grass. So he mows, fertilizes, thins, and removes the thatch, to rejuvenate growth—exactly the procedures leading to the high yields characteristic of crop plants and an immature, fast-changing ecological state. He then resents the abundance of grass clippings resulting from these measures!

It is thus something of a paradox that almost everything man wants in his lawn and garden requires contesting natural ecological trends, to favor productivity rather than maturity and stability. Fortunately, a homeowner can have the beautiful lawn he desires because he has at his ready command modern tools which permit him to maintain the particular ecological stage he cherishes.

Lawns can flourish in many climates. This is easy to demonstrate in a landmass as large as the United States–Canada which has an appreciable temperature gradient from South to North; a moisture gradient from rain forest to desert; and an altitudinal gradient from seaside to mountaintop. These and other variables impose their basic ecological influences upon the lawn, and cause lawn tending to be easier or more difficult as the case may be. A homeowner striving for the conventional lawn of constantly rejuvenated grass, grown in approximate monoculture, may find some guidance in the following ecological rules-of-thumb.

By and large plant populations will follow these trends: from less diversity in dry climates, to greater diversity where it is moist; from little diversity where the climate is cold, to great diversity where the weather is warm; and, of course, from little diversity where darkness abounds, to greater diversity where sunlight is bright. These basic factors—temperature, moisture and sunlight—govern the growth of any plant. Since their effects can only be modified to a very limited extent, they should help tell you what to expect when planning a lawn and its care in any given area.

Obviously a lawn is impossible in the desert (without irrigation); on the arctic tundra (except with special protection); or even within the Astrodome (without special provisions for light and other necessities). It is simply sound thinking, and only incidently good ecology, to recognize that basic constraints do exist, and that lawn establishment and its tending can be made easier by choosing grasses (and systems for their care) well adapted to the locale.

The disadvantage of monoculture is an ecological hazard man must constantly face up to in his lawn keeping. The greatest difficulty posed by having one kind of grass is that when disaster does strike, it is apt to be epidemic. A newly virulent disease will spread through a genetically-alike grass population like wildfire. A bad turn of weather may lay low all the grass in the lawn, if all the grass is identical. Lawnsmen get around this by deliberately introducing some diversity into the lawn, although limiting this diversity to kinds of grasses that are very similar in appearance and which respond to care in much the same

Kentucky Bluegrass

Oregon Lawn Fescue

Hay Fescues and Ryegrasses

The choice of seeds is wide; not only are they different in size (and therefore number per pound, some "going farther") but the plants they eventually yield have markedly different characteristics and different adaptations.

way. Thus two or three varieties of bluegrass may reduce the risk of disease (different varieties, having different heredity, are not all likely to succumb to the same race of disease). More often, lawnsmen will go a step further and include similar but entirely different grass species, which are even more likely to respond individually in the event of stress. Thus Kentucky bluegrasses are combined with fine or red fescues in lawnseeding mixtures for the cool, humid regions. The bluegrasses are great for good looks and sod formation in open areas and on good soil; while the fescues stand up better on poor soil, in droughty locations and in the shade. Yet bluegrass and fescue live compatibly together, enjoy the same general maintenance, and don't become disruptively patchy. Well-formulated lawnseed mixtures take advantage of the ecological virtue of diversity, without introducing greatly different plants that would give a discordant appearance, making the lawn look like a weed patch.

Lawns and Pollution Problems

A great deal is said these days about eutrophication—the rapid aging of waters accompanied by an explosive growth of algae. Organic and mineral runoff from the land feeds this cycle and speeds the aging process. Algal "blooms" are mostly attributed to soluble phosphorus in runoff water, stimulated secondarily by nitrogenous compounds. Some homeowners are hesitant to fertilize their lawns for fear of contributing to the eutrophication problem, but their fears are unfounded. Aside from rare instances of fertilizer spillage that washes into the drainage, a lawn has little chance of contributing to the eutrophication of nearby watersheds. In the first place, phosphorus applied to the lawn, even if soluble, does not remain in solution long but is fixed on soil particles. Many years are required for phosphorus to work itself down even a few inches into the ground on most soils. There is almost no movement of phosphorus into water draining from a lawn. The grass itself protects the soil from washing and physically carrying phosphorus into the drainage system. Most of the phosphorus responsible for eutrophication comes not from fertilizer but from urban waste.

Some nitrate does enter drainage water, for soil organisms are continuously nitrifying nitrogen and lightning produces some oxidation of the gas! But growing plants claim free nitrate so avidly that almost none is lost from the sod, even when a lawn is heavily fertilized. At the Lawn Institute, nitrogen fertilizer was applied to impoverished bluegrass in mid-winter, its influence measured the following spring. In spite of four inches of rain falling on frozen soil shortly after treatment, spring growth showed grass stimulation *only* where the fertilizer was applied; it had not washed even a few inches down the slope. And its influence was almost as intense where used in January, as on other grass receiving the same fertilization in spring. Certainly, most fertilizer nitrogen is immediately absorbed by lawngrass, or, in the case of slow-release fertilizers, remains immobilized in the sod for gradual feed-out.

Ecological Success with the Lawn

In the final analysis, success with a lawn depends on how well each individual grass plant flourishes. The lawn will need help in overcoming many adversities.

Adversity will be most prevalent in climates for which favorite lawngrasses are not particularly well adapted (such as in the "transition zone" of the border states, where the climate is neither very boreal nor tropical, and in which neither northern nor southern grasses are at their best).

Typically, grass plants in the lawn are abnormally crowded in order to give a carpet-like texture. Inevitably such crowding means a dwarfing of the individual plants, with fewer (often malformed) leaves and puny root systems that don't reach very deeply for water and nutrients. The "better" the lawn, the more crowded the grass plants, and the more special care is apt to be needed in order to supply sufficient nutrients and moisture, and to keep out pests.

Every lawn will have certain ecological niches not ideally adapted to grass growth. There will be places where soil pockets are poor, the land poorly drained and waterlogged much of the year, the habitat too shady, and so on. The best the lawnsman can do under circumstances such as these is to try to mitigate the adversity where it occurs, and to improve the ecological situation for the grass.

Homeowners increasingly demand a year-around performance from their lawns; who wants to be "in the mud," even seasonally? This may be contrary to the natural bent of the grass, since almost all species undergo seasonal dormancy. Yet a bluegrass lawn may be "pushed" in summer by fertilization and watering, until food reserves the grass was husbanding for autumn growth are exhausted. Or grasses that naturally go off-color in autumn may be kept green longer by generous nitrogen feeding at the expense of cold-weather hardiness. Not that extending seasonal performance of a grass is undesirable, but do keep in mind that whenever growth is forced abnormally, risks are entailed and compensations may be needed.

Lawngrasses are subject to stress simply because they are mowed. Left to grow naturally, the grass would retain much more food-making green leaf; tall-mowed grass is generally less subject to disease, weed invasion, or other risks that come with the weakening that low mowing inflicts. Fortunately, most newer bluegrasses and fescues have been selected for low growth, and are better adapted to low mowing than were their traditional predecessors. Of course, some species, such as the bentgrasses and bermudagrasses, just don't look well mowed tall. Nevertheless, most lawns have more trouble if mowed very low ("scalped"), than if mowed high. This is especially true for northern grasses planted to climates where the summers are long and hot, such as bluegrass in the border states, or any grass in a stressful habitat (such as in the shade).

Some lawns are subject to much wear. Turf that is a playground day after day is bound to show the strain. No matter how well tended, it will probably have to be renovated from time to time. The same is true for pathways. A lawn is meant to be used and enjoyed, and no "keep off the grass" sign is suggested. But recognize that wear is one of the afflictions lawns must endure, and constant trampling (even the running of the mower repeatedly along the same path) can cause soil structure to deteriorate, especially if the soil is wet.

Adversity is also inflicted on the lawn through ignorance. It is quite possible to do the right thing, but to do it at the wrong time. For example, fertilizing a bluegrass lawn just as the crabgrass is gaining ascendency in late spring (and the bluegrass, at least in the southern portions of the bluegrass zone, is heading towards mild dormancy) encourages crabgrass, not lawngrass. The same fertilization would be much better applied in autumn, when crabgrass is at the end of its growing season, and bluegrass just beginning the most advantageous part of its yearly growth cycle. Careless application of lawn products because of failure to follow label directions can cause difficulties as well. Too much of certain fertilizers can "burn" the lawn, either by direct contact, or from raising the salt index in the soil. Pre-emergence crabgrass preventers used excessively or repeatedly often restrict rooting of the lawngrass, or cause its thinning.

The following chapters will consider such lawn matters subject by subject. I merely point out here that any lawn is a dynamic system, continuously subject to ecological influences. These can be altered or compensated for as need be, but good judgment must be exercised to achieve the desired result. Don't feel that your situation is hopeless. Good lawns, of one or another type, can be grown in all sections of the United States and Canada, without extravagant costs or undue effort. Some regions, where one would think it extremely difficult to have a lawn, actually possess many advantages. Arid lands, even desert, are one such case (provided irrigation can be had; elaborate irrigation devices are now available which even operate automatically). In keeping with the ecological principles advanced earlier there is usually clear air (giving cool nights), bright sun (for abundant, squat growth), and few weeds (the natural restriction on ecological diversity), in deserts and arid regions. Once water becomes available, these are natural advantages. Even alkali soils can be leached of detrimental salts, and improved physically by amendments to permit the growth of grass under circumstances that were naturally quite inimical to lawn keeping. Modern grasses, tools, and techniques can so modify the ecology, almost anywhere, as to make having a good lawn not only possible but pleasurable.

COMMON MISCONCEPTIONS

ECOLOGY HAS LITTLE PRACTICAL BEARING ON LAWN MAINTENANCE. Far from it. When you avoid using crabgrass preventer on shaded parts of the lawn (because crabgrass won't grow in the shade), that's ecology! So is mowing grass tall, fertilizing in autumn, regulating watering, etc.—all to favor the grass over the weeds. More subtle is proper balancing of nutrients to restrain lawn disease, understanding the chemical antagonisms of one species towards another, increasing (or decreasing) fertilization to favor one grass over another (e.g., light fertilization may encourage fescue, heavy fertilization, bluegrass, in mixed populations of these two species). The choice of a lawngrass (the region it is suited to) is, of course, basically an ecological consideration, as is avoidance of competing nursegrass in a seeding mixture or restraining clover through nitrogen fertilization (rather than with a herbicide). All maintenance has ecological implications and efficient lawn tending requires understanding the ecology of your lawn.

LAWN MAINTENANCE CAN HURT THE ENVIRONMENT. Just the opposite. Encouraging the grass (by fertilization and judicious pest control) protects the soil and provides a reserve of plant tissue biologically useful in many ways. The well-intentioned environmentalist who refuses to buy a lawn fertilizer containing phosphorus is misled; compared to urban wastes, fertilizer contributes an infinitesimal amount of phosphate to the environment in the first place, and this small contribution is quickly fixed by the soil and the vegetation, contributing to plant growth that has many ecological benefits.

3

lawngrasses

WHETHER THEY ARE towering bamboos or creeping covers, grasses are unlike trees, shrubs, and other familiar flowering plants in that they do not grow from the tip. Instead, they elongate from the lower part of the abbreviated stem, or *culm*, which is ensheathed by the leaves. The sheath is the lower portion of the leaf that surrounds the culm. Thus it is possible to cut the tips of grass without impairing the formation of new leaves. Most grasses can be mowed at reasonably low levels without delaying or damaging new buds, as would happen with most other plants.

Under lawn conditions, bluegrass is not ordinarily allowed to grow tall enough to form seedheads, but trailing bermudagrass may mature so low that some seedheads escape the mower. Both species demonstrate the ground-hugging growth typical of lawngrasses, in contrast to the tall stalks of cereal grasses such as corn. In a lawngrass the core of solid stem, the *crown*, is greatly condensed, often hidden in the soil. From the crown arises a telescoped series of leaves, each progressively popping up through the sheath of the preceding older leaf.

In bluegrass, the buds aboveground form additional culms that are called *tillers*. Buds belowground usually become horizontal stems that worm their way through the soil, producing new plantlets where they finally turn up to the surface. These are the *rhizomes*, or underground stems. Bermudagrass produces tillers, but instead of depending solely upon rhizomes underground, it spreads most of its stems over the surface of the soil. These are called runners, or *stolons*. If a grass does not produce stolons or rhizomes, it is considered a bunchgrass; bunchgrasses become clumpy, rather than interlacing into a tight sod.

Almost as much of the grass plant lives in the soil as aboveground. The extensive fibrous root system in most lawn species amounts to several tons per acre. Normally, about half of these fine roots die and decompose each year, to be replaced by new growth. That, of course, is why grasses contribute so much to soil fertility—each year they thread organic residues throughout the topsoil. For more information about the soil-building value of grass roots, see Chapter 5.

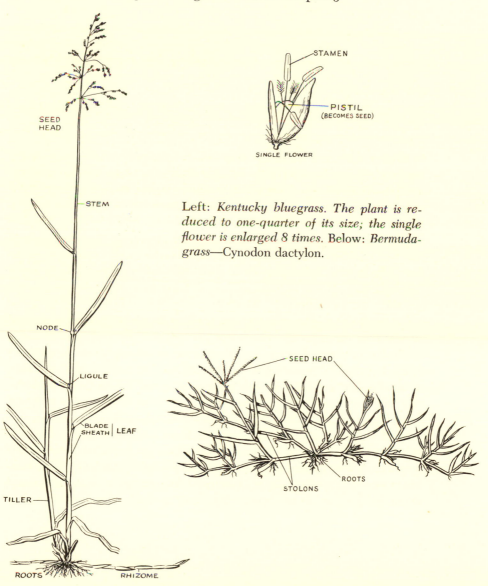

Left: *Kentucky bluegrass. The plant is reduced to one-quarter of its size; the single flower is enlarged 8 times.* Below: *Bermuda-grass*—Cynodon dactylon.

of them are killed by cold winters, and would be annuals in the North. Seeded bermuda sown north of St. Louis illustrates this group.

The major lawngrasses described in this chapter can also be utilized in arid regions, if irrigation can be supplied. Where water is in short supply, the lawnmaker must do the best he can with some of the dry-land or native prairie species, even though their texture is not as attractive. A few grasses for the arid zones are listed with the map (see page 23), especially wheatgrasses in the northern high plains; buffalo, grama, and lovegrasses farther south.

The Most Useful Lawngrasses

These are the major lawngrass species found today, either in seed mixtures or as vegetative planting material. They are well known for their widespread usefulness, though it is recognized that any hero can become a rogue if he intrudes where not wanted.

Northern Species

BENTGRASS (or browntop in England) (Principally *Agrostis tenuis* or *A. stolonifera* in Europe; the creeping bents of golf greens are mostly *A. palustris*; the velvet bents, *A. canina*.) Spreads by stolons and gives a soft, carpet-like, bright-green effect. The leaves are rolled in bud, with prominent ligule and veins. They are small, short, not very glossy, with a pointed tip, and densely clustered. The trailing stolons make dense colonies that stifle other grasses. Bent is best used in cool

Colonial bentgrass (Agrostis tenuis)

regions with ample moisture and fertility. It browns easily in hot, humid weather, especially when heavily fertilized, and is only for lawns receiving better-than-average care.

Prominent varieties of colonial bentgrass are: Astoria, Exeter, Highland, and Holfior. Creeping types include Penncross and Seaside from seed, and many golf-green bentgrasses such as Arlington, Cohansey, Congressional, Dahlgreen, Evansville, Metropolitan Toronto, and Washington which are planted vegetatively. Kingstown is the most prominent velvet bent.

BLUEGRASS, KENTUCKY (*Poa pratensis*; a few other *Poa* species such as Canada bluegrass, *P. compressa*, and woods bluegrass, *P. nemoralis*, are sometimes used in mixtures.) Kentucky bluegrass grows erect from graceful arching shoots that produce a soft, uniform, dark-green effect.

Left: *Close-up of a Highland bentgrass plug (separated to show runners and roots), mowed at ¾ inch.*

Right: *Section of Penncross Creeping bentgrass sod mowed ½ inch. Creeping and velvet bents are usually considered the ultimate in fine-textured turf, and are much used for golf greens.*

It spreads by rhizomes. The leaves are folded flat in bud with a smooth ligule much like a fingernail. Leaf tips are boat-shaped and feel like a small spoon when run between thumb and finger. Kentucky bluegrass is the most widely adapted lawngrass, although some of its varieties are restricted in use. It prefers good, neutral soil, high shade or full sun in the North, partial shade in the upper South. It is especially desirable where attention can be but moderate. High clipping is best, at least in the southern part of its range.

Scores of Kentucky bluegrass cultivars have now been selected or bred. In resistance to disease and for low, dense growth most of the recent ones are distinctly improved over traditional varieties and natural bluegrass. For relatively untended lawns where the grass must be self-reliant, the broad genetic base of the older varieties, or "wild" bluegrass, may have an advantage, as represented in the Arboretum, Kenblue, Park, and similar varieties. Similar to natural bluegrass, but selected for various attributes (such as improved vigor, color, etc.) are such varieties as Arista, Newport, Prato, Windsor, etc. Highly bred selections for low growth and disease resistance, much used for commercial sod growing as well as home plantings, are Adelphi, Baron, Bonnieblue, Fylking, Nugget, Pennstar, Sodco, Sydsport and many others (some of them even vegetatively propagated, such as A-20 and A-34). Merion was the first of the new breed of highly selected grasses, and is probably still the best known and most widely planted of the elite cultivars. It does suffer from diseases however, such as the newly important stripe smut, *Fusarium roseum*, rust, and others, although it is quite resistant to the ubiquitous leafspot that plagues the bluegrasses. Merion should receive a higher level of fertility than most cultivars. When it is well-tended, Merion is one of the most attractive bluegrass varieties (low, dense, of deep color) and is the standard by which newer releases are judged.

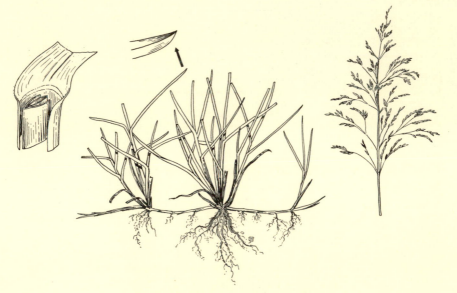

Kentucky bluegrass (Poa pratensis)

Note abundant rhizome production from this flourishing clump of Kentucky bluegrass.

Individual culms of bluegrass cultivars bred especially for fine turf usage. From left to right: Prato, Arboretum, Merion, Fylking, and Nugget.

Fylking bluegrass, a select variety that withstands low mowing well.

BLUEGRASS, ROUGH (*Poa trivialis*; often known by Latin rather than common name) Produces stolons and gives a soft, fine-textured, sometimes patchy, light-green effect, similar to that of bentgrass. The leaves of rough bluegrass are folded like those of Kentucky bluegrass. They

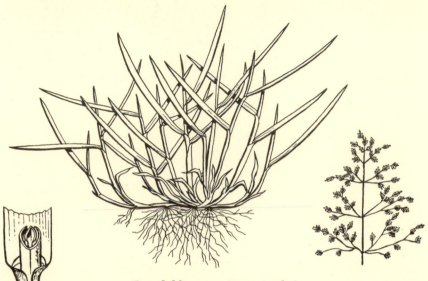

Rough bluegrass (Poa trivialis)

are bright-green and glossy. Rough bluegrass is shallow-rooted and cannot tolerate traffic, but it is useful and attractive in moist, shady locations. It can become patchy like bentgrass and should be given the same care as bent. It is also popular for winter seeding southern golf greens. There are no named varieties or selections of rough bluegrass.

FESCUE, RED OR FINE (*Festuca rubra*, the "creeping red" cultivars which supposedly are less dense but spread moderately by rhizomes, and *F. rubra commutata*, the denser "Chewings-type" cultivars which presumably spread less vigorously by rhizome. The distinctions are not constant and vary with growing conditions. Sheep fescue, *F. ovina*, is similar, used occasionally in dry sites.) Red fescue grows from a short rhizome with many tillers bunched from the crown and gives a wiry, hair-like, dark-green effect. Its thin, wiry leaves are usually curled inward at the edges, folded like bluegrass. The ligule is of short fuzz rather than a conspicuous "nail" as in bluegrass. The brownish, old leaf sheaths persist at the base of the culm. The growth pattern of red fescue is similar to that of Kentucky bluegrass, and the two grasses are

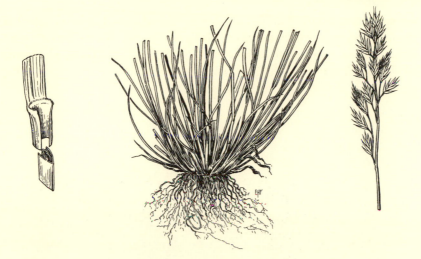

Red fescue (Festuca rubra)

excellent companions. Red fescue generally gives way to bluegrass on better soils, but outstrips it in shade and on poor sandy soils. It should be fertilized moderately since disease strikes severely on heavily fed stands; it is not suited to hot southern summers.

New cultivars of fine fescue are being bred and released almost as abundantly as bluegrasses. Traditional fine fescues for the lawn, in addition to unselected "creeping red," are Chewings, Illahee and Rainier. Pennlawn was an early disease-resistant variety from Pennsylvania State University, bred through the crossing of three parent selections. A more recent Chewings-type is Cascade. Dawson, Golfrood and Ruby are cultivars developed in Europe, the last seeming to endure continental summers better than most fine fescues and being well suited for bluegrass mixtures. Highlight and Jamestown are two of the denser, more attractive releases; Highlight (from Holland) is a brilliant color, Jamestown (from Rhode Island), low-growing and dark green. Wintergreen is a selection made in Michigan. Many other attractive fine fescue cultivars are under test, with seed supplies sufficient for commercial release being built up.

FESCUE, TALL (*Festuca arundinacea*; occasionally meadow fescue, *F. elatior*). This is a bunchgrass with little or no rhizoming. It produces a rough, frequently clumpy appearance. The coarse, broad-bladed leaf is rolled in bud, but the front of the collar has overhanging "ears" along the sheath slit. Tall fescue survives where summers are too difficult for better grasses. It endures neglect and is useful on playgrounds and athletic fields, where it should be planted densely to crowd and dwarf the individual plants, and not be mowed too closely. It has a sturdy root system. Meadow fescue is generally not as persist-

A plug of Pennlawn fine fescue (left) contrasted with Penncross creeping bent (right).

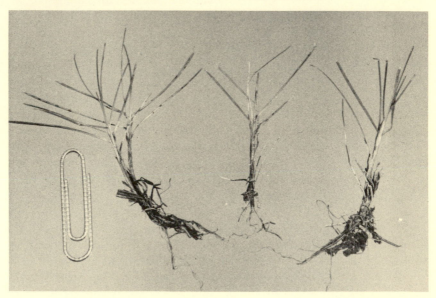

Individual plants of Jamestown fine fescue mowed 1½ inches.

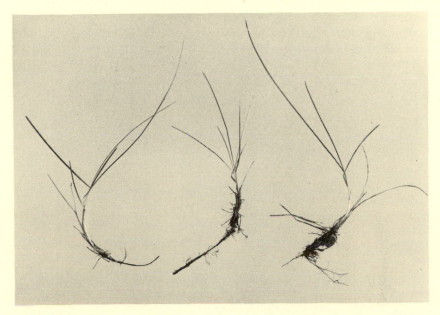

Individual culms of selected lawn fescues. Left to right: *Pennlawn, Wintergreen, and Highlight.*

Tall fescue (Festuca arundinacea)

ent as tall fescue, but is preferred in parts of California. Early varieties of tall fescue including Alta and Kentucky 31 are much alike, but newer, finer-leafed cultivars are being bred.

REDTOP (*Agrostis alba*). Grows in bunches of medium to coarse leaves that give a soft but clumpy effect. Redtop is a bentgrass with leaf rolled in bud and conspicuous smooth ligule. It has reddish seedheads. Redtop is often used as a nursegrass, and seldom endures more than a few years. It is not considered a desirable lawn species. Its chief

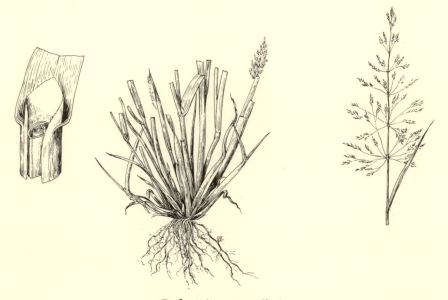

Redtop (Agrostis alba)

use is for quick temporary cover in difficult situations, especially in middle latitudes, and for moist locations, such as along seepage channels. Redtop is sometimes used as a wintergrass with bermudagrass in the South.

There are no named varieties of redtop. General-run seed often carries with it coarse grasses and weeds, and should be checked before sowing to fine turf areas.

RYEGRASS (*Lolium*; annual ryegrass is *L. multiflorum*, also called domestic or Italian ryegrass; *L. perenne* is perennial ryegrass.) Grows in bunches with medium to coarse leaves, forming a soft, open sod which may become clumpy. The two species of ryegrass intergrade, with the annual similar to tall fescue, the perennial more like bluegrass (except pointed leaf tips and no rhizomes). Both are bunchgrasses with shiny leaves; the annual has "ears" at the collar, rolled bud

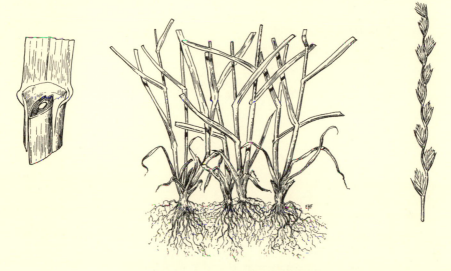

Perennial ryegrass (Lolium perenne)

leaves, round yellowish culms; the perennial has folded leaves, flattened culms, reddish at base. Ryegrass is quick-sprouting, aggressive, the annual form becoming clumpy if it persists; it is frequently used in inexpensive seed mixtures and is not a desirable lawngrass since its aggressiveness in mixtures holds back permanent grasses. Use annual rye for temporary cover when conditions are inappropriate for permanent seeding, or as a winter grass in the South. Perennial ryegrasses have gained favor with development of new "fine-leaf" cultivars. These are not quite up to bluegrass quality, but serve well where quick cover is needed. In small percentage, they can be used in mixture with bluegrass-fescue, and they are excellent for winter seeding in the South. Named varieties of ryegrass include Compas, Manhattan, NK-100, Norlea, Pelo, and Pennfine. Manhattan is derived by combining 16 hardy selections made by Rutgers University, most of which were picked up in Central Park, New York City. Norlea is a Canadian selection showing excellent winter hardiness.

TIMOTHY (*Phleum pratense*, a hay grass; brome and orchard are others.) Grows as a bunch grass with coarse leaves that give a rough, clumpy effect. The leaves of timothy are rolled in bud. They have a large, smooth ligule. The base of the culm is swollen and bulb-like. Timothy is a pasture and hay grass throughout the Northeast, but it

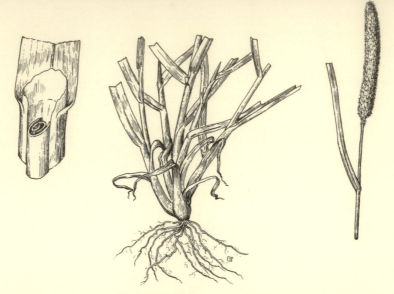

Timothy (Phleum pratense)

is unsatisfactory as a lawngrass, although dwarf cultivars are planted in athletic fields in Europe.

There are no lawn varieties of timothy in America.

Southern Species

BAHIA (*Paspalum notatum*). Produces stolons that result in a loose, medium-low, spreading turf of rather coarse appearance. Bahia leaves are rolled in bud, with a nail-like ligule. Bahias are reasonably tolerant of shade and salt spray and they are one of the few seeded grasses for the deep South. Because it roots deeply, it can be an economy grass in sandy soils where high quality is not needed. It withstands foot traffic well. Bahiagrasses form tough seedheads that are hard to mow, requiring regular mowing with a rotary machine from May to November.

Pensacola is a smooth variety, Argentine and Paraguay, hairy types,

Bahiagrass (Paspalum notatum)

and generally slightly coarser. Wilmington is a dwarf form. Argentine is the hardiest and most tolerant of the varieties.

BERMUDA (*Cynodon dactylon*; other species and varieties are some-times used, such as *C. X magenesii* [Sunturf], and *C. transvaalensis* [African or Ugandan]). Spreads by stolons and gives a medium-soft, dense, low, dark-green appearance. Bermuda leaves are short, flat, bluish-green, rolled in bud, the ligule and leaf margin at collar with long stringy hair. It has stiff, trailing stolons with clusters of small upright culms at intervals. The "crowfoot" seedheads come in season.

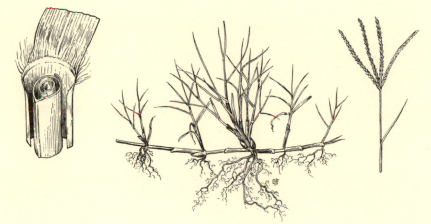

Bermudagrass (Cynodon dactylon)

Bermuda is a rampant grower for upper South. It cannot stand shade. It does best in neutral soils with ample fertility. Bermuda makes an attractive quick-growing lawngrass when cared for; its vigor means that frequent mowing is necessary.

Varieties or selections of bermudagrass are: common bermuda from seed; vegetative selections of finer texture such as Bayshore, Ever-glades, Midiron, Midway, Ormond, Pee Dee, Santa Ana, Texturf, Tifdwarf, Tiffine, Tiflawn, Tifgreen; Sunturf and U-3 are "hardy" vari-eties sometimes planted north of the usual bermuda zone. The "Tif" varieties are mostly sterile hybrids of Uganda grass, *C. transvaalensis,* and selections of *C. dactylon* made at the Tifton, Georgia, Experiment Station.

BUFFALO (*Buchloë dactyloides*). Stolon growth produces a stringy-leaved, loose, thin, grayish-green turf. The pointed leaves of buffalo

MALE, ON STALKS

FEMALE, LOW IN LEAVES

Buffalograss (Buchloe dactyloides)

are lightly hairy, often curled and turning to straw color in drought or cold weather. The ligule is a ring of hairs. Buffalo has separate male and female plants. It is used only where rainfall is insufficient to maintain more desirable grasses; especially the high plains from western Texas north to Montana.

Several varieties of buffalograss have been selected, but none primarily for fine turf purposes.

CARPET (*Axonopus affinis*; occasionally *A. furcatus*, and *A. compressus*). Stolon growth produces a coarse-leaved, loose, creeping effect. The frequent seedheads of carpetgrass are hard to mow. The leaves are folded and blunt. The ligule is a ring of hairs. The stem is compressed. Carpetgrass is used chiefly on acid, sandy, boggy soils where conditions are too poor for better species. Unselected seed of carpetgrass is suitable.

Carpetgrass (Axonopus)

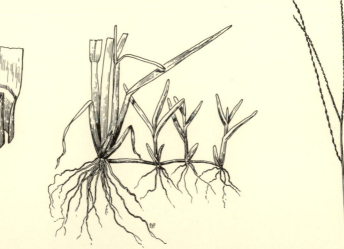

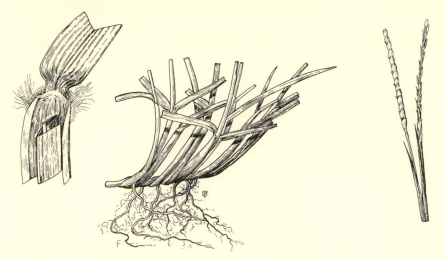

Centipedegrass (Eremochloa ophiuroides)

CENTIPEDE (*Eremochloa ophiuroides*). Centipede has a finer texture than st. augustine or carpetgrass, but it is coarser than bermuda and most zoysias. It has trailing stolons, blunt leaves folded in bud, and a hairy constriction at the collar. The occasional seedheads are single spikes. Centipede is excellent for poor soils with minimum maintenance. It will grow in sandy soils and tolerate light shade. It makes low, dense, attractive turf. Started either from seed or vegetatively planted. Oklawn is a selection of centipedegrass made in Oklahoma.

ST. AUGUSTINE (*Stenotaphrum secundatum*). Produces trailing stolons that form a loose, resilient turf with some upright leaves. The leaf blades are short and blunt, constricted at the juncture with the flattened sheath, and exhibiting a half-twist. The single-spike seedheads are coarse but infrequent. St. augustine is widely adapted to the South, enduring shade or sun and some salt spray. It is too coarse for a fine

St. augustine grass (Stenotaphrum secundatum)

lawn and suffers from chinch bugs and diseases. No seed is available, but this is one of the cheapest sods for Florida and the Gulf Coast.

Several selections of st. augustine have been made, especially in Florida, where both Bitter Blue, Floratam, and Floratine sod can be purchased.

ZOYSIA (*Zoysia matrella,* including *Z. japonica* and *Z. tenuifolia;* also called Japanese lawngrass, Manila grass, or Mascarene grass). The rhizomes and stolons of zoysia produce a tight, very resilient turf like a thick carpet. The leaf is rolled in bud; there are several long hairs at the base of the leaf blade. The seedheads come in single

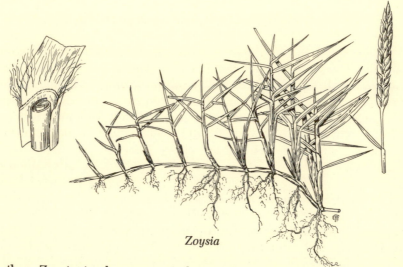

Zoysia

spikes. Zoysia is slow-growing but rugged. It adapts to full sun or partial shade. Like other southern grasses, zoysia is off-color during cold weather. It is one of the best lawngrasses, but in most areas it takes two to three years for complete coverage. Slow growth means less mowing.

Varieties or selections of zoysia include Meyer, a hardy selection for northern areas; Emerald, an attractive hybrid; many local "matrella" selections, such as Flawn, are vegetatively propagated and better for the South than is Meyer; "japonica" is available as seed.

Grasses for Climatic Zones

Although the primary climatic zones suited to specific grasses can be indicated by the map on page 23, local circumstances sometimes alter conditions enough to warrant the use of a grass from a neighboring zone. The difference between north- and south-facing slopes may be the equivalent of a distance 200 miles north or south, or 1,000 feet in elevation. Northern gardeners, with summer homes or lawns emphasized only in summer, might overlook the winter dormancy of bermuda or zoysia in favor of vigorous summer growth, at least as far north as the Ohio Valley.

Similar exceptions occur where mountains exert an influence. In the South, shade or high mountains often permit the use of northern grasses. For example, on Lookout Mountain at Chattanooga, Tennessee, bluegrass grows easily, but river-bottom Chattanooga is predominantly bermuda country. The higher elevations ranging from western California to northern New Mexico make that area good bluegrass land in spite of its location in southern and desert climatic zones.

Short distances sometimes make a difference in the amount of moisture naturally available. Southeastern Oklahoma has a normal rainfall of 55 inches, while the northwestern section has only 15 inches. The moist area can use most of the Gulf Coast lawn species, but the dry Northwest must resort to irrigation even to grow the northern lawngrasses. Without irrigation, native prairie grasses may hang on, but they fail to make a fine lawn.

One map cannot be detailed enough to pinpoint each variation in climate. The lawnsman must rely upon his own judgment and local experience in choosing grass.

Selecting a Lawngrass

The selection of a grass from among those which are climatically suitable should be governed by the intensity of care to be lavished on the lawn.

Especially attractive in the North is the well-kept bentgrass lawn. Given unceasing care, bent looks like velvet, its fine texture and tailored management being especially fitting for formal plantings. On the other hand, it is hardly the grass for a playground, or where mowing must be neglected. A bentgrass lawn is costly in dollars and in attention. To look its best, it ordinarily needs frequent mowing, watering, fertilization, fungicide treatment, and thinning of thatch. Unless bentgrass is so favored, there will always be blemishes and patchiness. As a minor component in a lawn of mixed grasses, bent can be a weed.

Not so formal or as tight a turf, but nevertheless equally attractive to most people in northern states, is the bluegrass lawn. Kentucky bluegrass is the chief constituent of a vast majority of American lawns.

Bluegrass, blended with varieties of red fescue, makes a rugged yet attractive and widely adaptable cover for the country north of San Francisco, Albuquerque, Atlanta, and Washington, D.C. Treated to occasional fertilization, especially in autumn, mowed with consideration, and weeded as need be, a bluegrass lawn satisfies most needs.

A third possibility exists in northern climates for rough, distant areas where cover is important but beauty secondary. This may be the children's play yard, or an exceedingly difficult slope where the sun bakes deep in summer. Here, some of the coarse, tough, hay grasses may prove suitable if they are not cut too closely. Especially enduring is the tall fescue group. (Alta and Kentucky-31 are familiar varieties.) Tall fescue is not to be confused with the narrow-leafed red fescues that are appropriate companions of bluegrass. Hay grass lawns will be forever coarse, never first-class; but they do serve a purpose for hidden corners receiving rough wear.

In recent years, there has been publicity about planting bermuda and zoysia in northern regions. Seldom can this be sincerely advocated, except where the turf is important only in summer. The most familiar hardy bermuda is U-3, recommended for the southern portions of the bluegrass zone; the customary zoysia is the Meyer strain. Both varieties must be vegetatively planted.

In the South, one might choose the selected (vegetative) strains of bermuda or zoysia for a first-class lawn. These require generous feeding and watering to do their best, plus frequent mowing of bermuda (zoysia is a slow grower). Fine-textured bermudas are the "bents of the South."

The average seeded bermuda lawn generally gets by with less intensive maintenance. Its attractiveness will reflect the amount of care given, especially frequent fertilization and mowing, and watering when drought strikes. Zoysias, too, are useful for "average" lawns, except that they require from one to three years after planting to grow into a tight sod. During this interval, weeds must not be allowed to compete with the zoysia; growth will be facilitated by generous feeding and watering. For the first two years, even with lawns ultimately receiving only routine care, zoysia should be treated with the greatest care.

Utility lawns for the South might be of centipede or st. augustine, but frequently are of neglected bermuda, which then looks ragged. Centipede is a "poor soil" grass, noteworthy for needing little fertility and often killing out when heavily fed. St. augustine is coarser, but is generally quite useful in the Deep South, especially for shaded areas. Seeded grasses, about as coarse as tall fescue in the North but fortunately not clumpy, include carpet and bahia. Carpet is frequently used in poor, boggy locations unsuited to other grasses. Kikuyugrass (*Pennisetum clandestinum*), an African species now widely spread through the tropics, has been used sparingly in southern California. More often it is regarded as a weed, difficult to eradicate, too coarse for fine lawns.

Legumes and Dichondra

Legumes, members of the pea or clover family, are good companions for grass. They develop bacterial nodules on their roots that trap nitrogen from the air and make it into nitrates usable by other plants. Clover has always been valued in unfertilized sward. Since lawn fertilizers have become readily available, however, clover is less vital and most people prefer lawns without the patchiness and contrasting texture which legumes introduce. White clover is the most familiar lawn legume, and becomes a weed where it is not wanted, especially on poorer soils and where moisture is abundant. It is a low-growing perennial, spreading by trailing stems.

Dichondra, a member of the morning-glory family, is used as a lawn cover in the South, especially southern California. It is often seeded with white clover, which makes temporary cover until the slower dichondra fills in. Dichondra is mowed, watered, and fertilized much like bermudagrass, so it is marketed along with grass seed. It is a broadleaf ground cover, however, and must be spared weeding with 2,4-D, although dalapon may be used.

Close-up of Dichondra, a favorite ground cover for lawns in the Los Angeles area.

Temporary, Quick Lawns

It is often unavoidable that a new house be completed at a season inappropriate for starting the permanent lawn. Still, weeds must be controlled, and a semblance of attractive cover established until the proper time for a permanent lawn seeding. One possibility, effective but expensive, is to sod. If carefully done, this is possible at almost any season, although most satisfactory when grass is in active growth (autumn and spring in bluegrass country, spring and summer in the South).

Increasing costs and modern impatience have outmoded "green manuring," the old practice of planting some temporary grass or legume to be plowed under at a later date for its organic value. But even without attempting a plow-down planting, the seedbed is best readied soon after final grading. A fairly attractive temporary cover can be sown, one not competitive with the permanent grasses coming later. This *is not* a time for planting cheap lawn seed and considering it expendable; some plants and some of the seeds will survive to become weeds in the finished lawn.

For northern lawns (which are best planted in autumn or early spring), legumes serve well as a summer cover when it is inappropriate to sow bluegrass seed. Clover or beans could be used; but this risks clover becoming a perennial not wanted in the permanent lawn, while species like soybeans are coarse and unattractive. A finer leafed legume successfully used as temporary cover is Korean lespedeza, an annual. It will not endure frost, although it does set seed which can sprout another year. If conditions are good for the bluegrass, lespedeza will soon give ground and offer no competition to an autumn or early spring planting.

In the South, where bermuda, zoysia, centipede, and other summer grasses are the typical lawn species, a seeding of a northern grass in autumn provides useful winter cover until warm weather allows sowing of the major type. Annual ryegrass is commonly used; it is then clipped close in April to permit the planting of sun-loving bermuda. Even when not clipped close it will disappear as hot weather advances. It never makes a permanent cover in the South.

Other northern species, such as bluegrass and fine fescue, can be used as a winter grass, but must be considered expendable, the same as ryegrass. Avoid the coarse fescues (Alta and Kentucky-31), since they may persist beyond the first winter as isolated clumpy weeds.

Grasses for Special Purposes

For reasons of esthetic interest, peculiar adaptability, or unusual types of utilization, grasses not commonly employed may be utilized. Thus in prairie environments, native prairie grasses (including species of *Bouteloua*, *Andropogon* and others) may be seeded on larger acreages to recreate a sort of untended, unmowed prairie reminiscent of the virgin landscape. In other areas, the soil may be too alkaline to sustain conventional turfgrasses well, although species such as salt-grass (*Puccinellia*) may tolerate this difficult environment. If your interests or needs lie in these directions, it is best to follow locally successful examples, and consult with authorities in the area (such as the state college and its extension agents).

With today's emphasis on recreation and the outdoors, even the small property owner may wish to establish specialized turf in his yard, for such activities as badminton, croquet, or a practice golf-putting green. Normally the maintenance of low-growing creeping bentgrasses in the North, or selected bermudagrasses in the South, ideal for such purposes when properly kept, is beyond the capacity of the homeowner. For one thing, a turf of this type needs mowing at least every other day during the growing season, as well as other special attentions. However, the development of new, low-growing cultivars of standard easy-to-keep lawngrasses, such as the bluegrasses, affords a compromise. Varieties such as Fylking and Pennstar adapt well when properly cared for, possibly in combination with an open-growing bentgrass such as Highland or Holfior, and endure well even when mowed to a height of about three-quarters of an inch. This is not the quality of putting surface equal to quarter-inch creeping bent-grass on a golf course, but it serves for practice and is quite suitable for most game activities. Keeping a bluegrass-fescue turf growing well, mowed this low, requires some extra effort, but not the special skills a golf superintendent uses in maintaining a golf green (topdressing, preventive spraying, precise watering, etc.).

REGIONAL FOCUS

THE HUMID NORTHEAST, PACIFIC NORTHWEST. Generally these are regions of heavy soils which receive enough rainfall to maintain good turf without irrigation. Eastern uplands have frequent mists and driz-zles, as do coastal Oregon, Washington, and British Columbia, the home for bentgrass. Bentgrasses do so well in the humid Northwest that they're a natural even for playing fields.

The Northeast is mainly bluegrass country, often blended with fine fescues in shady situations and on sandy, infertile soils. Bluegrass does so well here that there's little point in settling for less. You can plant play areas to coarse field grasses such as tall fescue, but it's often winter-killed in northern states.

Since bluegrasses grow best in cool weather, fertilize heavily in autumn and lightly, to maintain color, in hot weather. They do best on rich, well-drained soil, limed to near neutral pH. Since they are very tolerant of pesticides you can use crabgrass preventives, or weed selectively with 2,4-D and dicamba.

For very low-mowed bowling and putting greens, or for moderately short fairway turf, you may have occasion to use bentgrass. Colonial bents such as Highland are fine for the latter. Use creeping bents such as Penncross for the former. Bents are heavy feeders and need the equivalent of a pound of nitrogen per thousand square feet each month during the growing season. Apply a fungicide from time to time, especially before winter, to protect against snowmold. The trailing stems of bentgrass tend to thatch, and occasional thinning (vertical mowing) is advisable in early autumn or spring.

THE HUMID SOUTHEAST. Southern grasses do well in hot, humid weather but become dormant in winter. In the South there are more weeds to contend with, a longer season (and consequently the need to fertilize more), and in general more pests and problems. Lawns on the sandy coastal plain need frequent watering and fertilizing, especially if a heavy feeder such as bermuda is used. Mow frequently—most southern grasses are rampant growers. Mow bermudas low, and others intermediate to high.

WESTERN PRAIRIES AND PLAINS. West from the humid regions, and all the way to the Sierra-Nevada-Cascade Mountains, arid country occurs where lawns are not possible without irrigation, except at mountainous elevations. With regular watering, however, you can have an exceptionally fine lawn in what is a predominantly bright, fairly weed- and disease-free environment. Cool night temperatures mean you can grow the northern lawngrasses as far south as middle Arizona. The same maintenance outlined in the section on the humid Northeast applies wherever bluegrasses or fine fescues are grown.

In arid country, however, watering is paramount. At least an inch of water per week during the main growing season is a must. If regular watering is not possible, you might try dryland grasses, such as wheatgrass (*Agropyron*) from Nebraska northward, and buffalograss (*Buchloë dactyloides*) from Kansas south.

THE ARID SOUTHWEST. This region extends from San Francisco southward and eastward into Texas. In the San Francisco Bay area, you can use northern grasses successfully, especially perennial ryegrass. At mountainous elevations, use a bluegrass-fine fescue combination, or a bentgrass. The interior valley is basically subtropical, so select southern species.

Southern California is a hodgepodge of microclimates, with the temperate grasses often as well adapted as the subtropical varieties. With conditions not favoring either group strongly, choice of a variety will depend on whether you will use the lawn most in the cool or warm months. Bluegrass blends do very well most of the year and generally survive the summer. Bermuda survives, but in most places becomes dormant in winter. It tends to play out in a few years and become full of winter weeds. Eastward from California (except at high elevations) bermuda does best, with overseeding of ryegrass in autumn if you want green turf during winter.

In Arizona and eastward, seeded bermuda is quite common. Southern California has Santa Ana (good color and smog resistance), Tifway, Sunturf, and Tifgreen. Newport bluegrass does well in California, as do Highland bentgrass and Fylking bluegrass for fairway turf.

Pests are often a problem in the Southwest. Your lawn will live longer if given protection against fungi and insects. The most wear-resistant grasses for the region are zoysia, bermuda, and tall fescue; Kentucky bluegrass, perennial rye, and red fescue secondarily. Bentgrasses and dichondra should not be used for play lawns here. Sunturf, Santa Ana, and U-3 are among the more wear-resistant bermudas.

Generally Recognized Grass Adaptations

Acid soils—Most species unless soil is very acid, especially bentgrasses in the North; centipede in the South.

Close mowing—Bentgrasses, and to an extent newer bluegrasses in the North; bermudas in the South.

Dry soil—Prairie grasses (in arid regions not irrigated); fescues.

Fast growing—Ryegrasses in the North; bermudagrasses in the South.

Hardy to cold—Bluegrasses, fine fescues and bentgrasses in the North; zoysias and many bermudas in the South.

Low fertility—Fescues in the North; centipede, and to some extent bahia, in the South.

Moist areas—Bentgrasses (including redtop) and rough bluegrass in the North; carpetgrass in the South.

Prone to disease and pests—Bentgrasses in the North; st. augustine in the South.

Quick sprouting—Ryegrasses.

Slow growing—Zoysias.

Stands shade—Fescues, rough bluegrass, and to an extent, other species in the North; st. augustine, to a large extent bahia, centipede, and zoysia in the South.

Strongly recuperative—Bluegrasses in the North; bermudagrasses and bahias in the South.

Tough to mow—Ryegrasses in the North; zoysias, and to some extent bahia, in the South.

Wears poorly—Rough bluegrass in the North.

COMMON MISCONCEPTIONS

PLANT A LAWN LIKE THE ONE BACK HOME. Families moving from region to region may long for the familiar type of lawn. A change to a different climatic zone, however, as when retired northerners move South, makes it mandatory that different grasses, or at least different management, prevail. Every region has several lawn choices; choose a climatically suitable grass that will not require burdensome care.

WHAT'S GOOD FOR ONE LAWN IS GOOD FOR ANOTHER. Each grass species has its own personality, and two grasses may be as unlike in behavior as are cats and dogs. For example, grasses that produce runners have special problems; bentgrasses mat, while bermuda runners are aggressive invaders of flower beds. Or a species with coarse leaves, such as tall fescue, can never have the attractive texture of bluegrass and the red fescues. In the same way, each species has its own particular growth pattern, seasons when it responds characteristically, and its own particular ability to persist under certain mowing heights or regimens of fertilization.

ALL GRASSES APPEAR MUCH ALIKE, SO IT DOESN'T MAKE A GREAT DEAL OF DIFFERENCE WHAT IS PLANTED. It is true that growing grasses, densely crowded and regularly mowed, show little obvious differences (other than in texture and color). But there is considerable difference in their adaptability to particular environments. Cultivars of the same species, such as Baron and Fylking bluegrasses, Highlight and Jamestown fescues, are the most closely related in the classification scheme, and could be expected to respond similarly to any particular kind of care. Species, however, are more distantly related (such as the colonial bentgrasses, *Agrostis tenuis,* and the creeping bentgrasses, *Agrostis palustris*); their needs, and their response to a given type of care can be expected to differ more pronouncedly than with cultivars. Genera are even more distantly related, such as the bluegrasses (*Poa*) and the fescues (*Festuca*), and can be expected to have even greater differences and show more distinctive responses.

THE GRASS I PLANTED HAS CHANGED ITS CHARACTERISTICS. This is impossible to any great extent, although sports or mutations can occur, with the mutants eventually dominating the grass population (Tifdwarf bermudagrass, for example, was a sport out of Tifgreen). In most cases where lawn characteristics change, however, the grass originally planted has unobtrusively died out and become replaced by volunteer grass of which seeds or live-starts were already present in the soil. In the southern portions of the bluegrass belt, for example, it is not uncommon for a lawn planted to Merion bluegrass to gradually change over to natural bluegrass without the change ever being especially noticeable. Or any lawn may have obscure components that stand out at certain seasons when the majority grass population languishes and the minority enjoys a spurt of growth (such as timothy in a bluegrass lawn in early summer).

4

planning the lawn

EACH LAWN is individualistic, in some respects totally unlike any other lawn. Minor changes occur even within a few short steps across any lawn. Becoming familiar with a lawn's personality is the key to both success and economy.

No lawn need be a burden, financially or in terms of the time you have to give to it. There are many choices of grass, and effective levels of maintenance. Keeping a lawn can be fun when one recognizes in the beginning that there are Fords as well as Cadillacs among lawns; a more luxurious ride is obtained at greater cost in a Cadillac, but either gets you where you are going quite well. One should attempt no more than is convenient, or than can be cared for with certainty. Few homes need, and fewer owners can afford, a golf green for a yard.

If it is to flourish, a lawn must fit the soil and the climate; perhaps even more important, its treatment should match requirements of the grasses chosen. No one grass or mixture is best. Some grasses—bents for example—require much more attention than others. A southern lawn will not employ the same grass as a northern one. A play area needs different handling from the fine lawn out front. In general, a lawn should be well laid out to avoid time-consuming tasks such as hand trimming. Even lawns on spacious suburban lots of an acre or more should not require more than an hour or two of attention a week, if well-adapted grass is planted and if the owner is adequately equipped (primarily with a good mower of optimum capacity, a sturdy spreader and sprayer, and a few familiar hand tools).

After determining a budget of time and money to be dedicated to the lawn, consider an appropriate grass mainstay. In climates offering multiple choice, this decision can be reinforced by checking neighboring lawns to see which grasses have thrived under approximately the same care you will expend. Keep in mind that, since most homeowners seldom mow, fertilize, and water as correctly as they might, most lawns, no matter what the grass, could look better than they do.

A bit of discretion will be needed in deciding which grasses have been successful locally. Simply asking the next-door neighbor does not always bring the answer, since few persons recognize the grasses in their lawn. They may have sown a ryegrass mixture and credit the lawn to that planting, when, in reality, volunteer Kentucky bluegrass from chance seed in the soil has become the mainstay. The portraits of the major lawn grasses in Chapter 3 will help you to recognize the grass population of a lawn.

When building a new home, one is usually confronted with a reality such as this. It takes planning to effectively transform such an area into a finished lawn and landscape.

Chief Southern Lawngrass Choices

	Adaptation	Care
Bahiagrass	For the deep South, especially useful for utility lawns that can receive only average care; colonizes sandy coastal soils well. Fairly coarse, establishing economically from seed.	No special problems, although its loose growth permits weed encroachment when mowed close. Does not need a great deal of fertility, and usually not pesticide treatment. Tolerant to 2,4-D weed killers, but not to arsonate crabgrass killers.
Bermudagrass	Fast-growing, spreading by rhizome and stolon, not true to type from seed. Seeded bermuda is widely used in the upper South, vegetative varieties (finer textured) for golf greens and other specialty turfs throughout the South.	Requires a high level of maintenance, with generous fertilization and frequent mowing, much like bentgrass. Will not stand shade. Quite tolerant of the usual herbicides.
Centipede	A "poor soil" grass, especially in the upper coastal plain, tolerating shade reasonably well, but temperamental about soil and fertility conditions.	Survives and even thrives under low maintenance, but usually resents alkalinity. Phenoxy herbicides should be used with care, and arsonate weed killers avoided. Live starts can receive simazine-type weed prevention.
St. Augustine	Much used in the deep South, noted for shade tolerance. More recently afflicted with chinchbug and many diseases. Inexpensive.	Becoming costly to care for, requiring frequent preventive sprays, especially for chinchbug in Florida and along the Gulf. Can't stand arsonates and phenoxy herbicides, but tolerant of simazine (new sprigging).
Zoysia	A widely tolerant group, some varieties winter-hardy in the North, but mainly used throughout the South for better quality turfs that can receive moderate attention. Very slow growing.	Maintenance is not onerous, but mowing is difficult (requiring heavy-duty equipment). Occasional thinning helpful. Tolerates usual lawn pesticides; weeds are serious only with new plantings (tight sod takes 2-3 years). Billbug attacks.

A Realistic Choice of Grass

One should neither expect the impossible, nor feel that a good lawn is overly temperamental in its requirements. For most lawns, sturdy grasses of proved worth can be selected, usually in a mixture to cover a wider range of conditions than those for which a single species might be adapted. Thus Kentucky bluegrass blended with red fescue varieties provides for open areas of good soil (bluegrass), and the shaded droughty spots under trees (red fescue). Bluegrass supplies the backbone for the majority of Northern lawns, helped by the compatible lawn fescues that fill those niches where bluegrass may be at a disadvantage.

In any region, the better lawngrasses will make a first-rate appearance under reasonable care. They will also be tenacious under neglect. For the North the bluegrass-red fescue combination is basic, with bentgrasses left largely to the coastal slopes of the Pacific-Northwest, or to especially humid habitats such as leeward of the Great Lakes and the Appalachian ridges. In the South, all types must be considered in relation to the particular conditions. (See the above table.)

Climatic Considerations

Missteps in lawn tending are usually more noticeable in the difficult middle latitudes from Missouri to Washington, D.C. More leeway exists with bluegrass lawns farther toward the North and with the semitropical grasses in the South.

Comparing southern locations with more northerly ones, there is a doubled-up influence of temperature. While everyone realizes that "average" temperatures are warmer as one goes southward, there is superimposed upon this a more pronounced daily maximum, which intensifies heat effects. There is also, obviously, a more prolonged hot season. Summers may be really tough in the South for grasses that like cool conditions. It is no wonder that they peter out quickly in Georgia and Alabama; that bluegrass loves the shade in Tennessee, but not in Minnesota.

Plentiful moisture is another obvious climatic influence, often determining which grasses persist and which weeds invade. For example, where rainfall is persistent, bentgrasses, bluegrasses, and clovers are favored. (The bents are especially happy in acid soils, the clovers in alkaline soils.) In the dry plains states, buffalograss may occur only in swales where water accumulates after infrequent rains; on higher,

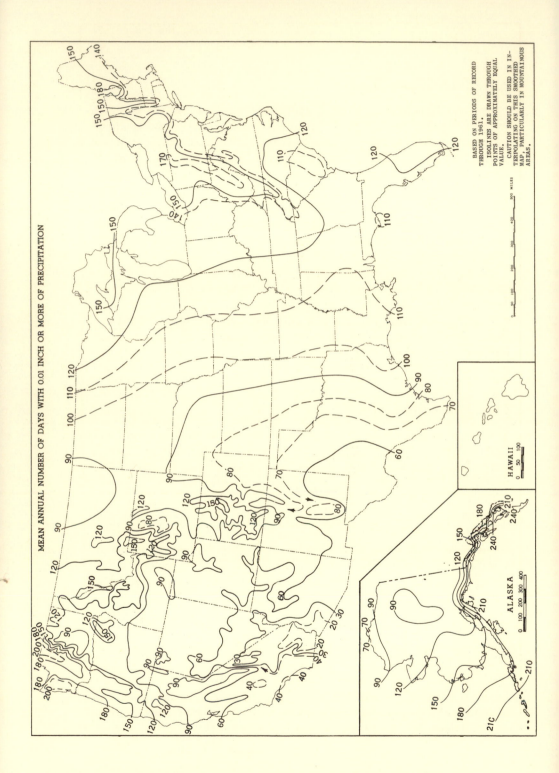

MEAN ANNUAL NUMBER OF DAYS WITH 0.01 INCH OR MORE OF PRECIPITATION

BASED ON PERIODS OF RECORD
THROUGH 1961.
ISOLINES ARE DRAWN THROUGH
POINTS OF APPROXIMATELY EQUAL
VALUE.
CAUTION SHOULD BE USED IN IN-
TERPOLATING ON THIS SMOOTHED
MAP, PARTICULARLY IN MOUNTAINOUS
AREAS.

HAWAII

ALASKA

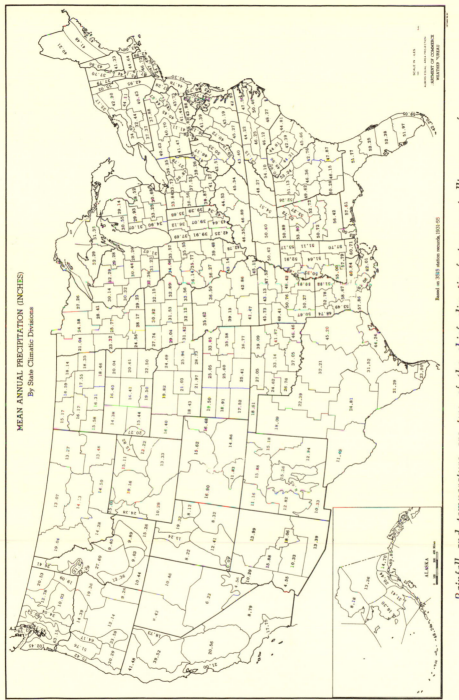

MEAN ANNUAL PRECIPITATION (INCHES)
By State Climatic Divisions

Rainfall and temperature are two of the chief climatic factors controlling ease of growing grass. Irrigation can substitute for rainfall, but summer temperatures (see page 54) limit success with northern grasses used in the South.

Based on 3515 station records, 1931-55

drier ground, other natural prairie grasses, better adapted to aridity, persist.

Total rainfall is not the only determining moisture factor. Evaporation and transpiration play important roles. The moisture that plants lose through their leaves increases greatly as sunshine and wind increase. A week of overcast, still weather may be worth an inch of rainfall. However, good air circulation is important to dry the grass blades quickly, and thus aid in the control of disease. This problem is often present on golf courses of creeping bentgrass that are made muggy by a dense surrounding of trees and shrubs.

The Climate at Lawn Level

Weather Bureau recordings are made at a height of five feet aboveground. That they do not necessarily reflect the problems where the grass is growing is evident from fragmentary research on lawn microclimate. One study in Tucson, Arizona, showed a temperature during the hottest part of the day of 109° F. at five feet; the soil temperature was 160°. Both soil and air remained over 100° for five hours. Certainly life at lawn level was under greater stress than human beings might have supposed.

Even clipping height makes a difference. In Missouri, average minimum soil temperature in late July was 91° in mowed turf; only 79° in unmowed sod. Bare soil reached 100°, while maximum air temperatures averaged about 90°. Watered areas were only a few degrees cooler; but bluegrass sod exhausted about half the total soil moisture (contained in bare ground).

While shade and slope directly control lawn temperature, by determining the quantity of sun rays striking a given area, they also have an indirect effect on the grass through their influence on watering. Shade, if uncomplicated by tree roots competing for water, conserves moisture. Slopes tend to shed water, since the run-off there is ordinarily greater and penetration less. A fine, loose mulch of clippings soaks up water before it can be lost; so too might a lawn that has been gone over with an aerator (a mechanical hole-punching machine).

Good Landscaping Is Helpful

A well-planned layout and proper tools help to make lawn care enjoyable. Intelligent landscaping prevents troubles or irritations that recur each time the lawn is tended. Eliminate blind corners and sharp banks that are not easily maneuvered with the mower. Avoid retaining walls against which a mower cannot clip closely (necessitating hand trimming). Plan a clean sweep of lawn, unmarred by obstructions. This makes possible continuous use of the mower in a straight path. Do away with mounds or depressions that become scalped or that accumulate water. Avoid using fences under which the mower will not fit.

In laying out shrub beds and borders it is always helpful to position them so that the mower can sweep around the edges without halting and backing (especially with the larger riding mowers). These graceful curves are usually preferable to sharp angles, with the long axis in the general direction of mowing rather than across it. In general, grasses and shrubbery don't mingle well and the grass becomes a weed if it spreads into border plantings. Since both grass and border plantings require their own particular modes of care, it is best to keep them separate and distinct by mechanical or chemical edging (see Chapter 11).

There may be other potential trouble spots. If foot traffic will inevitably cross the lawn from a door to the utility area or garage, recognize this shortcut from the beginning and establish a path of bricks, flagstones, or concrete. No grass can stand this continuous pounding. Similarly, on badminton courts, picnic areas, baseball diamonds, and the like, grass is bound to be worn away under continuous use. Either arrange for these facilities to be moved from time to time, allowing grass to recuperate, or put them in an out-of-the-way corner where the inevitable bare spots will not be an eyesore.

Do not be discouraged if your lawn is not immediately the most beautiful on the block. Building a good lawn takes time, especially with such slow-growing grasses as zoysia. In northern regions, bluegrass seedlings are slower to appear than the so-called "nursegrasses" such as ryegrass, redtop, or tall fescue, but they eventually make a superior lawn.

Trees in the Lawn

The roots of some plants have a repressing effect on neighboring plants. Perhaps the most familiar example is the influence of black walnut roots, through their secretion of juglone. Many plants, including fruit trees, may die within the zone of walnut root contact. Certain desert plants similarly hold the competition in check in an environment where water is scarce. There is speculation that grass influences grass; we know that quackgrass inhibits legumes such as alfalfa and that decomposing ryegrass may slow other plant growth. There may be many such subtle biological influences. Bluegrass, fortunately, is not bothered by walnut's juglone; in fact it seems to be benefited, perhaps because the competing species are then held in check under the walnuts.

Aside from the possibility of such secretions, trees and grass vie with each other in other ways. Only a small amount of grass occurred in primeval forests; there was neither sufficient light nor appropriate soil conditions. When man felled the forests and churned the duff, exposing mineral soil, grass came in. This does not mean that grass and trees cannot grow in harmony. They can, if the trees are not so thick that they cast complete shade or take moisture and plant food needed by the lawn.

Usually, trees amenable to trimming should be trimmed high to allow sunlight to filter through the branches to the grass. However, you wouldn't want to remove low branches of most evergreens, or of specimen trees such as beech. Enough fertilizer and water must be provided to supply the needs of both grass and tree. Light feeding at stepped-up intervals and heavier-than-usual watering may be needed throughout the growing season. With trees notorious for surface roots, such as elms and maples, weekly watering during drought and at least monthly feeding may be called for. While it is almost impossible to keep tree roots from mingling with grass, fertilizer applied to the surface will be garnered in sufficient measure by the grass before tree roots can get it.

Tree Leaves

Deciduous trees shed their leaves each autumn. Small leaflets, such as from locusts, seldom accumulate in smothering quantities. In open situations with only a few trees, the chances are that winds and normal wear will scatter tree leaves before they mat over the grass.

Where leaves accumulate in deep layers or heavy windrows, grass smothering can occur. The leaves may be raked, then hauled to the compost pile (preferable to burning). Many modern rotary mowers are equipped to chop fallen leaves into a loose mulch. The mower is run over leaves on the lawn, using the required attachment. The fragmented leaves then settle among the grass blades. If the layer of loose fragments is not over a couple of inches thick, it will settle down and decompose sufficiently before the next growing season to avoid smothering the grass. In fact, the organic contribution should benefit the lawn. Since most leaves have a high carbohydrate content, it is wise to scatter a nitrogenous fertilizer over the leaf mulch to prevent a deficiency of nitrogen during the time decay organisms and grass roots both need it.

Saving the Trees

When lawns are being made, care must be taken to protect tree roots during grading operations. If the soil is dug away from the roots, the life of the tree is in danger. An established tree can rarely withstand more than a few inches of additional soil piled over its root system.

If deep fill of one to three feet is necessary, it is the custom to construct wells around the tree. A layer of crushed stone and gravel is placed over the original soil level to permit air and moisture to reach the root system. Enough soil to maintain grass completes the fill outside the well. (Twelve inches of soil should be ample.) Construction of tree wells is expensive, and the soil fill may drain down into the graveled area and prevent air from reaching the tree roots. Local expectations of success and the value of the tree must guide one in determining whether or not a tree well is likely to save the tree and be economically worth the effort.

By the same token, in lowering the grade, not much surface soil (containing a large volume of tree roots) can be sacrificed without at least debilitating the tree. Better to leave soil mounded upward in a gentle contour toward the tree than drastically to cut away the root system. In such a contingency it may be preferable to sacrifice the tree or replant it elsewhere.

REGIONAL FOCUS

A well planned lawn should be at its peak the second and third years after planting. Lawns containing bentgrass, named varieties of bermuda, or other matting species, may need special attention to prevent their going downhill. Occasional thinning of such stoloniferous grasses, by vigorous raking before mowing, or with thinners and aerifiers, may become necessary. In fact, the grasses named need greater care in general—extra attention to feeding, watering, disease, and pest control, if they are to look attractive.

The familiar bluegrass-red fescue lawns in the North, common bermuda and centipede in the South, get along well with moderate attention. Fertilization should follow local needs, dictated by soil and climate. Where summers are abnormally warm for the northern grasses, such as in the border states, the bluegrass lawn should not be fertilized heavily in summer, and should be mown tall (preferably two to three inches with traditional bluegrass cultivars). Watering is not vital to the life of such a lawn (even if a bluegrass lawn turns brown, it will revive again when rains come). Watering is used to keep the lawn green during a drought, and remember that excessive watering and feeding in summer favors weeds more than lawngrasses.

At the latitude of Tennessee, and in the Piedmont from Georgia northeastward, lawnmakers may find it necessary to live with a combination of bermudagrass and bluegrass; it is difficult there to keep bermuda out of a lawn. Maintenance practices should favor the bluegrass—autumn seeding and autumn feeding, high mowing in summer; the bermuda will take care of itself.

In much of the South it is customary to overseed a bermuda lawn each autumn with northern winter grass. Most frequently, annual ryegrass is used, since it provides a big seed able to push a seedling through the declining bermuda. The new turf-type of perennial ryegrasses would be more attractive. Bluegrasses, red fescues, and bentgrasses can also be established in common bermuda, though it is difficult in the tighter growing forms and in zoysia.

COMMON MISCONCEPTIONS

TREE LEAVES, SUCH AS OAK LEAVES, ARE TOXIC. While some leaves may have soluble tannins that discolor walks and painted surfaces, seldom are these of sufficient strength to influence grass or soil. Oak leaves do not make soils acid, as is commonly supposed; the soils turn acid under conditions where oak trees normally grow. Don't worry that substances leached from leaves will harm your grass.

TREE SHADE PREVENTS GOOD GRASS. In very dense shade, such as beneath beech and maple trees with low branches, shade can limit grass growth; bermuda is not tolerant of shade. However, most grass can exist on a fraction of full sunlight. Where summers are especially hot, shade may be an advantage. Usually it is lack of fertility, or a combination of infertility and lack of moisture under trees, or increased disease in the shade rather than shade itself, that limits growth of grass. Providing fertility and moisture, and mowing the grass tall (so that it has added leaf to make up for less sunlight), should enable the growing of shade-tolerant turf under the usual lawn trees.

LAWN PLANNING NEEDS ONLY MINOR CONSIDERATIONS IN HOUSE BUILDING. The success of a lawn, indispensable for an attractive house, will depend upon how well the grass selected thrives in the environment provided. Seed should be as carefully chosen as any permament furnishing of the house, to fit the climate and the conditions discussed in subsequent chapters. Just as one wouldn't heat a modern house with a potbellied stove, neither would one surround it with a hayfield.

"IF I ONLY LIVED IN X LOCATION, I COULD HAVE A REALLY GOOD LAWN EASILY." Although some locations are more ideal than others for maintaining a lawn, all have some advantages and disadvantages—"the grass often looks greener on the other side of the fence." For example, total annual rainfall may look great for lawn keeping in a certain location on the map. But the map doesn't point out that the summers are longer and hotter there, and that more moisture is used; nor does it indicate whether the rain falls when it is needed in summer, rather than uselessly in winter; nor whether it falls infrequently as cloudbursts, rather than gently and more often (thus soaking into the soil rather than running off). "Ideal" climates may well have more weeds, more diseases, more winterkill, more burdensome mowing, and so on.

5

lawn soils

SELDOM DOES the lawnsman start with the rich, crumbly soil ideal for quickly developing a tight, uniform turf. Hauling in topsoil (the generally darker, organically rich, upper few inches of native ground) is expensive, and really good topsoil may not even be available. But knowledge of the native soil and ways to improve it make possible the building of a good lawn on almost any ground. Gradually, through the years the lawn itself will greatly improve its soil.

What Is Soil?

There is no standard mixture; soil differs all over the map. It is not like a chemical formula with exact amounts of known ingredients that can be mixed to specifications anywhere in the world. Not only do a variety of chance ingredients occur, but time, climate, history, and the various soil organisms enter into the picture.

Soil is tangible; a person can feel its particles. These are mostly decomposed rock fragments from which certain soluble components have been lost. The main ingredient can be imagined as rock dust. If the particles are relatively large, more than 1/500 of an inch in diameter, they are called *sand*, and a soil containing them is called a sandy soil. It feels gritty when smeared. Soil particles smaller than sand, but still large enough to settle out from water in an hour or so, are considered as *silt*. These typically smear as a rough, irregular surface. Very small soil particles, less than 1/10,000 of an inch, are termed *clay*. They produce a smooth, slick smear.

Seldom is a soil completely clay (or silt or sand), but even a modest fraction of clay particles mixed with silt produces a sticky substance most persons think of as clay. *Loams* are crumbly mixtures, not very sticky but not so quick to dry as sand; they usually contain a sizable percentage of silt particles. If we had our choice for good plant growth, loams would almost always be chosen.

In addition to rock fragments, most soils have an extremely important percentage of organic material, or *humus*. It may be as much as 7 per cent in good prairie loam, 3 or 4 per cent in Kentucky's bluegrass counties, or almost nonexistent in deserts, sandy coastal plains, or in the familiar subsoils exposed by excavations.

Humus is the great leavener of soils; it makes sandy soils more retentive of moisture and nutrients, and loosens sticky clays to a tillable consistency. It also feeds the soil organisms—billions of them in each teaspoonful of soil, and in themselves a living pool of fertility.

Classification of soils according to texture. Loams contain a balance of the primary textural types—clay, silt, and sand. The percentage of each of these components for the various categories of loam can be read by following the indicator lines to the percentage reading on each edge of the triangle.

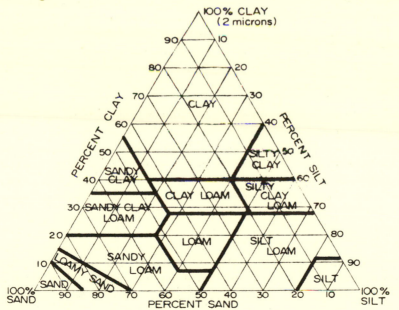

The soil you start with, whether good or poor, is a product of its history and environment. Planted with grass, most soils improve.

This is why composts, manures, and grass roots (old ones die as new are produced) improve soils so much. In an acre of bluegrass sod, there may be over three tons of roots, of which 2 per cent consists of nitrogen. Since half of the rootlets may die and be replaced each year, they become important builders of soil and reservoirs of nutrients.

Nature furnishes constant additions of organic matter wherever rainfall is adequate for the growth of plants whose parts will eventually decay. Decay releases both nutrients for more plant growth, and "gums" which aggregate the soil and hold it porous. Breakdown occurs more rapidly under warm temperatures than cool; southern soils are therefore likely to be lower in organic content (humus) than northern. Sandy soils generally contain little humus.

Soil Structure

Perhaps more important than the size of soil particles, or *texture*, is their *structure*, or the way they are held together. A soil with good structure has adhesive material binding the particles into clusters, so that the soil crumbles. A crumbly soil retains this structure even when wet, retaining pore space between the crumbs. Water penetrates readily, and as it drains it "sucks into" the pore passages air vital to roots. In soils of poor structure the particles slide past each other, compacting and eliminating most pore space. These soils soon become compact and impervious to water and air. The yellow, stunted appearance of plants after floods indicates what an airless, waterlogged environment for roots can do.

Soils with poor structure, even when fertile, do not produce thriving plants. A good soil should be nearly half solid soil particles, half pore space. A soil with appreciably less pore space than this will tend to waterlog, draining poorly. Organic matter, the leavener, supplies the aggregating gums that improve soil structure. It is in this way that grass builds the soil, as its minute rootlets work organic residues all through the upper layers. Witness the fertile prairies, deep with dark topsoil.

The bottom side of a Baron Kentucky bluegrass sod section. Note the good rooting (which makes the sod hang together so well), and the friable soil in the root zone.

Water Infiltration

Texture of Soil	Infiltration Rate, Inches of Water Soaking into Soil Per Hour		
	Level Ground	Moderate Slope	Steep Slope
Sand	1.0	0.5	0.3
Sandy Loam	0.5	0.3	0.2
Loam	0.25	0.18	0.12
Clay Loam	0.15	0.10	0.07
Clay	0.10	0.08	0.06

Soil texture and structure determine the ability of water to soak into the lawn quickly or slowly. Where infiltration is slow, most rain will be lost as runoff during heavy showers. Rapid infiltration is usually accompanied by rapid soil drainage, too, so such soils must be watered frequently. Of course, slope affects infiltration rate markedly.

Drainage and porosity are indirectly improved by organic matter, too, when it acts as a stimulus to beneficial soil organisms from bacteria to earthworms. A century ago Darwin realized that earthworm tunnelings may, little by little, churn fifteen tons of soil to the acre each year. Earthworms are most numerous in soils containing ample humus. A striking instance of the usefulness of earthworms in preventing excessive build-up of organic residues (thatch) at the soil surface under turf can be seen at Bingley, England (the British Sportsturf Institute). An area adjacent to where earthworms are normally active has been treated with arsenate for many years, eliminating the worms. The thatch there is detrimentally thick, but where the earthworms are active, organic residues have been consumed and mixed into the soil. The same has been found true in Illinois.

It has also long been realized that calcium (lime) improves the structure and porosity of soil. That is part of the reason for liming soils which are very acid. It also helps to explain the beneficial effect of gypsum (calcium sulfate) on the slaking alkali soils of arid climates, which are loaded with sodium instead of calcium.

Slaking soils have poor structure because the individual particles do not adhere, and are thus free to slide past each other, eliminating pore space. These soils "puddle" and "crust" at the surface. When watered, the unaggregated particles "melt" into a soupy mix that soon blocks all pores. When this dries, it may harden to such an extent that seedlings cannot push through the crust. Because it resists puddling longer, a pebbled surface is better for a seedbed than one which is finely pulverized.

Baron Kentucky bluegrass, noted for vigorous rooting and rhizoming. Here the root system of sod only a few months old has been brushed free of soil. These underground parts are great soil builders.

Natural Influences on Soil

Clayish soils typically shrink on drying, swell on wetting. This change can amount to as much as ten per cent of the soil volume. Alternate wetting and drying can be assumed to have a beneficial influence in loosening or "cultivating" the soil from within. The wetting-drying cycle also has a biological influence, causing weeds to sprout after wetting, then killing them in subsequent droughts that are not severe enough to bother the deeper-rooted perennial grass.

Natural soil cultivation is promoted even more by freezing and thawing. Frost churns soil to the depth of its penetration, undoing last summer's trampling. Many a football field would be less the domain of spurge and knotweed, which are favored by tight soils, if the mechanical benefits of winter freezing and thawing could somehow be extended through summer.

Man has endeavored to duplicate winter loosening by punching holes in the soil with aerating machines. Presumably the soil is thus bettered for roots—air and moisture penetrating deeper for root "breathing" and growth. Aeration also encourages microorganisms that break down organic materials to operate at a faster pace, thus releasing more nitrogen into the soil.

Soil Fertility

Although most of the elements required for the formation of plant tissue are abundant in air and water, many others are needed for plant growth, some in large quantities. More than a dozen elements must come from the soil, if only in minute amounts. Probably a great many others are also essential, but in such small quantities as to be undetectable at present.

The nutrient elements of major importance are nitrogen (N), phosphorus (P), and potassium (K). Nitrogen fluctuates with the organic content of the soil; the phosphorus available to plants is usually 0.03 per cent to 0.1 per cent; potassium ranges from almost nothing in leached soils to 2.5 per cent in good prairie loam. These major nutrients are always given in percentages in N-P-K order on fertilizer bags, as required by law. Thus when a fertilizer analysis reads 20-10-5 it signifies 20 per cent nitrogen, 10 per cent phosphorus (usually as the oxide P_2O_5), and 5 per cent potassium (as the oxide K_2O). The remaining 65 per cent, known as the carrier, is considered inert, although it often contains valuable secondary nutrients such as calcium, sulfur, or magnesium.

Even though they may be called secondary and presumed adequate in most soils, calcium, sulfur, and magnesium are used by plants in appreciable quantities. Certain other elements such as copper, cobalt, manganese, zinc, molybdenum, chlorine, and iron are required in such small amounts that they are termed *trace elements*. In some instances, a trace element such as iron may be "tied up" by a soil imbalance, as under high alkalinity in the western prairies, or on limed centipede lawns in the South. This means that the element is in the soil, but not available to the plants. The iron probably can be freed more effectively by improving acidity than by adding iron salts. Chelated compounds, such as those of iron, can be sprayed on trace-element-deficient plants as a fairly lasting source of the missing minor element.

Phosphorus may become tied up on very acid or very alkaline soils. It seems paradoxical that on certain soils phosphorus, as with trace elements, can be made available to plants by adding lime or sulfur rather than more phosphate. Balance counts for more than nutrient quantity. Even at an ideal degree of acidity, phosphorus is "fixed" in insoluble forms in the soil; surface applications work down through the soil column at a snail's pace, in contrast to the ready penetration of most nitrogen and potassium.

The interaction of soil particles with organisms and the various

These crocks illustrate the great difference soil can make: crock 18 has grass planted in subsoil; crock 19, in topsoil, both samples taken from the same hole. Subsoil can be greatly improved with fertilizer, etc.

nutrient elements is so complex that even experts are not certain what goes on. How nutrients are held and released by clay particles, substituted one for the other—as when calcium and potassium are released by the hydrogen of organic acids created by plant growth—is too involved to detail here.

As a rule, soils with a high percentage of humus and small particles such as clay are very reactive because of the tremendous total particle surface to which nutrients can fasten. It has been estimated that a thimbleful of clay would have an internal surface equivalent to many

Soil Nutrients Utilized by Kentucky Bluegrass
(based upon two tons of dry clippings per acre).

These minerals are essential for plant tissue formation, and even
those normally occurring in very limited amounts are vital
to plant physiology.

Nutrients	Lbs. Per Acre
Nitrogen	60.00
Phosphorus	20.00
Potassium	60.00
Calcium	16.00
Magnesium	7.00
Sulfur	5.00
Copper	0.02
Manganese	0.30
Zinc	0.08

square miles. The larger the internal surface, the greater the possible reservoir of nutrients. Hence sandy soils can be expected to need fertilization more frequently than clays and loams, since they hold nutrients neither so voluminously nor so long.

The importance of proper balance has already been mentioned. Too much of an element is almost as disastrous as too little. If the crop growth is continuously stimulated with a single nutrient, such as nitrogen, without replenishment of others, deficiencies are likely to show up in later years; that is, unless the elements are replaced through organic accumulations (such as clippings left on the lawn), or complete fertilizers that contain all major nutrients plus accessory ones in the carrier. Of course, organic fertilizers, composts, or the grass clippings left on the lawn all return the very things that were extracted from the soil to make plant tissue. Fertilizers also tend to have an acidifying influence.

Soil deficiencies can often be detected by the appearance of the plants. The most common deficiency with grass, lack of nitrogen, is indicated by slow-growing yellowish plants, although iron deficiency may have somewhat similar symptoms in the alkaline plains or on light soils in the South. Clover may suffer from lack of molybdenum, and other plants, from low zinc in the Coastal Plain; but by and large, deficiency diseases other than occasional iron troubles are not reported

A good way to improve soil structure is to mix in organic additions such as compost or peat. Porosity is generally increased and grass roots grow deeper.

for lawns. Lawnmakers are fortunate that good lawngrasses are not prima donnas.

Soil Tests

A number of commercial companies and state agricultural colleges offer soil-testing services. The homeowner can also procure kits to make his own analysis. Most soil tests give satisfactory indications of phosphorus and potash abundance. Nitrogen readings are rather meaningless, since nitrogen is steadily exhausted and will always prove an advisable addition to the lawn.

One of the simplest soil tests is for acidity or alkalinity. This reads as pH, a scale based upon the logarithm of the acid ions. 7 is neutral: numbers lower than 7 indicate acidity, and above 7 alkalinity. A soil measuring as low as pH 5 is quite acid, and above 8 unusually alkaline. Generally best for most grasses is a pH between 6 and 7, although lawngrasses are tolerant of a wide pH range. Bent, centipede, and carpetgrass tolerate considerable acidity; Kentucky bluegrass, bermudas, zoysia, and the fescues do best in mildly acid or neutral conditions. As a general rule, if the pH tests lower than 6, liming is in order. If the pH is as high as 8, acidifying fertilizers or an application of sulfur or gypsum should be helpful. Centipedegrass is unusual in preferring acid conditions, pH 4.0–6.0. On neutral or alkaline soils it frequently becomes blanched (chlorotic) from lack of iron.

A side influence of low pH is that acid soils favor other fungi over bacteria. Since bacteria are the notable nitrogen fixers in the soil, liming acid soils may well help improve nitrogen fertility.

REGIONAL FOCUS

Soils vary with climate. From Manitoba and Texas, east to the Atlantic Coast, enough rainfall occurs to soak through the soil, washing away soluble materials. In general, the eastern part of this zone has more regular rainfall, with greater leaching and more impoverished acid soils, at least in the uplands. As a whole, the region was characterized by forests when white men first came. Forest soils are typically low in fertility, soluble nutrients having washed out; in many areas they are also of poor structure through loss of organic matter, or irregular deposition of clay-like components in the soil profile. Yet, with some attention, most forest soils are very productive, as witness the eastern and southern Piedmont and the Ohio drainage system west of the mountains. Mostly they require lime, fertilizer, and care to avoid structural breakdown from tilling when wet; they improve under grass when encouraged by generous fertilization.

Within this humid zone are intergrading subdivisions. Soils of Canada and the most northerly states accumulate more organic reserves. Since warm weather, the stimulus for biological activity, is less intense and briefer there, grass needs somewhat less fertilizer and water. Southern soils have been subjected to more severe decomposition, resulting in red and yellow oxides and low organic content. Southern lawns, helped as they are by favorable growing weather, support grass well, and with attention readily build up the soil.

From the Mississippi Valley westward the climate becomes progressively drier, the land having been originally in prairie grass rather than forest. Not enough rainfall occurs to leach away fertility from the rich topsoil, which is generally of good structure. Lack of consistent rainfall is all that restricts excellent plant growth here. This is largely overcome by irrigation of lawns.

Sometimes high alkalinity occurs in arid climates where surface evaporation is great and salts rise in the capillary water. Then good soil structure may fade, producing some of the adobes or alkali soils. This is especially characteristic of the deserts and basins west of the Rockies. It often becomes necessary to apply acidifying chemicals such as sulfur and gypsum, and to irrigate thoroughly to leach away excessive salts.

From San Francisco Bay northward along the coast, there is again a humid zone. Here, the greatest rainfall on the continent originally produced tremendous forests. Conditions are analogous to those of the humid East, with regular rainfall making grass-growing easy when the soils, impoverished through leaching, are limed and fertilized. Across the mountains into eastern Oregon and Washington the conditions are like those of the plains or desert.

COMMON MISCONCEPTIONS

THE LAWN SOIL SHOULD BE LEVELED BY ROLLING. Rolling when the soil is wet, or with a very heavy roller, can compact the soil, causing harm. If the soil surface is uneven or pitted, a surer way of correcting the trouble is to scatter weed-free or sterilized soil (top dressing), no thicker than one-fourth of an inch at a time. This will sift into the depressions. Most grass that heaves because of frost in winter settles back into the soil; in any event root breakage has already occurred, and smashing the plant back into the ground will be of little help.

THE SOIL IS TERRIBLE; A GOOD LAWN IS OUT OF THE QUESTION. Seldom is any soil completely perfect—or useless. Learning the major soil deficiencies and coping with them should permit an excellent lawn without bringing in topsoil. Lawns on difficult soils may need a little extra attention, as discussed in subsequent chapters, but they are far from impossible.

THE LAWN SHOULD BE LIMED EACH SPRING. Not unless a pH test or other reliable signs indicate so. Where soils are already neutral or alkaline, this might upset soil balance, making other nutrients unobtainable by the grass. Also, some lawngrasses (centipede, carpet, bent) prefer acidity, so that liming favors the weeds instead of the grass.

TOPSOIL IS A CURE-ALL. The structure of topsoil is usually better than that of subsoil, and its fertility is perhaps greater (but not enough so to avoid fertilization). But topsoil is generally full of weed seeds that may be more trouble to fight than it would be to build up the relatively weed-free subsoil through frequent fertilization, liming if needed, and perhaps the mixing-in of amendments such as organic materials (e.g., peat, compost, treated manure or sewerage, etc.). Sometimes infertile (but dark-colored) muck is peddled as topsoil: it is essentially worthless and apt to be weedy. If you buy topsoil, check its source, and be aware of the weed hazard.

6

lawngrass seed

SEEDS CONDENSE a whole generation of plant life into a minute dormant fragment, capable of wide travel before it grows into a new plant. The seed carries concentrated food to launch the new seedling. (Man avails himself of this food when he eats wheat, corn, beans, peas.) The small living embryo in the seed is quiescent until proper temperature, moisture, and access of air pronounce the time ripe for bursting through the leathery seed coat to strike root.

In some seeds the coats are nearly impervious, requiring many days of soaking before the embryo is stimulated. Other seeds apparently carry inhibitors that must undergo aging or chemical modification before the embryo can be released from its sleep. Seeds have lain dormant for decades, even centuries, without loss of viability, while awaiting favorable sprouting conditions. On the other hand, many seeds, especially if they were not sufficiently dried before storage, lose viability in relatively few days. That is why seed producers must take pains in the curing, cleaning, and warehousing of seed. Years of experience have demonstrated individual requirements and the need for precise laboratory testing and retesting of germination as the seed progresses through commerce.

Nature's scheme for perpetuating species by seed is man's convenience. The easiest way to establish a lawn is by seed. The planting of lawns from sprigs or plugs is much more expensive and laborious.

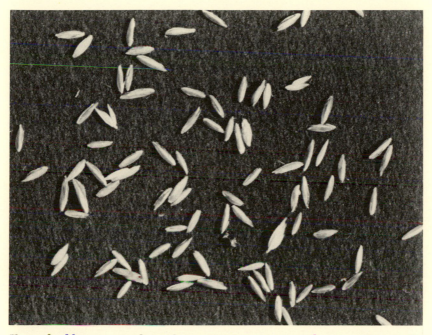

Kentucky bluegrass seeds as they come to market, nearly two million to the pound.

When one plants cuttings, the same hereditary characteristics are perpetuated in the new grass as were in the old. This is simple asexual propagation, of the sort familiar in "slipping" a geranium or in budding or grafting fruit trees and roses. But when seed is formed there is usually some hereditary change. This is because a male cell (pollen), from the anthers of the small grass flowers, reaches the female portion of the flower, the pistil. In the majority of grasses, this union of pollen with the egg of the pistil results in seed with the mixed heredity of two parents. Thus, most grass seeds convey unpredictable minor variations that would not occur if the same grass were reproduced from sprigs or plugs.

A few lawngrasses, notably Kentucky bluegrass, do not necessarily require fusion of sexual cells. The pistil produces a viable seed without direct contribution from the pollen. On the average, about 85 per cent of bluegrass seed develops this way, and such offspring should be identical with the female parent. The other 15 per cent would be expected to show the typical reassortment of characteristics that comes with sexual reproduction. Because of the limited sexuality in bluegrass,

Good sprouting from a bluegrass seed lot of excellent quality.

it is possible to perpetuate desirable selections if any off-types are eliminated (rogued) in the fields; one would then feel fairly confident that in future seed the parent variety would predominate. Whether this is entirely desirable for grass seed will be discussed shortly.

Approximate Number of Seeds Per Pound of Lawn Grass

	Millions of Seeds Per Lb.*	Suggested Lawn Seeding Rate Lbs./1,000 sq. ft.
Bahia	0.17	4–5
Bent, Colonial	8.50	1–2
Bermuda	1.80	2
**Bluegrass, Kentucky	2.20	2
Bluegrass, rough	2.50	2
Buffalo	0.06	variable
Carpet	1.30	3–5
Centipede	0.41	few ounces
Fescue, red	0.62	3–4
Fescue, tall	0.23	6–8
Redtop	5.00	1–2
Ryegrass	0.23	4–6
Wheatgrass, Fairway	0.32	4–6
Zoysia	1.30	1
Clover, white	0.70	1–2
Lespedeza, Korean	0.23	4

* According to W. A. Wheeler and D. D. Hill, **Grassland Seeds**, New York, D. Van Nostrand, 1957.

** Newer cultivars of Kentucky bluegrass selected for seedling vigor (which is encouraged by large seed with much stored food) may have only half this figure.

Seed size varies greatly among the grasses. Size, of course, determines the number of seeds in each pound. The accompanying table gives seed numbers per pound for the major grasses. It is obvious that, should certain kinds be inexpensive by the pound, it does not necessarily follow that they are economical by the seed. For example, with Kentucky bluegrass seeds almost ten times as abundant per pound as are ryegrass, each seed (or potential plant in a lawn) would be only half as expensive, even were the price per pound five times as much. The spread is even greater with bentgrass.

Seed technologists are able to recognize different seeds quite readily. They are even able to distinguish many varieties or cultivars, such as natural Kentucky bluegrass from Merion. The homeowner need not learn to recognize seeds, since the law requires their accurate listing on every seed package. Authorities sample marketed seed to see that labels and information tags are reliable.

Buying Seed

Most lawn seed is sold in attractively packaged, convenient units. The average purchaser, lacking the familiarity with seeds that his rural ancestors may have had, relies upon the packager for choice and quality. Lawngrasses of quality cannot be mass-produced as conveniently as high-yielding grains and agricultural grasses; the cost of lawngrass seed by the pound is usually more. Unfortunately, the human tendency to shop for the lowest price has forced seedsmen, who would rather do otherwise, to sell "cheap" seed mixtures.

Although the picture on the seedbox may be most attractive, results will depend upon the kinds of seeds inside, and may be entirely unrelated to the picture. The only way to be certain of a satisfactory seed mix is to look for the ingredient listing that is required on the package. Species appropriate for the climate, as discussed in Chapters 3 and 4, should predominate. If the mixture contains very little of the permanent grasses and much annual ryegrass or coarse bunchgrass, it may not be worth planting. Under budget restrictions it is better to get a smaller amount of quality grass than heaps of a worthless mixture.

The seed listing on the package shows not only the different types of grass contained, by weight percentage, but also the germination percentage, purity, and weeds. None of these is as serious a consideration as is the proper choice of grass. Weeds, for example, are so restricted by law and so thoroughly removed in seed cleaning that few troublesome ones are ever packaged. Weeds in a lawn almost always

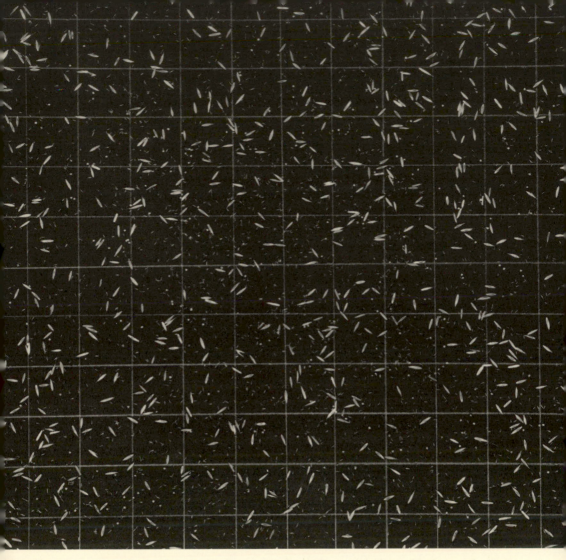

Distribution of a seed mixture at about three pounds to the thousand square feet. The grid is marked in square inches. The large seeds are fescue and ryegrass, the small, elongate ones, redtop, and the small, round ones, clover. This would be a very poor choice for a lawn, although acceptable for roadsides in some locations.

result from residual seed in the soil or chance introductions, rather than introduction with the lawngrass. As a matter of fact, the weeds typically harvested along with the seed are almost always field species that stand little chance of survival in a mowed turf. Naturally, the smaller the weed content, the better; but the selection of grass type is more important, for one is, in effect, planting weeds if he plants undesirable grasses.

Germination and purity figures are more for the trade than a clue to the consumer. Seed is sold according to germination standards accepted by the seed trade, and usually formalized in state requirements. Seed on the retail shelf is subject to checking by control officials. Some grasses normally carry a higher designation than others, but the consumer may take for granted that the germination will be satisfactory, or the seed will not reach the seed-store shelf. The same is true of purity. This designation merely signifies the number of living seeds of the *specified grass*, as against the *chaff* and superfluous seeds termed "crop."

Crop content can be a serious cause for concern. Permitted for listing as crop without specific identification, if in very small percentage, are various perennial grasses useful (or at least not harmful) in the farm pasture, but which can be quite a pest in a lawn because of their coarse, weedy appearance. Timothy, orchardgrass, tall fescue, bromegrass, annual ryegrass,—even redtop and rough bluegrass where they are not wanted—are typical examples. Along with such "weeds" as annual bluegrass, velvetgrass, quackgrass, and nongrasses, such as nutsedge and wild onion (which may or may not have to be named as weeds, depending upon the particular state seed law), these are the most serious "weeds" likely to be introduced in lawn seed. Plant species that are weeds by state seed law are usually not so serious as crop, because noxious ones cannot similarly pass unnoticed. In any event they seldom persist in mowed turf and most are easily controlled with herbicides.

Almost all states require retesting of seed for germination, usually at nine-month intervals. Unless the seed has been badly mishandled, germination is unlikely to fall off appreciably. Major grass seeds are long-lived. Once moisture in Kentucky bluegrass is reduced to around 7 per cent—or 10 per cent in red fescues—germination seems to be well stabilized. Properly stored, Kentucky bluegrass can be held for many years with little or no loss of viability. As a matter of fact, germination usually rises the second year. Red fescues are a little more sensitive to high temperatures, especially in a moist atmosphere. But if seed is sufficiently dry, as it normally is at retail, neither freezing nor moderate heat harms it. If it becomes damp, sprouting may be initiated, a one-way road on which there is no return. Seed is best stored in ventilated locations where humidity and internal heat cannot build up.

Other things being equal, the heavier the seeds, the better their germination and the more vigorous the young seedlings. Thus Kentucky bluegrass that weighs 26 pounds to the bushel should start faster

Prominent "Weeds" that Occur in Commercial Lots of Lawn Seed, According to Species and Percentage of Lots in which Recorded (from Seed Technology Sampling).

	Bluegrass	Fine Fescue	Bentgrass	Ryegrass	Redtop	Tall Fescue
No. Samples	777	335	478	90	55	46
Dicotyledons						
Buttercup	—	—	—	6%	—	—
Cat's-ear	—	4%	—	—	—	—
Chickweed, Common	0.5%	—	—	—	—	—
Chickweed, Mouse-ear	5%	—	24%	—	5%	—
Cresses (Cruciferae), misc.	0.8%	—	—	2%	—	2%
Dandelion	2%	2%	—	—	—	—
Dock	1%	—	0.6%	8%	—	26%
Hawkweeds	—	—	0.2%	—	—	—
Henbit or Dead-nettle	0.7%	—	—	—	—	—
Lambs-quarters	0.4%	—	—	—	—	—
Lespedeza	—	—	—	—	—	2%
Pigweed	0.1%	—	—	—	—	—
Pineapple-weed	0.4%	—	2%	—	—	—
Plantain, Broadleaf & Narrow	2%	—	1%	—	16%	2%
Sheep Sorrel	4%	5%	—	9%	—	9%
Shepherd's-purse	5%	0.3%	4%	—	—	—
Speedwell or Veronica	2%	—	6%	—	—	—
Verbena	0.1%	—	—	—	—	—
Vetch (Vicia)	—	—	—	1%	—	—
Winter Cress (Barbarea)	—	—	—	—	—	2%
Yarrow or Milfoil	0.1%	—	—	—	100%	—
Wood Sorrel (Oxalis)	0.1%	—	—	—	—	—
Monocotyledons						
Annual Bluegrass	20%	2%	3%	17%	—	—
Barleys (Hordeum)	—	3%	—	4%	—	2%
"Bentgrass" (Agrostia)	8%	10%	—	1%	—	—
Bromes & Chess, Various (Bromus)	1%	14%	—	28%	—	80%
Goosegrass	0.1%	—	—	—	—	—
Orchardgrass	4%	15%	—	2%	—	78%
Quackgrass	—	1%	—	—	—	—
Rushes (Juncus)	—	—	22%	—	20%	2%
Sedges (Cyperaceae)	6%	2%	—	—	25%	26%
Tall Fescue	0.4%	4%	—	9%	—	—
Timothy	6%	0.3%	1%	1%	75%	7%
Velvetgrass	7%	11%	20%	42%	—	2%
Wild Onion	—	—	—	—	—	9%

Contaminants Sometimes Carried in Lawn Seed, But Not Overly
Serious Because They Tend To Disappear Naturally.

I Prominent lawn weeds

Common Name	Botanical Name
ox-eye daisy	Chrysanthemum leucanthemum
popcornflower	Plagiobothrys hispidulus
ragwort or groundsel	Senecio
scorpionweed	Allocarya
snapdragon	Antirrhinum
sneezeweed	Helenium
sowthistle	Sonchus
spurry	Spergularia rubra
sweet clover	Melilotus
trefoil	Lotus uliginosus

Common Name	Botanical Name
(a) Dicotyledons	
buttercup	Ranunculus
lamb's-quarters	Chenopodium
lespedeza	Lespedeza
pigweed	Amaranthus
vervain	Verbena
vetch	Vicia
wood sorrel	Oxalis
(b) Monocotyledons	
rushes	Juncus

(b) Monocotyledons

Common Name	Botanical Name
alkaligrass	Puccinellia
beardgrass	Polypogon monspeliensis
bluegrass, big	Poa ampla
bluegrass, bulbous	Poa bulbosa
bluegrass, Canada	Poa compressa
bluegrass, woods, etc.	Poa nemoralis, P. palustris, P. scabrella, etc.
bristly dogs-tail	Cynosurus
calamagrostis	Calamagrostis
fescue, meadow	Festuca elatior
fescues, various annuals	F. myuros, F. octoflora, etc.
fescues, various perennial	F. capillata, etc.
hairgrass, silver	Aira
hairgrass	Deschampsia
junegrass	Koeleria
mannagrass	Glyceria
needlegrass	Stipa
poverty oatgrass	Danthonia spicata
sedges, various	Cyperaceae
vernalgrass	Anthoxanthum
water foxtail	Alopercurus geniculatus
windgrass	Apera

II Additional species sometimes contained in lawn seed

(a) Dicotyledons

Common Name	Botanical Name
avens	Geum
bedstraw	Galium
black-eyed susan	Rudbeckia hirta
burnet	Sanguisorba
campion, white	Lychnis alba
catchfly	Silene
chervil	Chaerophyllum
cinquefoil	Potentilla
corn cockle	Agrostemma
deptford pink	Dianthus armeria
downingia	Downingia
fiddleneck	Amsinckia
fireweed	Epilobium
flax	Linum
fleabane	Erigeron
hawksbeard	Crepis
hedgehyssop	Gratiola
hedge parsley	Torilis
jagged chickweed	Holosteum umbellatum
klamath weed	Hypericum
lettuce, wild	Lactuca
mullein	Verbascum

than seed weighing 21 pounds. There is more food, more charge, in the heavier seed, and less chaff. The less chaff weeds, and crop the better. High-quality seed has been thoroughly cleaned, with only a small percentage of "inert" materials (chaff and dust), and a fraction of a per cent of weeds and crop, remaining.

Seed Treatments

Occasionally lawn seed is dusted or coated with a fungicide. This is done more often to protect the sprouts when they appear than to protect the seed during storage. Undoubtedly seed disinfectants control any harmful fungi that may be present, but it is doubtful that such treatment would be worthwhile on home lawns. In almost all instances good germination will result from ample sown good seed. Seedling diseases (damping off) are infrequent, and are carried in the soil rather than by the seed (an exception perhaps being *Pythium* attack on ryegrass used for winterseeding in the South). Seed treatments used for farm-crop seeds, such as mercurial compounds sometimes found to be hazardous to the environment, are not utilized for lawn seed.

There have been attempts to hasten grass seed sprouting. Again, nothing very practical has been found. Some of the slower varieties, notably Merion Kentucky bluegrass, have been started indoors, then planted outside. The seed is mixed with damp soil, vermiculite, peat, or some other suitable medium, or is simply piled loosely in a polyethylene bag after soaking. Warm indoor temperatures speed sprouting. Kentucky bluegrass may be swollen and ready to sow outdoors in a few days. Seed in which sprouting has been initiated must be sown within a few days, no matter what the outdoor weather. The procedure can bog down in mud; and even under the best of circumstances there will be a lot of extra handling, as well as difficulties in sowing damp seed.

The Lawn Institute has undertaken tests to determine whether or not preliminary soaking of seed, and then drying, would prove helpful; or whether washing the seed with solvents such as alcohol and gasoline might remove any inhibitors. Neither seems advantageous. It is surprising that bluegrass seed will survive many days immersed in water. A fair percentage of seed held as long as three weeks under water still germinated.

Gibberellins and other growth regulators have been effective in stimulating growing plants, but have offered almost no advantage as seed treatment. Dusting or soaking in gibberellin solution does not hasten germination of good seed much beyond that obtainable with adequate moisture and temperature. In certain instances, as when moisture was barely enough to trigger sprouting, the gibberellins did seem to make a difference. However, it appears that sowing good seed in a well prepared seedbed with a mulch is still the most practical way to start a lawn.

Essentials for Sprouting Grass Seeds

There are three essentials for seed sprouting: warmth, moisture, and air. Air is assured by shallow sowing in a tilled seedbed. Moisture can be regulated, rainfall failing, by sprinkling and mulching; continuous humidity is needed for quickest sprouting. Thus it is usually temperature that determines germination rate.

Not all grasses respond alike to temperature. Some have far higher requirements than others for initiating any sprouting at all. Southern grasses and crabgrass will not germinate until late spring, when the soil warms to around 60° F.

By contrast, northern grasses, such as Kentucky bluegrass, red fescue, and bentgrass, will sprout (slowly) when temperatures are not much above freezing. Tests at the Lawn Institute showed appreciable sprouting in Kentucky bluegrass in about five weeks when temperatures were constantly below 50° F. At higher temperatures (86° alternating with 60°), the same seed sprouted in five days. There is no hard-and-fast demarcation, but it is obvious that bermudas and crabgrass will not sprout when weather is cool. In contrast, the familiar northern species may sprout almost any time, although much more rapidly when days are moderately warm.

The better lawngrasses tend to sprout and grow somewhat more slowly than the usual constituents of inexpensive seed mixtures. An impatient homeowner feels he is "getting something for his money" when ryegrass and redtop show green in half the time it takes Kentucky bluegrass to sprout. But quick sprouting is no indication of permanence; it is usually the opposite. One of the easiest ways to set back permanent grasses is to include a sizable proportion of fast-sprouting nursegrasses in a seed mixture. These usurp the space, nutrients, and water, giving the slower red fescues and Kentucky bluegrass little chance to take hold. Such aggressive, short-lived species might more appropriately be termed "robber grass" or "smother grass" rather than nursegrass. Fortunately, with newer emphasis on mulching, nurse species are seldom needed for their main role of stabilizing soil.

Seed Sprouting Rates

Seed	Rate of Sprouting	Ideal Temperature, F.	Visible Seedling Stand (under ideal conditions*) in Days
Bluegrass	Medium-slow	60° Night, 75° Day	15
Fine Fescue	Medium	60° Night, 75° Day	10
Bentgrass, colonial	Medium-slow	60° Night, 75° Day	15
Bentgrass, creeping	Medium	60° Night, 75° Day	12
Ryegrass	Fast	60° Night, 75° Day	6
Tall Fescue	Medium-fast	60° Night, 75° Day	8
Bermuda, de-hulled	Medium (unhulled seed— slow)	68° Night, 95° Day	12
Centipede	Slow	68° Night, 95° Day	barely visible early
Bahia	Medium-fast	80° Night, 95° Day	8
Zoysia	Slow (unless acid- treated)	68° Night, 95° Day	15

* Under unfavorable conditions, such as low temperature not much above freezing, sprouting goes on so slowly that months may be required before there is much "show of green."

Some seeds, such as buffalo and bermuda, can be purchased either with or without hulls. When the seed has hulls, sprouting is delayed, since moisture must soak through this coating and the seedling break out. For faster sprouting, say to get the jump on weeds in the spring, seed without hulls may be preferable. Naturally it is going to cost more, for in addition to the labor of dehulling, there will be many more seeds in a pound.

Some seeds cannot be mechanically dehulled, but can have the seed coat "burned" away by dipping in acid. This can be done with zoysia to aid sprouting.

Zoysia is one of the slower types, and much of the seed will lie dormant for many weeks. Bahia is a reasonably fast sprouter for the South, as are the legumes such as lespedeza and white clover. Buffalo and bermuda are among the fastest sprouters when dehulled.

With northern seeds, the coarse, impermanent species are among the fastest sprouting; fine fescues, rough bluegrass, and bentgrasses are more or less intermediate. Kentucky bluegrass, although hardly any slower under favorable conditions, is usually considered a slow starter. Some of the newer varieties (Fylking, Baron) have been touted for quicker sprouting, while Merion is notoriously slow.

The Advantages of Variability

In earlier paragraphs it was pointed out that natural stands of grass, unselected for uniformity, tend to perpetuate variability through at least a percentage of sexual crossing during seed formation. Much seed used to come from semiwild stands, consisting of plants that had survived unpampered through the decades. Kentucky bluegrass harvested from the pastures of Kentucky and the western district (Missouri north into Canada) is of this sort. It contains a great many slightly variable types.

From time to time, man singles out selections or deliberately makes crosses and isolates superior plants from the progeny. Thus Merion Kentucky bluegrass, and the many other varieties listed in Chapter 3, were chosen because someone felt they provided certain advantages. This is much the same process by which new varieties of wheat, oats, or other agricultural crops are chosen. The selected variety is then perpetuated in isolation, away from grass of the same species that may tend to cross with it.

In lawngrass, however, the situation is not quite parallel to that in crops. With agriculture there is a need for complete uniformity, so that all of the crop can be harvested with the same machinery at the same time, and have like chemical characteristics for marketing and processing. For grass in a lawn there are advantages to variability. Any lawn has a tremendous range of microenvironments, small and subtle differences due to slopes, shade or sun, mowing variations, fertilizer and watering discrepancies, slight depressions or mounding, better or poorer soil pockets, tree-root competition, and traffic. With such variability, does it not make sense to sow an array of similar but genetically varying grasses, presuming that at least some will be adapted to localized differences? All turf should not then be susceptible to a single disease and succumb to an epidemic.

This is one of the more compelling reasons for including broadly adapted and proved species, as the hard core of a marketed seed mixture, perhaps embellished by varieties of special attribute. A single selection offers greater risk; it may go along nicely for a few years, until new diseases catch up (this happens with wheat, and new varieties must be developed constantly). Or volunteer grasses may gradually change the population from the selected variety to a mixture that might as well have been sown in the first place.

When a new variety is planted alone, one should be as certain as possible of its requirements, and provide the necessary maintenance for it. Sometimes the preferences of a new variety are not entirely clear, and have to be learned through experience. Thus, when Merion Kentucky bluegrass was first released, it was not realized how serious rust disease could become, nor that Merion required more fertilization than natural bluegrass. It had been admired for leaf-spot resistance and the fact that it was dense and low growing.

New varieties are usually tested intensively where they are selected, then sent around the country for further scrutiny under differing climatic conditions. If reports are favorable, seed provided by the originator ("breeder seed") is sent for wider propagation to an isolated area, usually under irrigation in the West. The breeder seed is multiplied under careful supervision, to provide "foundation" seed. This in turn is released under surveillance to other growers, whose crop will be "registered," and this goes in its turn to farmers who will grow for the retail market. If this final product is checked by government authorities who will certify its varietal trueness, it can be marketed as "certified" seed. While certified seed guarantees genetic purity, the foregoing discussion points out that this may have disadvantages, and other cultivars may have to be blended to make a mixture of greater variability.

This same reasoning supports seedsmen's compounding of lawn mixtures rather than marketing single species. If variability within a species increases the range of adaptability for a given grass, inclusion of two or three compatible grasses within a mixture should cover a wider range of possible habitats and lawn abuses. We have already mentioned the Kentucky bluegrass-red fescue mixture, in which the bluegrass is particularly useful for open areas on good soil, red fescue varieties for shade and poor soil. The average consumer could not be expected to determine just which location in the lawn would be most suitable for each and sow them separately.

COMMON MISCONCEPTIONS

WEIGHT IS A SUITABLE GUIDE TO SEEDING RATE. The number of seeds in a pound of grass seed may vary tenfold or more. Obviously a pound that contains only two hundred thousand seeds will not go so far as one of bluegrass with over two million seeds, or bentgrass with seven million. It is the number of potential plants, not the total weight, that is important.

THE GRASS PLANTED ORIGINALLY CHANGES IDENTITY. If the type planted disappears, conditions did not favor it. What appears in its stead comes from seed or sprouts in the soil, and is not a change in the kind sown.

NURSEGRASSES ARE NEEDED TO GET BETTER GRASSES STARTED. This can be disproved on any roadside or lawn. Nursegrasses usurp space and nutrients that the permanent grass should have for a fast start; they later die out, leaving voids for weeds. Stay away from the so-called nursegrasses.

A SINGLE, HIGHLY SELECTED GRASS IS MOST SUITABLE. This may be true for the expert who wants complete uniformity and is prepared to satisfy the wants of a single cultivar (including protection from disease). But for most lawns a mixture of varieties that are similar in appearance and require similar types of care is a better risk and is more easily cared for. Mixtures provide genetic variability sufficient to adapt to a wide range of local circumstances, and to better resist the onslaught of a given disease or other calamity.

preparing the seedbed

THE VITAL STEPS in preparing a suitable seedbed are few or many, simple or elaborate, as soil and local circumstances vary.

The General Layout

Good surface drainage should be encouraged by sloping the grade of the seedbed to eliminate puddles of standing water. A gentle slope away from the house is best. Slopes with more than one foot rise in three feet are undesirable because they hinder mowing, and encourage gullying and such rapid run-off that water hasn't time to seep into the soil. Each location has its special problems, but in general, gradual slopes are preferable to level terraces with abrupt cuts at their extremities. Long sweeps of lawn also lend an air of spaciousness and facilitate mowing.

If the soil has a history of waterlogging and the lie of the land is such as to hinder drainage, it may prove profitable before a lawn is completed to lay agricultural drain tile at about twenty-foot intervals, a few feet below the surface. Professional help may be needed to lay tile properly, with an accurate, consistent slope and appropriate outlet. It is fortunate that tiling is not often needed. On established lawns that need improved drainage, a French drain can often be used with less disfigurement to the lawn than is caused by digging a trench to lay tile. A French drain is simply a narrow slit-like cut in the ground only an inch or two wide. It is filled with porous material such as gravel, and serves to conduct soil water away from higher levels to a lower outlet. The drain is scarcely visible after a few days for grass growth quickly overtops the cut.

Around new houses a clutter of broken bricks, board trimmings, sand, and plaster may be mixed in with the soil as the mass is bulldozed to grade. All such detectable trash should be retrieved and spots of sand and spilled cement thoroughly scattered before further conditioning of the soil. Sometimes the moving of soils or the incomplete mixing of organic additions results in soil layers. Layered soil impedes both water percolation and grass-root penetration. For example, plant roots cannot enter a tight clay "hardpan" if the good topsoil above it has not been partly worked into it. Water will also stop at an abrupt layer of sand where it is kept from further seepage by large-pore "air bubbles" blocking its descent. Sand layers left from construction and soils of contrasting texture and structure are best avoided as fill. Rotary tillage, with machines that churn the soil, is good insurance against layering in the top few inches of seedbed, as is deep discing with tractor and agricultural disc plow.

Soil of the Seedbed

If cost were not a factor, soils might be mixed to order, as is done for golf greens. Prepared soils are usually compounded from sand, loam, and organic matter. As much as 80 per cent sand and 10 per cent of each of the other ingredients may prove practicable where compaction from traffic is a problem and where regular watering can be maintained, as on the golf green. This would be extreme for a home lawn,

Soil very receptive for seeding. Nature has prepared the seedbed through winter freezing (note the frost cracks and pocks).

Today most seedbeds are cultivated mechanically. Loosen soil and break up clods, but don't cultivate so much as to adversely affect soil structure.

although compounding to the specifications of a horticultural potting soil (about seven parts loam, three parts peat, and two parts sand, plus various fertilizers) might be possible for small areas.

For the average home, such preparation is out of the question. Probably the most practical procedure, where improvement is needed, is to mix about an inch of organic material (such as compost, peat, weedless manures, or even straw or sawdust) into the top four or five inches of seedbed, stirring it thoroughly. Use plenty of fertilizer, too. Nitrogen is especially needed to decompose materials rich in carbohydrates, such as sawdust (about one pound of nitrogen to each 100 pounds of sawdust or straw). Adding minor amounts of sand is relatively useless, since this will simply bind in clay as does sand in making concrete.

Using Subsoils

One hopes that during home construction and grading, the topsoil was pushed aside and later replaced. But if not, poor soils exposed by digging the foundation may have one advantage. Through the ages topsoil has accumulated crop after crop of weed seeds; soil from several feet deep, though infertile and of poor structure, is weedless. A subsoil lets grass get started without competition, and the grass will grow lustily when it is amply fertilized and watered. Buying topsoil chances getting weedy scrapings from an old agricultural field. Although weeds can be overcome in time, they are a nuisance and an expense. Building from subsoil may be preferable.

Grass itself furnishes over 50 pounds of renewable roots yearly in the top six inches of each 1,000 square feet of lawn. Slowly the lawn improves itself. But planting can't wait; for speedy improvement, humus should be mixed into the initial seedbed. Sticky subsoil needs the improved structure provided by humus, although mixing in less than a one-inch layer will show little effect.

Of course, not all subsoils have the same problems. Within one state there may be both gluey subsoils and others which are relatively easy to handle and improve. About the worst is a heavy clay from deep down, essentially the stuff used in brickmaking. It always seems either too wet—sticky and not manipulatable—or too dry—hard and bricklike.

With such subsoil there may be only a few days during the year when the moisture is just right for tillage. If at all possible, choose these days to work one or two inches of organic residues (compost, peat, weedless manures, sludges, even grass clippings, leaves, sawdust, shredded cobs, or similar locally abundant organics) into the top four or five inches of seedbed.

A tractor with disc or a powerful rotary tiller will churn the organics into the dryish clay. It won't be easy, but a reasonably uniform mixing is possible. If high-carbohydrate materials are mixed in, such as unweathered straw, ground corncobs, or fresh sawdust, an extra 10 to 20 pounds of nitrogenous fertilizer should be added with the organic matter, in addition to the regular complete fertilizer.

A complete garden fertilizer containing nitrogen, phosphorous and potassium about equally such as 12-12-12, or better, a specific analysis designed for the locality and type of soil, should be mixed into the tilled surface, about 20 pounds per 1,000 feet. Or something proportionately higher in phosphate (even superphosphate alone, 16 to 48 per cent P_2O_5) might be preferred at this stage. This is the last chance to get phosphorus down into the root zone, for phosphorus does not move through the soil as readily as nitrogen or potassium.

On better subsoils, seedbed preparations are not so burdensome. Reasonably tillable subsoils can be as effective as topsoil if ample fertilizer is used. On such subsoils, and on topsoils, there is considerably more leeway with tillage, and smaller amounts of organic matter may be needed, or none at all.

Occasionally there are special problems. In some locations, as on Long Island or in Florida, fine sands may become as tight as clay. This occurs when small grains of essentially uniform size combine with gummy materials that "set" the grains together almost like concrete. As we have seen, the incorporation of humus into soil is the magic that improves both sand and clay.

The steps in preparing a subsoil for seeding are summarized as follows (topsoils and better subsoils require the same general sequence, except that organic additions may not be needed, nor are the requirements so exacting):

1. Rough grade to provide gentle slopes with good surface drainage (perpetually waterlogged soils may need tile drainage); remove debris.
2. Thoroughly mix organic additions (preferably a layer an inch or more thick) into the soil when it is moderately dry so as not to compact it or form clods.
3. At the same time mix in about 20 pounds of phosphorus-containing fertilizer per 1,000 square feet, or whatever a soil test indicates is desirable; lime if needed.
4. Do final grading, leveling, breaking up of large lumps; on loose soils roll lightly, or allow a period for settling before completing the final touches.
5. Apply additional surface fertilization at time of seeding.

Liming

Although fertilization has been stressed, liming is almost equally important in certain regions where soils are acid. The map gives a rough indication of acid regions. Over much of the East, lime would

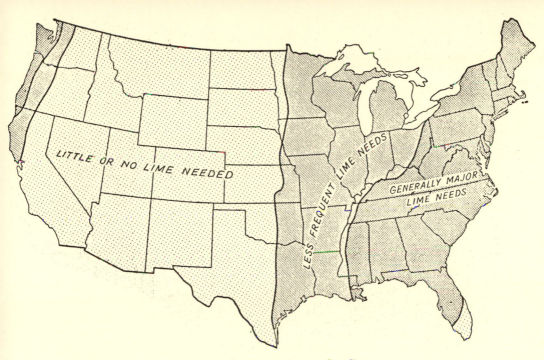

Regions Needing Lime (Generalized)

be useful, but a pH test is the only sure indicator of whether or not it is needed for a given lawn. The table on page 94 shows that one Minnesota county seems not to need lime while another requires a great deal.

It is safe to assume that lime will be useful when the pH is below six. A hundred pounds of ground limestone to 1,000 square feet should raise the pH about one unit, although required rates are higher on very acid and heavier-textured (clay type) soils than on mildly acid or sandy ones. Ordinarily, liming is not needed more than once every four or five years. Successive small additions, until the correct pH is reached, are preferable to a single large application that might cause temporary soil "indigestion."

Hydrated lime is a concentrated, treated limestone; it should be used with greater caution, at least on growing grass, since it may burn unless flushed from the foliage. Hydrated lime reacts with some fertilizers to waste a portion of the nutrients, and it may inactivate certain chemicals. It should be applied separately from the fertilizer, although mixing it into the fertilized seedbed will cause no difficulty.

The Final Touches

Common sense will indicate the number of rakings and draggings (as with a chain-link mat, tractor-drawn harrow, or mounted rake)

Miscellaneous Examples of Lime Requirements of Agricultural
Soils. Acidity corresponds roughly to the amount of rainfall.

Area	Percent of cultivated land acid enough to require lime
Iowa, state	33
Iowa, northeastern	67
Kansas, southeastern	71
Kansas, central	41
Minnesota, Mower County	62
Minnesota, Stevens County	2
New York, western	91
North Carolina, state	nearly 100
Oregon, coastal counties	80
Oregon, eastern counties	0
Wisconsin, state	64

necessary to level and properly grade a finished seedbed. Sprinklings, in default of rain, might well precede the final raking, so that filled-in areas are thoroughly settled. This last raking will loosen the surface if it has crusted, making it receptive again for seed. Sufficient passes should be made so that tractor tracks or footprints no longer indent the soil appreciably. On most seedbeds rolling is not necessary; rolling flattens a desirably roughened surface and may recompact clay soils if they are damp.

Where soils crust, several things can be done to help new seedings. Don't beat soil to a dusty consistency during the preparation. A pulverized soil seldom makes as desirable a seedbed as one which is mildly lumpy, with soil chunks from the dimension of peas up to golfball size. Several rains or waterings will likely be needed to pack a coarser surface, whereas a single watering might crust a dusty one.

Water only lightly with a fine spray until grass is established. Pounding by large drops in a heavy downpour blasts the surface, causing slaking and crusting. A mulch after seeding affords protection. Mulching not only facilitates quick, reliable grass sprouting (Chapter 8), but protects the soil against slaking, lessens soil wash, and contributes organic residues upon decomposition.

It goes without saying that equipment should be kept off the seedbed when the soil is soggy. Working a wet soil can make clods and can compact soil under tractor wheels so that the benefit of cultivation is undone. If the seedbed has been traversed by heavy equipment, such as vans bringing supplies to the home, it should be recultivated three or four inches deep before seeding.

Soil Sterilization

One of the newer frontiers in lawnmaking is treatment of the soil before seeding to eliminate pests of various types. These may be insects and nematodes or, more commonly, weed roots and seeds. Killing the living remains of such troublesome invaders as bermudagrass (in northern lawns), quackgrass rhizomes, unwanted creeping bentgrass colonies, or any persistent weedy growth resistant to selective herbicides, is especially beneficial.

Soil sterilization is normally practiced after the seedbed has been worked. Depending upon the kind of sterilant used, the seedbed must "air" from a few days to several weeks before seeding. Treatment varies with the chemical used; instructions accompanying the product should be followed to the letter. Sometimes a poor, weedy lawn is sterilized without cultivation, the new seed being sown later among the dried remains of old vegetation, which then serves as a mulch (see Chapter 9).

A list of sterilization chemicals is given in Chapter 15. Most of these are risky for the inexperienced lawnmaker to use, and if soil is to be sterilized (a fairly expensive procedure), it might well be left to the professional. Unless skillfully done, there is not only danger of imperfect treatment but also the chance that ornamentals adjacent to the lawn area may be injured, or that the soil may be poisoned for prolonged periods by overapplication or spillage.

Under ordinary circumstances, soil sterilization will probably not be needed. Only when soil infestations of one kind or another get completely out of hand, making it impossible to grow grass with ordinary care, is this drastic and expensive measure necessary.

Grub-Proofing

Another possibility at the time of seedbed preparation is chemical treatment against insects. This, too, is seldom necessary, although on top-grade lawns in areas known to be infested (as by Japanese beetle, whose grubs eat grass roots) it might be a useful precaution.

Arsenates (lead arsenate, calcium arsenate) were once widely recommended for grub-proofing, and indeed do an effective job. Large quantities must be used, however, on the order of 25 pounds of chemical to 1,000 square feet of seedbed.

More recently a number of organic insecticides have been developed, including several of the chlorinated hydrocarbon type, which are extremely effective at light rates. Two effective insecticides for lawns are chlordane and dieldrin (Chapter 16), but one or both may be restricted by state law as a result of the antipathy to "hard" insecticides similar to DDT (even though, in the soil, a long-lasting material such as chlordane should prove completely without hazard to the home or to wildlife).

REGIONAL FOCUS

Seedbed preparation follows essentially the same principles no matter where practiced, corresponding more to local sources and the condition of the soil than to region. Climate and rainfall influence soils, and consequently determine indirectly the need for liming (in humid regions) or sulfur acidification and iron additions (on alkali soils of arid lands).

Humid region soils are apt to need liming more than those of areas with lesser rainfall. The coastal counties of the Pacific Northwest; most of the Appalachians and Coastal Plain of the East, from New England south to Louisiana; and many uplands east of the Mississippi where limestone does not outcrop, will particularly profit from an application of lime. The same soils need generous fertilization as well.

Soils of the Coastal Plain, from eastern Texas through the southern parts of the Gulf States and as far north as eastern New Jersey, are mostly sandy and will not be easily damaged by equipment or tillage when wet. Northeastward from the Ohio Valley through New England one must be more careful, in the mechanics of seedbed preparation, not to squeeze the life out of heavy soils when wet. Their preparation is almost always easier in autumn than in the sogginess of early spring. Soils of prairie lands from parts of Indiana westward usually have sufficient native organic content so that soil structure is not easily damaged. Adobes of the Far West offer about as much of a problem as the unaerated deep clays from foundation diggings in the East; although they hold fertility and moisture well, achieving proper moisture content for tillage is difficult, and improvement of their structure is a prolonged, gradual evolution.

In the South, lawns are often planted from sprigs or plugs. Although seedbeds in such cases should be cultivated and fertilized, preparations need not be so painstaking as for seeding: but regular watering beginning immediately after planting must be assured.

In the North, where bluegrass lawns are planted with minute seeds running about two million to the pound, the seedbed should be as close to perfection as possible. Final leveling should be precise; the surface texture should be crumbly, so as to catch and hold the seed in soil crevices and not crust or wash upon wetting. All the necessary ingredients should be in the soil before the seed is planted and the mulch applied.

COMMON MISCONCEPTIONS

THE MORE A SEEDBED IS TILLED, THE BETTER. Soil tillage is necessary to prepare a seedbed; but after loosening the soil, extra tillage is a waste of time and may even be harmful. Pulverizing soil breaks down its structure, and a fluffy or dusty seedbed risks crusting, washing, irregular subsidence, uneven emergence of seedlings, and is unpleasant to work. This is one of those rare instances where less work is more productive.

IF THE SOIL COULD ONLY BE STERILIZED! Complete sterilization, fortunately, is impossible; without "contaminating" microorganisms, most of them beneficial, the soil would be out of balance, probably with poorer structure and unsatisfactory fertility. In the complex soil world, "some bugs eat other bugs," keeping harmful organisms in check. Fumigation may be temporarily successful, as in nematode control; but these pests may reinvade stronger than ever if organisms that feed on them are killed.

WET SOILS OF SPRING MAKE THE BEST SEEDBED. It is true that seeds need moisture for sprouting, generally ample in spring. But wet soils are also cold soils, and if waterlogged they do not provide the air needed for germination. Clay and loam soils generally make a superior seedbed in autumn when they foster quicker sprouting.

THE SEEDBED SHOULD BE ROLLED FIRM AND LEVEL. Fluffy seedbeds may need some rolling to point up soft and firm areas and to reconsolidate overly loose soil. Rolling will not hurt sandy soils, especially when dry. But it is best not to roll heavy soils, especially if wet. Rolling compacts the soil, and eliminates pore space, the very thing cultivation was meant to overcome. The surface is smashed flat, eliminating the crevices between soil chunks so desirable for seed to nestle into. Water tends to run off rather than soak into a compacted surface. Unfirm spots can be detected by noting their settling after a soaking. An uneven seedbed should be leveled by raking loose soil into depressions, rather than by squeezing down high spots with a roller.

8

sowing seed

IT IS EVIDENT that in a seed we have a remarkably tenacious spark of life. Good seed can be sown at almost any time of the year without harm, and lie dormant in the soil if conditions are unfavorable for sprouting. It is usually better to sow a lawn in the bluegrass zone while soil is workable in late autumn, even if temperatures are too cold for sprouting, than to await the usual soggy conditions of spring when it might be difficult to make a satisfactory planting.

As a rule it is best to plant a grass just ahead of the season that favors it most. For bluegrass, fescue, and bent this means autumn, with early spring the next best choice. For southern grasses that require warm temperatures, planting usually is best in spring. The grass can then get a good start, competing well with weeds, before the trials and tribulations of an unfavorable season come upon it.

The rate of seeding will vary with the seed. Those types that contain relatively few seeds to the pound should be sown heavily. Species such as tall fescue (which must be crowded to look presentable) or ryegrass (when used as a southern winter grass) might require five to ten pounds per 1,000 square feet. At the other extreme, bentgrass, with perhaps seven million seeds in a pound, may get by with only a few ounces, if such a slim quantity can be distributed accurately (usually impossible unless extended with inert materials). Kentucky bluegrass and bermuda, the two most used seeds for the North and South, are

A nicely leveled soilbed ready for seeding.

somewhat intermediate; mixtures based primarily upon these grasses are sown two to three pounds per 1,000 square feet, or perhaps more lightly if uniform distribution can be achieved and a good soilbed is prepared.

Spreading and Planting

Sowing can be accomplished as Granddad did it, broadcasting seeds by hand. With a little practice, grass seed can be allowed to sift lightly through the fingers during a flick of the hand, casting the seed in a wide arc that settles in a thin layer on the seedbed. Some gardeners prefer to use the shaker-top boxes in which lawn seed is often marketed.

If the seed is given bulk with an extender, there is more leeway in

The surest means for uniform dispersal of seed is the use of one of today's excellent spreaders. This whirlwind type casts seed widely and covers up to a 10-foot band with each pass.

A gravity-drop spreader distributes seed in bands with precise margins, but is slower than whirlwind types because a narrower band is covered.

tossing it; plainly visible amounts will not then contain excessive seed, nor will spillage and poor casting be so wasteful. Seed may be mixed thoroughly with approximately an equal amount of any dry material of similar particle size for bulk. Cornmeal, vermiculite, pulverized organic materials, sifted dry soil, even sand or fertilizer will extend most lawn seeds satisfactorily.

The centrifugal or cyclone-type seeder is convenient and reasonably accurate. Seeds from the hopper dribble at a set rate onto a whirling plate which casts them in a fairly uniform pattern over a wide path. The width of the seeded path will vary with the seed mixture, and the operator will have to judge how close together adjacent passes must be. Allow sufficient overlap for one strip to feather surely into the next. For economy it is hard to beat the old sack-model, cyclone-type seeder slung over the shoulder. It is a sowing device familiar to farmers of a past generation.

In sowing by hand or with a centrifugal seeder, traverse the seedbed in one direction with half the seed, then move at right angles to this with the second half. This avoids skipped spots and evens out the seeding. One effective technique is to spread half the seed, then drag or rake lightly before applying the second half.

Uniformity in seeding is most accurate with drop-from-hopper

On fluffy seedbeds and surfaces that are not sufficiently "pebbly" to allow the seed to sift between soil chunks, tumble the seed into the soil by dragging either a mat or an inverted leaf rake over the sown seedbed.

spreaders in which an agitator circulates seeds over regulated hopper openings. The seeds then fall to the ground along the path of the spreader. Precision machines can be adjusted to distribute as little as one pound of seed per 1,000 square feet, something difficult to do by hand or with centrifugal seeders. The better spreaders have simple rate devices and setting instructions that adjust the openings for the major types of seed. A mixture based primarily upon bentgrass takes a smaller setting than bluegrass, while fescue or ryegrass needs a larger one.

In using these distributors, overlap the wheel tracks. Because the hopper is set in a slight distance from the wheels, the wheel should ride well within the previous track in the next pass. Here too, an even coverage is better assured if half the seed is spread in one direction, the other half at right angles.

"Planting" the seed is not necessary on rougher textured seedbeds, but is a good precaution in areas where seed remains perched on a dusty surface, prey to washing (if the soil puddles) or enticing to birds. Tumbling the surface so that the seed becomes embedded within the top one-quarter inch hides the seed in most soils; it also causes seed to sift into crevices between soil chunks where it is ideally situated for sprouting. This can be accomplished by dragging a section of chain mat or link fence over the seedbed, or by pulling a flexible tine-leaf rake upside down so as not to shift the seeded soil unduly.

On established lawns there may be occasion to bolster thin turfs with additional seed, or perhaps to upgrade the lawn by introducing the more desirable grasses. For this purpose use half the recommended rate. Contact with the soil can be facilitated by first raking away matted grass, fallen leaves and other debris. Scuffing the soil surface with a sharp-tined rake will provide lodging for the seeds; so will slicing with a disc (set the discs straight so as not to turn the sod) or punching holes with aerifying machines. In winter, nature helps with frost pocks and crevices. Chapter 9 on Renovation discusses the reseeding of older lawns in more detail.

Rolling the seedbed is often advised. There is no harm in this if the soil is dry and the roller light. But in most instances rolling is not necessary. The first watering will work the seeds down into cracks between soil crumbs, and pack the soil sufficiently about them. Heavy equipment on moist clay compacts it, undoing the benefits of tillage. Use of a heavy roller can also mash the surface tight, causing rain or sprinkling to run off rather than soak in, thus chancing erosion and seed loss.

Although some seed will find suitable lodging for growth in the cracks of this crusted soil, it is preferable to loosen the crust with a rake before sowing.

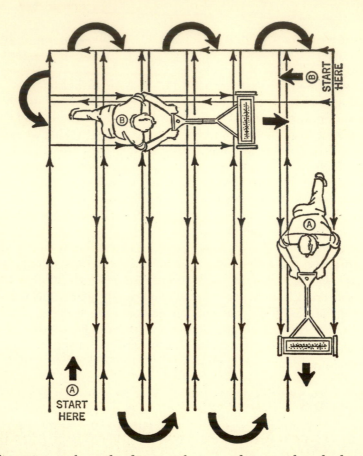

In dispersing seed or other lawn products, overlap spreader wheel tracks to avoid skipped strips.

Mulching the Seeding

While newly sown seed sprouts without difficulty if sprinkled frequently, the surest growth comes with mulching. A mulch can be of any suitable material, scattered over the surface after the seed has been sown. It protects the soil, retains moisture at the soil surface and around the seed, and guards seedlings against extreme fluctuations of weather; on lawns it must be loose enough to allow rainfall, air, and some light to reach the sprouting seeds.

The most generally used mulch was formerly clean straw, which is difficult to procure in urban areas nowadays. "Clean" means relatively free of grain heads and weeds. A bale of straw usually covers at least 1,000 square feet. It should be spread three or four intermeshed straws deep, not piled up in smothering mounds. Except in windy locations, the straw will stay put without additional anchoring, becoming partially stuck to the soil from being walked over during its laying. On steep slopes or windy sites, straw can be tied down by running strings between stakes driven into the soil, or with woven netting.

Hay or grass clippings can be used like straw, as can sphagnum moss (the long stringy stuff, not pulverized peat). The latter should be soaked beforehand, since when it is dry and light from a new bale it blows easily in the wind. Some experts fear that sphagnum may encourage disease, since it holds moisture so tenaciously. In my experience, this offers scant hazard, and in dry climates its water-holding capacity is welcomed. Sphagnum should not be spread as deeply as straw; one-eighth to one-quarter inch is ample. Similar are the pulp slurries offered by forest products companies for hydromulching extensive surfaces such as roadsides and golf courses. In some instances these may be available for home use, although they are costly to apply on a small scale.

Netting serves as a mulch and also anchors loose straw against the wind.

A plastic cover over a new seeding is like a greenhouse; it holds moisture beautifully, but may get too hot in bright sun, killing newly sprouted seed. Watch plastic-covered seedlings carefully.

Other mulches may be available locally. In tobacco country, tobacco stems are often thrown on the new lawn, contributing potash as well as mechanical protection. Loosely woven onion-sack netting may be purchased specifically for covering a new seeding (Erosionet). Wood chips or shredded bark can be used. An excelsior mat is manufactured for large-scale mulching, such as on roadsides, and is very effective for lawns where it can be procured. Coarse sawdust or ground corncobs might help, but they are rather light and tend to float away. Both of these can also be a drain upon nitrogen, since microorganisms that are decomposing them compete with the soil for nitrogen supplies. A little extra nitrogen on the surface will compensate for this.

Even small pebbles may serve as a mulch where they are not so large and irregular as to kick up in future mowing. A polyethylene film cover can provide a "minature greenhouse" over the new seeding, keeping moisture in and gullying out. The plastic must be removed shortly after the grass sprouts, and it must be ventilated on sunny days so that the temperature under it doesn't much exceed 100° F. (lethal to sprouting seedlings). Polyethylene sheets can be held on the soil by large nails or wire wickets pressed through the plastic into the ground around the margins. Since polyethylene costs several cents a square foot, it is more likely to be used for patching trouble spots than for large-scale mulching. People and animals show deference to a plastic-covered area that they would not accord mere grass or straw. The same is true for fiberglass mats, at one time procurable for turf mulching.

If the soil is damp before seeding, or is wetted down immediately after, a mulch will retain moisture for prolonged periods, depending, of course, upon time of year, wind, temperature, and cloudiness. Almost invariably, a mulched seeding will be many days ahead of its unmulched counterpart. Even a booster seeding into old crabgrass (after crabgrass has died) will benefit from this mulch of old vegetation and will sprout well ahead of bare areas seeded at the same time. This is the principle behind chemical knockdown or scorching of old vegetation in lawn renovation (Chapter 9).

Watering the New Seeding

In the early stages of lawn establishment, gentle, frequent sprinkling is called for. Once the seedbed has been wetted, light sprin-

An excellent stand of young grass sprouted quickly under a fiberglass mat mulch.

kling or misting is all that is needed to keep the seed environment moist enough for good germination. Later, when the seedlings are up and the roots strike deeper, watering can taper off; but with a newly started seeding in dry weather, showering may be needed several times a day. On dull days, with little wind, cool temperature, and high humidity, sprinkling will be less important. The final criterion is the condition of the soil; don't let the surface dry out even one-quarter inch deep if you can help it.

Just as it is undesirable to press the soil with a roller, so is it inappropriate to batter it down with water. Heavy watering breaks down soil structure, puddling the surface into a mud pie which cakes almost like concrete upon drying. Such a crust impedes sprouts trying to push through, and restricts the air (vital for germination and root growth) as well as the ready entry of water.

Mowing a New Lawn

The new seeding should get its first haircut when it has grown about twice what will be its customary mowing height. Three-inch Kentucky bluegrass seedlings merit trimming; two-inch bermuda or zoysia. Of course, this presumes that the seedbed has dried sufficiently to permit a mower to be used. Obviously, it would be better to let seedlings grow a bit taller than to track up and tear a soft seedbed.

Since young seedlings are not deeply rooted, be certain that the lawn mower is properly sharpened to avoid pulling them up. Once mowing is started, repeat it as soon as another similar increment of growth has occurred.

When seedlings are old enough to have undergone several mowings, they are old enough to receive booster fertilization and weed control. These are not mandatory, but fertilization will hasten growth. Regular mowing will take care of many of the weeds, and robustly growing grass will squeeze out others.

REGIONAL FOCUS

Cool weather comes more quickly in autumn the farther north one goes. Thus in the northern states and Canada, all preparations for seeding should be completed by early August and the seed sown that month. In latitudes from Ohio to Iowa, bluegrass lawns are best seeded from late August into early September. A little farther south, from Missouri through Kentucky and Tennessee to Virginia, seeding might be delayed until well into September, when cooler weather and more ample rainfall are apt to prevail. It becomes a chore to maintain sufficient moisture in a seedbed until at least one drenching has replenished soil moisture exhausted during summer.

There are a number of advantages to autumn seeding, aside from its being a favored season for northern grasses. Rainfall is apt to be gentler, less the thunderstorm type, and increasingly adequate in the autumn. At least evaporation is diminishing rather than increasing as is the case in spring. Soils are usually workable, not sticky, as they would be in most springs. Weeds are on the decline rather than on the increase. Bright days make the soil surface warm enough to encourage sprouting, while the nights are crisp enough for husky energy-conserving growth; wet soils of spring are usually slow to warm. And finally, the lawnsman is likely to have fewer competing gardening activities in autumn than in spring.

If, for one reason or another, it proves impossible to sow the lawn in early autumn, seeding before the soil freezes is still preferable to spring sowing. But it should be late enough for cool weather to prevent sprouting; the seed will come up in spring. Very young grass, caught by winter, may be heaved by the alternate freezing and thawing of the soil. Cold weather alone seldom kills plants, but the roots may be damaged by this mechanical lifting.

Failing an autumn seeding, seed as early as is possible in spring. If the soil has been worked previously, is level and ready, seed may be cast upon frozen ground in February or March. It will usually catch in frost crevices and pockets, and as soon as temperatures rise sufficiently it will sprout. If the soil must be worked and leveled, there is no alternative to waiting for days that are warm and dry enough to permit tilling.

Late spring or early summer seedings of northern grasses offer considerable risk. Where summers are bland and rainfall at least fair, such seedings will very likely succeed. Weeds are apt to be troublesome, however, although certain herbicides such as the crabgrass preventer siduron, or post-emergent bromoxynil spray, can selectively control many weeds without injury to the grass. In the warmer portions of the bluegrass zone, late spring and summer seedings seldom are successful. There is insufficient time for the grass to become strong enough to withstand the tribulations of summer drought, heat, and weeds.

In the bermuda zone the reverse is true. Late spring and early summer seedings have the best chance, with a long growing season ahead. Successful planting is possible any time through the summer. Autumn seeding is a doubtful practice, since there may not be time for southern grass to become sufficiently established and hardened to survive the winter with certainty. This is especially true of the more northerly bermudagrass. Bermuda can be allowed to grow tall just before it turns off-color, so that it mulches itself for protection through winter.

Planting and caring for dichondra, a familiar lawn cover in southern California, is not much different from treatment of the finer bermuda-grasses. Since dichondra grows little during the cooler season, its sowing is best in spring or summer; winter seedings sometimes are combined with clover to give a temporary cover, the clover usually dis-appearing the following summer under close mowing. Dichondra can even be seeded into old bermudagrass, and be encouraged to crowd out the bermuda eventually under a regimen of generous autumn and winter fertilization and frequent summer watering. Dichondra can be planted in full sun or partial shade, but should have the intensive attention generally accorded bermudagrass or bentgrass; it is not for an "economy" lawn. It can stand some freezing, and has survived with little damage in as cool a climate as the mountains of North Carolina. Dichondra will cover from only one-half pound of seed per 1,000 square feet, but distributing this small amount is difficult, so that it is usually bulked with several quarts of sand or pulverized organic mate-rials for easier sowing.

COMMON MISCONCEPTIONS

SOAKING SEED SPEEDS PLANTING. Seed germinates fastest where tem-perature and moisture are most favorable. At certain seasons this may be indoors. Seeds can be "preplanted," then cast upon an outdoor seedbed after they have begun germinating. But soaking in itself does not quicken germination. Seed soaked, then dried sufficiently for use in conventional applicators, will not sprout any sooner than the equiva-lent unsoaked seed.

NEW LAWNS NEED WINTER PROTECTION. Occasionally homeowners feel that a newly planted autumn lawn should be covered or protected through winter. Such is not the case. A covering would more likely smother the new grass, or hold moisture that encourages disease, rather than prove helpful. Grasses appropriate for the climate can withstand winter cold (although southern grasses planted north of their usual range might benefit from a layer of straw; this helps to prevent drying out more than it protects against cold).

SPRING IS THE PREFERRED SEASON TO SOW GRASS. In bluegrass country, autumn has a great many advantages that spring does not possess.

Nature points this out, in that seed is set through summer, starts growth with the rains and cooler weather of autumn. With southern grasses, or in the exceptional northern locations where summers are not so beset with heat and weeds (and the onset of winter comes quickly and violently), spring sowing is appropriate.

SEED PROBLEM SPOTS HEAVILY. Heavy seeding may aggravate uncorrected troubles. If lawn grass has failed, the cause should be determined before seeding anew. Frequently additional fertilization or soil improvement is needed more than additional seed. Crowding many seedlings into space that couldn't sustain few, results in spindly, weak plants. The usually recommended rates of two or three pounds per thousand square feet for mixtures based primarily upon bluegrass, and not more than double this for larger seeded grasses, will prove ample.

IS QUICK COVER A SIGN OF SEEDING SUCCESS? It signifies good sowing technique, and quick protection of the soil, nothing more. And it may imply a serious setback to the permanent grass. Nursegrasses such as annual rye sprout quickly and usurp space needed for full development of the slower permanent grasses such as bluegrass. Studies show that more than about 20 per cent nursegrass cuts markedly into the fine grass population, and when it dies out, little or no permanent grass is at hand to take over.

9

renovation

MODERN RECEPTIVENESS to technology makes lawn renovation increasingly feasible. Labor-saving equipment and convenient products are commonplace today, by rental if not by purchase, making practical renovation operations which only a few years ago would have been impossible. There have not been sudden breakthroughs, but gradually new techniques have taken hold, putting theory into practice. Most important are machinery to thin, scarify, and rework an old lawn surface; knock-down chemicals (anti-pollution emphasis, however, make some of them hard to come by); and a stable of thoroughbred lawn-grass varieties to serve all tastes and purposes. This accumulation of new products and knowledgeable practices usually makes the renovation of tired turfs feasible without the more expensive "major surgery" of plowing the old lawn and replanting it.

Planning Renovation

Renovation calls for reducing or eliminating undesired vegetation in order to establish that which is wanted. Lawn ecology reminds us that if renovation is to be successful, it must be executed in a way that matches grass needs and habitat. Human taste and judgment, however, are also important factors to be considered. No single grass or combination of grasses suits all tastes and all anticipated modes of

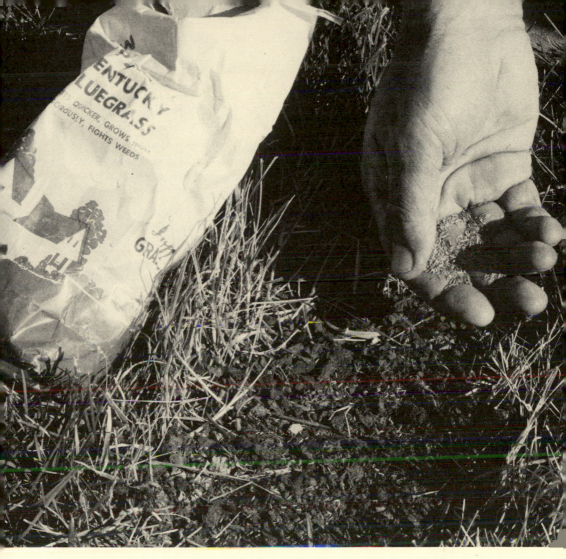

A simple type of renovation is reseeding a "bad" spot in the lawn by hand.

care. As with any lawn planting, a realistic appraisal should be made of what kind of grass is best adapted to local realities. There is no point in planting bentgrass, for example, where sufficient care and adequate humidity cannot prevail. Nor should elite bluegrasses be sown where they cannot be accorded at least moderate fertilization. The homeowner may have preferences, too, such as the broader blade of Baron or Merion bluegrass, or the delicate leaf of Fylking or Pennstar. Probably a combination of select bluegrasses and fine fescues will be used for renovating the majority of lawns north from Tennessee. In the South, vegetative plantings can be made with southern species after the preliminaries have been completed.

Ridding the Lawn of Unwanted Vegetation

Marvelous new herbicides, having been developed for chemical knock-down, are used mainly in agriculture, however, rather than for home use. In fact, it is difficult to find some of the more useful chemicals in garden stores. But they are increasingly used on the farm, especially for such purposes as no-tillage corn growing (in which old meadow, analogous to lawn sod, is chemically thwarted before the corn is row-seeded to grow without interference). True, many farm chemicals can be hazardous around the home, but the products mentioned here can be safely employed if directions are followed carefully. If your lawn is mostly unwanted vegetation, with nothing to be saved, a preliminary chemical knock-down makes renovation a good deal surer and simpler. But it is a step that can be skipped if you feel shy about using chemicals on the lawn, or cannot conveniently procure the products.

Two chemicals are especially useful for knocking out old vegetation —the arsonates (or cacodylic acid), and paraquat. Both substances scorch and kill all green leaf that they hit, but are not hazardous to roots or tree trunks protected by bark. The outstanding feature of these chemicals is that they are immediately inactivated by the soil, and when used at the light rates recommended will not toxify it; seeding can take place almost immediately, just as soon as the old turf has turned brown and died (within a day or two). Arsonate solutions are usually marketed under the trade designation Phytar (Ansul

Chemical knock-down prior to scarification in turf renovation. The browned grass in the foreground has been sprayed to restrain competition for new overseeding.

Chemical Company); Chevron (Standard Oil of California) produces paraquat. Unfortunately, as this is written, neither are readily available to homeowners, but only through agricultural outlets where label clearance has been obtained.

Other knock-down chemicals include dalapon (Dow), an excellent systemic killer of grasses and some broadleaf plants; and amitrol (Amchem), lethal to most vegetation hit (restricted from use on food plants). Both, however, leave some residual toxicity in the soil until microbial breakdown is complete; reseeding may be inadvisable for three to six weeks after spraying. A phenoxy weed killer such as 2,4-D can be combined with dalapon if broadleaf weeds are abundant in the old lawn. Some of the other agricultural chemicals, such as the triazines, have such long-lasting toxicity in the soil for many lawngrasses, that they should not be recommended for use around the home. But a venerable poison ivy and brush killer, ammate (Du Pont), and an old time "sterilant," calcium cyanamide (American Cyanamid), can be utilized much in the same way as the arsonates and paraquat. The amount of these two materials required, however, is considerable when compared to more modern chemicals.

Not all formulations are of equal strength so be certain to follow product directions explicitly, observing the recommended safety precautions. Sprays rather than granulars are generally more economical and effective, coating the vegetation thoroughly with a minimum of useless soaking into the soil. Light rates are quite effective; for example, as little as an ounce of paraquat with a quarter-ounce of wetting agent in a three-gallon hand-pump sprayer will probably be sufficient for a smallish front yard.

Making the Lawn Receptive for Overseeding

With or without chemical knock-down, mechanical scarification is necessary for effective renovation by overseeding. Scattering new seed over an old turf without some effort to properly seat it, is not an efficient way to establish new grass. Seed sown in such a manner lies on top of duff and litter, where it remains insufficiently moist to sprout, and not in close enough contact with soil for rooting. Its chances are even less if the old vegetation is not knocked out first, since any new seeding would have to compete with larger, well-rooted plants. Thus it is almost essential that the soil surface be scratched up.

A generation or two ago such scarification would have been a muscle-building endeavor for a boy on the business end of a sharp-tined rake. A few assiduous souls will still scratch thatch out of their lawn

Preparing a tired old turf for bolster seeding in spring.

with a rake (if it is a small lawn), but by-and-large technology has taken over. Powered machines that slice or cut into the turf can usually be rented from equipment outlets or garden centers. They are variously called "vertical mowers," "power rakes," "dethatchers," "turf thinners," and so on. The majority have toothed blades much like a buzz saw set vertically at a spacing of about an inch or less, on a horizontal axle that can be lowered or raised to cut as deep as needed (even shallowly into the soil). Some models have flexible tines rather than serrated discs, and, of course, even aerifiers (which punch holes into the soil) accomplish a certain amount of thatch removal and scarification.

A scarifier may be run over the old lawn in two directions to create a checkerboard of surface scratches and loose soil. The degree to which this should be carried out will vary. If the old lawn has been killed back chemically, or if none of the existing grass is being preserved, scarification can be quite thorough and deep, with several passes over the lawn stirring up the soil almost as much as if it were disced with a tractor. But if some residual grass is to be preserved, scarification should be less intensive—sufficient to remove thatch and expose some soil, but not so abusive as to tear up vegetation. Whatever the degree of seedbed preparation, new grass seeds will do best if buried shallowly.

Overseeding with Improved Grasses

Distributing seed uniformly is easy with any of the better seeder-spreaders. Three or four pounds to the 1,000 square feet of a bluegrass-

Motorized scarifying machine being used to make soil receptive to seeding without plow-down cultivation. Once over with the scarifier and the soil surface is ridged with striations and loose soil.

fescue blend is usually recommended, but half this amount would suffice for an overseeding in which old grass is to remain. Fertilizer can be spread at the same time; non-burn sorts based upon ureaform are especially appropriate, and do not raise the salt index sufficiently to interfere with quick sprouting. A final combing or working to tumble seed into the soil is recommended, or should there be weed-free topsoil available, a light scattering over the new seeding would do as well. Incidentally, topdressing is an excellent way to help control thatch. Where a lot of old turf remains, a very close mowing (scalping) helps reduce competition for the new seedlings. Unless the surface has turned dusty, rolling will not be needed nor should mulching be necessary.

Finishing Up

As was noted in earlier chapters, seed will not sprout, and established grass will not revive well without moisture. Water a renovated lawn as assiduously as you would a brand-new seeding. After a thorough soaking, frequent light waterings will keep the surface moist and encourage quick sprouting. Here, also, technology comes to the lawnman's aid, with a wide assortment of excellent sprinkling devices (Chapter 12). Self-installable plastic systems and wave sprinkler heads have now brought underground watering systems within the reach of modest incomes. As will be mentioned in the same chapter on watering, such a system can be laid out on the lawn surface to prove coverage, then be trenched into position with nothing more than a spade. Whatever the facilities, try to keep the overseeded lawn regularly watered until the new grass is well established. In warm weather this should be within the month.

Elimination of the old turf creates opportunities not only for new grass, but for weeds as well (from weed seed residual in the soil). A temporary upsurge of weeds is to be expected, most of which will disappear in competition with the grass and under regular lawn maintenance. It is well to avoid most pre-emergence crabgrass preventers (except perhaps siduron, which seldom bothers newly sprouting grass), and withhold broadleaf weed treatments until the new grass is old enough to have had a mowing or two.

Although renovation may seem a lengthy procedure, it need not be burdensome. From chemical knock-down through weed-control one has at his beck and call machines and easily applied products. Even if renovation is tried, costs should prove considerably less than complete lawn remaking. And some of the steps discussed may be elimi-

Top quality seed being spread to chemically treated, scalped turf, in renovation program.

nated under certain circumstances. Not only should lawn renovation improve the thickness of the turf, but it also provides the opportunity to introduce newer varieties of the top lawngrasses.

Aerification

With professionally-tended turf, aerification—the punching of holes into the soil—is frequently practiced. This is done more to reduce soil compaction, encourage deeper rooting, and facilitate water insoak, than as a renovation procedure. Nevertheless, a measure of rejuvenation follows aerification, and if the practice is accompanied by over-seeding, it could be considered as a mild renovation measure. That aerification can alter the botanical composition of the turf is proven by the sprouting of annual bluegrass near the aerification holes where the turf is opened on a golf green, especially if timed poorly so that the permanent grass is not growing aggressively at that season.

In a sense, aerification amounts to soil cultivation of a permanent turf without materially disturbing the grass. Theoretically, it would seem a very attractive measure to take. In actual practice, few benefits seem to accrue from aerifying the average home lawn, which ordinar-

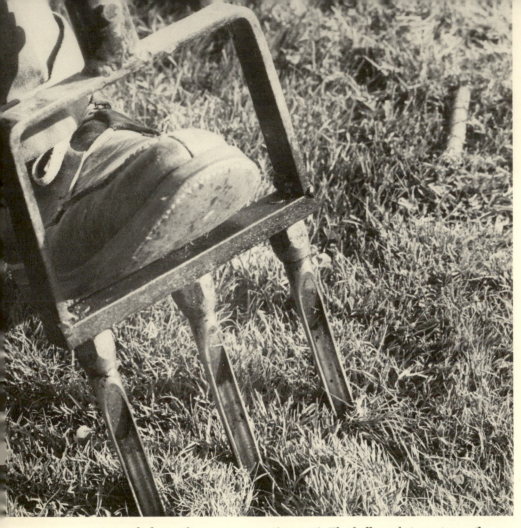

A simple but tedious way to aerify a turf. The hollowed tines eject soil cores.

ily is not suffering any great degree of soil compaction. Accompanying the punching of holes into the soil will be a certain amount of thatch loosening, which may aid in its decomposition. On slopes, the holes punched into the soil may provide small reservoirs for holding water, enabling greater insoak of rain. But since aerification is a fairly expensive operation, most homeowners would prefer to see a greater response than is ordinarily witnessed. In terms of greener grass, a few cents worth of fertilizer ordinarily does much more than lawn aerification. Many of the less expensive aerifiers offered for rental, or used by many landscaping houses, do not punch holes very deeply into the soil. Research in California has shown that aerification holes should be many inches deep, preferably up to ten inches, in order to materially improve grass rooting. That rooting is then improved is proven by the fact that the aerifier holes soon fill with fresh, actively growing roots. Without these cavities providing for oxygen exchange fairly deep within the soil, there would be no rooting there.

The best aerifying machines have a hollow tine which pulls a plug of soil out of the hole being made. These plugs are typically cast out behind the machine, and when raked or dragged about tend to break up and act as a soil topdressing for the turf. This in itself can be quite helpful for thatch control. Equipment makers have rushed to market with various types of "spiking" machines, some of which are merely attached to a garden tractor or lawn mower. These are really little different than the scarifiers mentioned for renovating. The points of the spikes seldom penetrate very deeply into the soil, and in doing so, compress the soil as well as creating depressions in it (in much the same fashion that a sheepsfoot-roller is used to consolidate soils in road building). The spiking machines might be quite useful for thinning thatch and rejuvenating the turf, but don't expect very much from them as a means for relieving soil compaction. Their use, accompanied by overseeding, would be preferable to overseeding without any soil treatment at all, however, for the indentations made by the spikes should provide a suitable niche into which new lawnseed could settle and find chance to sprout.

REGIONAL FOCUS

Lawn renovation may be contemplated anywhere as a means for upgrading the quality of the turf, but it is especially useful in climates where the fine turfgrasses find the going difficult. Thus in the transition zone between the North and the South, in the varied habitat of southern California, in fairly dense shade, or anywhere where lawn-growing conditions are less than ideal, an original planting may not last, at least as a monoculture, for very many years. One assumes under such circumstances that fairly frequent replanting will be necessary. In an extreme case, lawns in the shade of trees may have to be replanted each autumn, taking advantage of the time of year when the trees are leafless, and can be expected to be lost the following summer. This is no different from the annual winter seeding of southern lawns to avoid the brown, unattractive appearance in winter.

Aerification, alone or as an accompaniment to renovation, is mainly needed on heavily trodden areas such as frequently used athletic grounds, in arid regions where the typically alkaline soils tend to compact readily, and in southern regions where winters are not sufficiently cold for the soil to experience the "natural aerification" which a freezing cycle brings. There should be little call for aerification of the average home lawn anywhere, and certainly not on the sandy coastal plain soils from Cape Cod southward along the Atlantic and Gulf coasts, and locally elsewhere.

COMMON MISCONCEPTIONS

RENOVATION IS THERAPEUTIC FOR THE LAWN. The answer is both "yes" and "no." It is rejuvenating and stimulating, and a means of introducing better grasses, if these are your objectives. But just as it provides the chance for overseeding to gain a toehold, so it provides the opportunity for weed seeds to be exposed sufficiently to sprout and grow. In most instances, renovation is a measure of last resort, an easier means for remaking the lawn rather than plowing the whole thing up, but less sure in its results than the creation of an ideal seedbed.

A LAWN SHOULD BE REGULARLY AERIFIED. The idea has appeal because the procedure is psychologically impressive. It seldom shows any advantages, however, on lawns that receive only normal use, although it may help to make irrigation more efficient on heavy soils in the Southwest. Spiking lawns, by making shallow indentations into the soil surface, has little to recommend it other than the thatch control it may offer. But even mechanical dethatching has only a temporary effect; a year later the thatch is apt to be just as heavy as ever, unless the conditions which caused its original build-up have been altered.

RENOVATION IS AN INDICATOR OF POOR LAWN KEEPING. An occasional renovation is certainly no substitute for proper consistent lawn care, and in favorable environments, it might indicate carelessness. But where lawn-growing conditions leave something to be desired, renovation is more likely to be the business-like, sensible recourse rather than a reproach to one's lawn keeping. Although everyone would like to have a permanent lawn which persists "forever," this need not be the universal desiratum. In the crabgrass belt, for example, some lawn custodians might be content with crabgrass in summer, and an annual renovation each autumn just to provide a good green cover from autumn until spring. Vacation homes may require only seasonal lawns, for summer in the North (generally best planted in autumn, even though sprouting may not be until spring); for winter in the South (accomplished through annual winter seedings in October or November). Renovation is a procedure useful both for upgrading permanent turfs, and for adding greater flexibility to the lawn-keeping program where, for whatever reason, a regularly-tended fine lawn cannot be maintained.

10

starting lawns vegetatively

THE PROPAGATION of a plant by rooting pieces of the parent is as old as horticulture itself. Almost every greenhouse and nursery practices this technique with selected cultivars. The same is possible with lawn-grasses.

Turfs are reproduced vegetatively by: *sod*, large sections of turf that are lifted and relaid; *plugs*, small biscuits of sod; or *sprigs*, individual stems that are separated from sod, usually with a few leaves and roots. *Stolons* are actually any trailing stem branches. In commercial turf-grass parlance, the word "stolons" generally refers to the shredded fragments of softer grasses such as bentgrass (or sometimes bermuda). These can be mass scattered, covered with a bit of sifted soil (topdress-ing), and watered continuously to start a new stand. *Sprigs*, on the other hand, are stem sections generally of stiffer grasses such as zoysia, individually selected and planted.

The chief disadvantage of starting a lawn vegetatively is its costli-ness. Nor is it as simple as seeding, for it requires fresh materials that are cumbersome to store, and ample labor for immediate planting. With the living grass there is always the possibility, too, of introducing insects, diseases, or noxious weeds that would not be carried by seeds.

On the other hand, there is the assurance that a lawn vegetatively planted will be identical with the parent turf. Furthermore, if sod, plugs, or sprigs of good quality can be secured economically, a lawn can be established quickly. This is especially true with sod, because the ground is completely covered at once.

All things considered, vegetative planting is recommended mainly for special varieties that will not come true from seed or with grasses for which there is no ready source of seed. Given time, seeding can make a smoother, more uniform turf than most sodding, at less expense, although sodding does have the advantage of producing an "instant lawn."

In practice, vegetative planting becomes almost regional or occupational. Traditionally, it has been done more in the South than in the North, probably in part because of inexpensive labor in the past, and in part because the preferred grasses for the South have seldom been available as seed.

Sodding Northern Lawns

New, speculative "model" houses in the North, which must have lawns immediately to encourage sale, are generally sodded. New cultivars are increasingly being offered as sod, and the busy homeowner who is dissatisfied with his lawn can have it quickly re-established through nursery purchase. Golf greens, requiring strains of bent or bermuda of exact characteristics not obtainable through seed, are usually planted with stolons but may be sodded. Slopes and waterways that need quick soil protection are frequently sodded.

The familiar something-for-nothing sodding consists of slapping down, as economically as possible, turf gathered in some nearby pasture. As a result, weedy, low-quality sod ends up in many front yards. Fortunately, this practice is diminishing, and a respected professional sod industry has developed in which great pains are taken to provide a weed-free, viable sod of known genetic quality. But, unfortunately, some sod is simply purchased by a "man with a truck," the sod taken from bluegrass fields near a population center. Even if sprayed for weeds beforehand, it almost invariably contains odds and ends of vegetation and abundant weed seed in addition to the bluegrass. If the bluegrass thins, as it may if not promptly laid and reasonably tended, the weeds assert themselves.

Oftentimes sod lies rolled, awaiting marketing and laying, until it is completely yellow. It is a tribute to the remarkable tenacity of bluegrass that it can come back to make any kind of lawn at all after such treatment.

Contrary to expectation, bluegrass sod cut thin—about three-fourths of an inch—transplants better than thicker sod. Most of the rhizomes

A typical strip of Baron Kentucky bluegrass sod.

are in this top three-fourths of an inch, and new roots grow from crowns and stem nodes rather than from existing roots. When there is a thick layer of soil with the sod, the sod seems to stay self-contained, while thinner sod strikes root more quickly into the new seedbed on which it is laid. The only advantage of thick sod (aside from acquiring a little extra topsoil with it) is its greater water-holding capacity. A thin sod dries more rapidly and needs regular watering until it becomes established. Therefore, thick sod may be more able to outlast neglect.

Considerable skill is required for lifting sod. A homeowner can seldom remove it with a spade and lay it elsewhere smoothly and uniformly. Sod-cutting machines, which cut standard widths at set depth, are more efficient. The strip thus loosened is sectioned at intervals and usually rolled by hand for trucking.

No great skill is needed for laying sod if it is trimmed uniformly and all rolls are of equal thickness. The soil should be prepared, carefully leveled, and amply fertilized beforehand as with any seedbed; failure to do so will jeopardize this expensive undertaking. Then strips of sod are unrolled, nestled one against the other in staggered fashion as bricks are commonly laid, firmed into place, and perhaps topdressed with weed-free soil to fill in chinks. If the soil was not fertilized beforehand, the new sod should receive a surface feeding.

A newly sodded lawn is usually rolled to firm the sod into the soil and to mesh strips tightly against one another. It should then be watered thoroughly. In good growing weather, especially spring and autumn for bluegrass sod, the new turf will be able to fend for itself almost immediately. It should, of course, receive regular watering for at least several weeks, and thereafter the same attention that any lawn would receive. Within a few weeks it will be securely rooted to the soil beneath.

Sodding Considerations

The many newly originated bluegrass and fescue varieties have given great impetus to the sod industry. Sod carefully grown from top-flight, weed-free seed is commonplace even in garden centers formerly unlikely to stock perishables. Thus good seed is available as living grass, its sprouting and early growth completed for you through the services of a sod grower. Naturally, sodding is more costly than seeding; the growing and handling must be compensated for. On the other hand, sod provides an "instant" lawn while several weeks are needed to gain full cover from a seeding.

Carefully grown sod produced on land free of pernicious weeds provides the same fescues, bentgrasses, and bluegrass that you would sow to your own lawn. "Bargain basement" sod, like cut-rate seed, may be another matter. You could be introducing into your lawn for the first time such pests as quackgrass, billbugs, grass diseases, or seeds of annuals such as crabgrass which may already have been controlled on your own property.

However, almost all soils contain some weed seeds, and even if you seed your own lawn, nuisances like spurge, purslane, knotweed and shepherd's purse will probably sprout from residual seed in the soil. We have seen that none of these weeds are carried in well-cleaned lawnseed. These and familiar farm weeds such as pigweed, lambsquarters and velvetweed, although often abundant in young turf, mostly disappear in competition with the grass and because they can't stand mowing. Any remaining weeds are fairly easily eliminated with modern-day weed killers. The only exception are perennial pest grasses such as nimblewill, timothy or quackgrass; special pains should be taken to see that these are not brought into the lawn because it will be difficult to eliminate them later.

A common misconception is that sodding a lawn need not be as painstaking as sowing seed. Actually, the soilbed should be equally well prepared for either kind of planting, and neither seed nor sod will thrive on a rock-hard base into which it cannot root. Some authorities feel that a seedling rooted directly into endemic soil has some advantage over a transplanted grass started elsewhere. But this should not be a significant factor if sod is properly laid on a prepared soilbed, rolled firm, and kept watered for the several weeks needed until it is firmly rooted. Lawngrasses regenerate about half of their roots each year, and as long as there is no barrier (like a layer of humus) at the base of sod, the grass should root well. The old roots of transplanted sod cease to function, and new rootlets penetrate the soilbed.

Plugging Bare Areas

In northern climates, sodding is not the only alternative to seeding. Sprigs or plugs can be used, just as they are in the South, to patch bare spots. However, planting in this fashion is laborious. Rhizomatous or stoloniferous grasses spread from the introduced plugs or sprigs to colonize adjacent soil. Probably the easiest way to replant small grassless areas is to cut sod plugs from parts of the lawn where they won't be noticed. Hollow-handle plugging devices are available which accumulate about two dozen biscuits of sod before they start spilling out the top. When the handle is full, simply move to the bald areas and punch holes of the same size into the bare soil. Each time a hole is punched, the soil will force a sod plug out at the top; this is then laid by hand in the hole. The plug can be firmed into place by stepping on it.

Mass Planting Stolons

Occasionally lawns, as well as golf greens, are planted to bentgrass or bermudagrass cultivars. A typical golf green procedure is to shred sod (or purchase fragmented stolons), and scatter the pieces upon soil prepared as if for seed. A light topdressing of sifted, sterilized soil is spread, and the whole area rolled. It should be kept moist until the grass fragments have rooted. This happens in a few days if the soil is kept continuously moist. A more recent technique is to scatter stolons

Gathering plugs of grass with hollow stem plugging device.

on the prepared soil, throw a chain mat over them, then walk over the mat (thus firming the stolons into the soil) while scattering topdressing through the open links. In this way a worker can proceed across a soft seedbed, section by section, without leaving indented footprints.

Planting Southern Grasses

Although sodding is practiced in the South, planting smaller grass fragments is more economical and more frequent. Both plugs and sprigs are used, sprigs perhaps more commonly. These quickly grow into a complete turf in the propitious southern climate. This is especially true of bermudagrass, which, under favorable conditions, makes a complete cover in a few weeks. However, zoysia, a slow grower, may require a year or two to form a tight turf started from sprigs or plugs. A familiar practice in middle latitudes is to introduce zoysia plugs or strip plantings into an existing inadequate turf and let these gradually expand through the years. Most of the time zoysia is aggressive enough in summer to eventually crowd out northern species and to dominate the lawn population.

Special selections of bermuda, various zoysias, and st. augustine grass are the chief southern species which are vegetatively planted. Centipede is sometimes started in this way, and other species may be occasionally, although they are more easily grown from seed.

Homeowners planting their own lawns may purchase sprigs or plugs, make plugs from their own sod, or tear apart sod to make sprigs. Sprigs are often marketed in polyethylene bags. Zoysia so packaged will keep for many weeks if refrigerated. However, it is best to plant sprigs as soon as received. Drop the sprigs into a bucket of water so that they won't dry out before planting. The bucket can be carried down the rows as planting progresses.

Sprigs and plugs need the same favorable growing season, ample fertility, and regular watering required by seeded grasses. Don't presume that because growing plants are utilized, they can withstand early neglect any more than can newly sprouted seedlings.

Plugs are handled in much the same manner as described for bluegrass in the North. The plugs are from special plantings made in paper cups, or are cut with plug cutters, or sectioned into small chunks from larger sods. The resulting sod biscuits are hand-planted at spaced intervals in a prepared seedbed, and encouraged by watering and feeding to expand by rhizome and runner until a complete turf is knitted.

Plugs give greater assurance of survival than sprigs, since they already have roots established in a small chunk of soil. On the other hand, plugging is more expensive; one pays for soil as well as grass,

Plugging tool and a sample of the sod plug removed.

and plugs will not plant nearly so much lawn as an equal volume of sprigs. Plugs ordinarily require more time to develop rhizome or runner growth than do sprigs, possibly because stem tips are severed when the plugs are taken. Evidently, it also takes considerable time for growth to bridge the gap between the soil of the plug and the seedbed. Plugs are slower to become "at home" than are sprigs planted directly into seedbed soil.

Sprigs are sometimes obtained by running sod through a shredder. Better quality sprigs are produced by carefully pulling sod apart by hand after the soil has been washed away from the root system. The individual sprigs can be cut to proper length, or may consist of unsevered shoots. Newly planted sprigs should be firmed into soil, and must be watered regularly. Within a few days, bermuda and st. augustine sprigs will be rooted and growing; slower zoysias may take several weeks.

Bermudas are much like the bents of the North in that they root

Holes are made in a turfless area to accommodate plugs taken from growing sod. Simply insert the plug in the hole and press down with the foot.

Hand planting grass plugs.

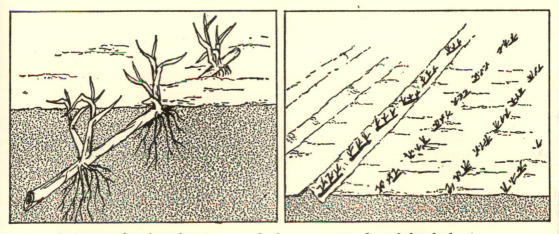

Sprigs may be planted in furrows, the lowermost joint buried, but buds of upper joint exposed.

easily. Stem fragments scattered on the surface, perhaps topdressed or partially disced into the seedbed, will strike root and spread if kept moist.

Zoysia should be more carefully planted. Usually sprigs must be inserted by hand into shallow trenches or at spaced points across the new lawn. Zoysia sprigs customarily contain three or four joints, or nodes. One node is inserted about an inch below the soil surface, and the stem is inclined so that the node at the opposite end is above-ground with the leaves showing. Sprigs thus planted will suffer little loss if regularly watered. Zoysia, especially, should receive fertilization and regular weed control after the sprigs have started growth, to hasten the spread of this slow-growing species. Even in parts of Florida with a twelve-month growing season, sprigged zoysia takes a year to make a tight lawn turf.

COMMON MISCONCEPTIONS

PLUGS KNIT TO A SOD MORE QUICKLY THAN DO SPRIGS. Strangely, even though the planting of plugs would seem to result in less disturbance and setback to the grass than sprigs, which have the roots torn loose from the soil, in most instances lateral growth from sprigs is more rapid than from plugs. Evidently shoots, rooting in the seedbed soil, are stimulated to immediate elongation, while plugs, in their own biscuit of soil, remain temporarily self-sufficient.

SOD WILL GIVE A FINER LAWN THAN SEEDING. Fine sod, expertly laid, can result in an excellent turf. But sodding is expensive, and may not have as smooth a surface as would a seeding. It often contains some unwanted weeds or off-type grasses. Some experts feel that better grass rooting is obtained when seed is started in native soil than when sod is introduced from a foreign location. The chief advantage of sodding is the speed with which a grass cover can be obtained.

SELECT CULTIVARS REVERT TO COMMON TYPES. Except in very rare cases where mutation takes place (such as Tifdwarf bermuda being a mutant out of Tifgreen, discovered in several locations), a vegetative planting will come true-to-type. Not uncommonly, volunteer grass beginning from just a few residual seeds or "starts" in the soil can expand and dominate the grass population if the planted cultivar is not as well adapted.

11

mowing and mowers

THE EARLIEST MEANS of controlling vegetation was probably fire; the earliest "mower" about the home was livestock. Then, with the advent of technology, sickle and scythe were devised for mowing grass. It is not uncommon today in tropical countries to see lawns mowed with the large bush knives called machetes.

In more recent times a variety of mechanical mowers has been invented, based either upon the whipping principle of the sickle or the scissors-like slicing action of sharp edge against edge. These have permitted easier keeping of formal ground cover, while also raising our expectations of what mowing should accomplish.

A. J. Downing, writing in 1849 in *Landscape Gardening and Rural Architecture*, advises: "Beauty depends upon *frequent mowing*. Once a fortnight at the furthest . . . a broad-bladed English scythe, at nearly parallel to the surface . . . a clever mower will be able to shave within half an inch of the ground without leaving any marks."

Such "new" advice little more than a century ago indicates how recently regular mowing has become accepted. Today, in America, it is taken for granted that every lawn will be mowed, and a man may be judged by his lawn's tidiness.

Height of Cut

The reason for mowing is not so much to keep grass short as to keep it even. A newly mown lawn is attractive, whether it is clipped to one inch or two inches. In either case it will have to be mowed again soon, when new leaves exceed the old and the surface exhibits an irregular, unkempt appearance.

Taste in mowing varies tremendously. Admirers of golf turf may feel that they prefer the very short clipping required for a green. Many people think a lawn is attractive because it has been closely clipped, when other attentions have made it attractive in spite of close clipping. Homeowners make extra work for themselves by demanding a low cut. Mowing too close leads to weak grass and invites weeds.

The influence of mowing upon the lawn is becoming more appreciated, and higher mowing is not the anathema it once was. There was a time when lawnmowers couldn't be set much over an inch high; today a lawnmower that will not adjust easily in the range between one and three inches is in the dark ages of design.

What is the effect of mowing on the individual grass plant? That a portion of each leaf is almost invariably severed is apparent. And, as with any plant, frequent trimming fosters bushiness; in other words, removing the tips stimulates budding from below. Under mowing, the longer, more robust culms and leaves normal to unmowed grass are replaced by a greater number of shorter tillers. By and large, this contributes to turf attractiveness, although not necessarily to the endurance of the individual grass plant. Constant low clipping encourages dwarfed culms and shallow roots. Under low mowing, as under close grazing, the shoot count will increase even while the sod may be weakened.

When over a third of the green leaf surface of grass is cut away, root growth slows or stops. Tests on Kentucky bluegrass indicate that root growth can be inhibited for as much as a month by a single scalping. If the lawn inadvertently has become excessively long, it is better to reduce cutting height gradually in a series of successively closer mowings, than to cut it back all at once (a practice which could prove lethal in spring when food reserves are being exhausted by new growth).

It is evident that with almost all lawn grasses, high clipping results in greater root growth than low clipping. Greater root growth usually lessens the care needed by a lawn; shallowly rooted grasses dry and succumb to drought more readily than a deeply rooted turf which can

Dr. Eliot Robert's solution culture work shows clearly that mowing height greatly influences depth of grass rooting.

fend for itself longer. Higher mowed turf is also its own best weed control.

In keeping a lawn, one strives for a balance between a turf so closely clipped that it needs constant babying, and a completely neglected hay-field. Mowing height can be predicated largely on how much effort and expenditure the lawnsman wants to put into watering, weed control, and similar ventures. Lawns that are "just like a carpet" generally have so many stunted plants, so tightly packed, that they seldom survive without regular watering, feeding, and control of pests. The individual plants are on "the ragged edge." If your lawn is not of putting-green texture, there are certain compensations. At least you don't need a full-time yardman. Moreover, turf clipped two inches high can be attractive by almost anyone's standards.

Mowing height also influences microclimate. Tall grass is a better insulator of soil than short grass. Keeping the soil cooler on hot days not only helps the grass, but may influence the atmosphere about the home. A lawn is considerably cooler than paved drives or patios that radiate heat.

Seasonal Considerations in Mowing

No matter what the climate, there will be seasons of luxurious growth alternating with seasons of at least partial dormancy. Thus, the frequency of lawn mowing moves in cycles. Provision must be made for the season of most luxurious growth; to have inadequate equipment when it is needed is one of the biggest irritants in maintaining a lawn. More time is spent in mowing than in doing anything else to the turf, so don't stint in providing yourself with the means for handling the job pleasurably even when grass grows its fastest.

The time when mowing should begin in spring and stop in autumn varies with climate and kind of grass. The only safe rule is to mow when the grass needs it. This means when additional leaf growth approaches half again normal clipping height. Mowing might well begin on bermudas and bents when the grass has grown an additional one-quarter to one-half inch, and on bluegrass, fescue, and st. augustine whenever one inch has been added. Of course, these goals are not always achieved, since rain or soggy soil may upset any schedule. But it is better to be equipped for frequent mowing that produces short clippings, than to cut off a lot infrequently, shocking the grass and creating clipping-disposal problems.

If summers are hot and dry, Kentucky bluegrass scarcely grows, and can sometimes be left for several weeks without mowing. On the other hand, an unusually cool, moist summer may make it necessary to mow at least weekly all season. Normally, bluegrass grows most vigorously in spring, and may need mowing twice a week during its peak period; the rest of the season, once-a-week mowing usually is ample.

Bermudas are rapid growers during warm weather. To look their best in summer they require mowing twice a week as long as fertility and moisture are adequate. Zoysia, on the other hand, grows very slowly. Though it merits once-a-week mowing for greatest attractiveness, it frequently can be let go two or three weeks without harm.

Maintenance practices through the growing season have tremendous influence on mowing. The stimulus of fertilization is obvious. The effect of watering may be twofold, for in addition to promoting growth, sprinkling can at times lower summer soil temperatures enough to keep grasses such as Kentucky blue from going dormant.

The lawnkeeper is often advised to clip the lawn close going into the winter. The reasoning usually offered is that long grass mats down and smothers new growth. Although rampant growth of trailing grasses may mat at any season, it is unlikely that a bluegrass-red fescue lawn, at normal clipping height, will develop troublesome smothering. In a test where bluegrass was purposely left completely unmowed, the turf seemed in no way harmed, although the dead, brown leaves did insulate the ground against quick warming in the spring and delayed greening for a week or two.

As noted, grass blades scorch in hard winter weather. Invariably there is a nubbin of green hidden within the brown sheaths. If the dead leaves are clipped, the green shows through. Perhaps it would be wiser to mow close as winter breaks rather than before it sets in. Where winter is mild, with occasional frosts that discolor the turf, fast-growing grasses, such as bermuda, revive at once in the warmer days that follow frost. A clipping exposes new leaf growth almost immediately. Zoysia does not revive so rapidly, nor do most of the other southern lawngrasses. With all lawngrasses, northern and southern, a closer-than-usual clipping as spring growth begins will brighten the lawn, removing the old discolored leaves, and letting the new blades show more quickly.

The Clippings

It is debatable whether lawn clippings should be removed. Long clippings from infrequent mowings remain perched on the surface, unsightly until new growth tops them. If they are so coarse as never to settle against moist soil, they may be a long time in decomposing and a perpetual source of discoloration each time the lawn is mowed.

If clippings are short, they settle into the grass and become hidden by new growth before turning brown. Grasses with upright rather than trailing stems, such as Kentucky bluegrass and fescue, seldom create any problem with short clippings (although with denser cultivars clipping may have difficulty sifting into the sod). On trailing species, such as bent, bermuda, and zoysia, layers of "thatch" sometimes build up: the trailing stems weave a mat that holds clippings and dead stems above the soil where they will not readily decompose. Because zoysia tissues are notably resistant to decay, this mat can become so tight that it sheds moisture like shingles; rainfall and irrigation water run off rather than sink into the soil.

At times clippings may prove to be a useful soil insulation against summer heat. For the most part, however, undecomposed clippings are of little benefit to a lawn and may, indeed, be a hazard. There is speculation that they serve as a reservoir for disease. However, a bluegrass test lawn in Ohio showed no increase in disease when clippings were left on it.

A powered sweeper for picking up lawn clippings, leaves, or removed thatch.

The prime objection to clippings lies in their unsightliness. Meticulous lawnkeepers usually gather them for the sake of appearance, in spite of the undoubted fertility value of decaying clippings. Many modern mowers, both of the rotary and reel types, are designed to collect clippings.

Incidentally, when clippings are removed, they can be put to good use in the garden. Shrubs profit from a layer over their root zone. And a mulch of clippings holds weeds in check while insulating sprawling tomatoes, for example, against soil splash and fruit rot. If you have a compost pile to make humus, grass clippings make a valuable contribution.

Fertility Value of Clippings

Because blades of grass contain nutrients from the soil, they have potential as an organic fertilizer. When clippings decompose on the lawn, the nutrients packed into the grass are once again returned to the soil. During the course of a year, clippings may recycle minerals equivalent to one or two average fertilizations. The following table shows the fertility value of the clippings from a well-tended lawn during a growing season. These nutrients can be replaced with fertilizer, but for the economy-minded there is much to recommend leaving clippings on the lawn. Decaying clippings also keep the soil surface aggregated, improving to some extent the penetration of rain or irrigation water.

Nutrient Recovery from Clippings of a ¼-Acre Lawn
in a Single Year (yielding ½ ton dry clippings).
Some nitrogen may change to gaseous form
and be lost during decomposition of clippings.

		Lbs.
Nitrogen	(N)	30
Phosphorus	(P_2O_5)	10
Potassium	(K_2O)	25
Lime	(CaO)	10
Magnesium	(MgO)	2
Sulfur	(S)	2

The Lawn Mower

Recent years have witnessed a revolution in lawn mowing. Almost no one powers a lawn mower any more by pushing; even the smallest suburban lot sports a motorized unit. Millions of power mowers are sold each year in a highly competitive market. With model changes that remind one of automobile merchandizing, the mower industry has catered both to the convenience of the customer and the good of the grass. The biggest boon for the latter is the introduction of mowers that can clip high, with simple, quick adjustments of mowing height.

Some of the basic features of mowers merit review. Motors, power ratios, gear assemblies, and other mechanical details usually are adequate in the models of any reputable manufacturer. Style, size, maneuverability, whether gasoline or electric, riding type or walk-behind, and similar features are largely matters of personal preference, to be chosen for the location where the mower is to be used and according to the funds available.

Reel Mowers versus Rotary Mowers

How does a reel mower compare with a rotary mower? Rotaries out-sell reels many times over, so they must have advantages. A rotary mower has a horizontally moving, high-speed blade which cuts vegetation by impact, as would a scythe or sickle. A reel mower has fixed blades, part of a turning cylinder (reel), which moves down and back against a stationary bedknife at the base of the mower.

Reel mowers, theoretically, should cut cleaner than rotaries, and they do if they are sharp and well adjusted. Then the sharp blade of the reel, playing against bedknife, exercises a scissors-like shearing action. Contrast this with the impact-cutting of a whirling rotary blade that relies on momentum. Impact-cutting always chances some fraying of the grass. A perfectionist might anticipate slightly more "gray hair" on his

A typical reel-type mower well suited to low, neat clipping.

grass from a rotary mower than from a well adjusted reel. Ryegrasses especially fray when the leaf is cut by rotary impact.

Rotaries generally travel on four wheels, reels on two. Reels thus tend to dip into depressions while rotaries tend to hold a uniform plane position. The reel mower can be expected to follow the contour more exactly, giving a more uniform height of cut from soil to leaf tip. The rotary has a greater tendency to clip longer over depressions, shorter over small mounds or ridges, showing deep green (long) grass contrasting with thin (semiscalped) spots. By the same token, small swales are more evident with reel mowing than with rotary.

A flying rotary blade can be hazardous, and small objects can be hurled from a rotary machine with the speed of a bullet. A toe in a whirling reel is bad enough, but the blade of a rotary packs more potential destructive power than a reel. Most mowers have suitable guards and offer no great danger unless carelessly handled. Certainly the housing should afford protection against entry of feet and from flying rocks struck inadvertently.

There are practical advantages to a rotary mower. It is generally more versatile, and can chew up tall grass that either clogs or escapes a reel mower. In most rotary models cutting height is more easily adjusted; many reel mowers cannot be set two to three inches high, and require resetting of wheels as well as roller.

Rotaries are mechanically simpler and somewhat less expensive initially. They require less skill to adjust and maintain. The homeowner can sharpen his rotary blade, but must send reels out to be sharpened. This is perhaps the biggest drawback to reels, for to do the cutting job well they must be in perfect adjustment. Sharp reel blades adjust barely to miss the bedknife, just as the blades of scissors slide by one another.

Rotary mowers don't jam on small twigs as easily as reel mowers, and thus are not so frustrating under trees. Some also function as leaf mulchers. Many rotary mowers chop clippings small enough to make raking unnecessary, but unless ejection is immediate, may simply mash clippings into a sodden pulp under the housing.

For the meticulously tended lawn, a reel mower is advocated. Yet the practical advantages of the rotaries for the average lawn are attested to in their markedly greater sales.

Less Frequently Used Mowers

Sickle bars have long been familiar for cutting hay and grain. Small units for the lawn are quite effective, although they are more cumbersome than reels and rotaries. They may shake themselves into frequent disrepair.

Flail or hammer-knife mowers find limited use. They have loose-hanging cutting blades which sever grass by impact as does a rotary, but pivot from a reel-like cylinder rotating at high speed. Centrifugal force keeps the blades extended. So far, these mowers have not proved too practical, largely because it becomes tedious to sharpen the many separate blades and to obtain as neat a cut as with other mowers. But for rough mowing, where hidden stones or debris can be expected, less damage is suffered when an object is struck.

Gasoline versus Electric Mowers

There are some advantages and disadvantages to both gasoline and electric motors for mowers. A purchaser must decide which features are most important to him. Electrics are free from exhaust smells and noise, and silence is fast becoming "golden," as public reaction to noise pollution increases. Chicago passed an ordinance, for example, restricting noise from lawn mowers and similar motorized equipment in residential areas to 74 decibels in 1972, declining to only 65 decibels by 1978, measured at a distance of 50 feet. Many power mowers in use will not meet that requirement. Electric motors are also generally foolproof, long-lasting, seldom need servicing, and require no gasoline or oil. They start readily in all weather. However, an electric cord trailing behind is a nuisance, and so far no really lightweight batteries with prolonged charge have been developed for models not using an electric outlet. Among trees, for homes without outdoor outlets, and on big lawns, electric mowers are at a disadvantage.

Gasoline motors are noisy, sometimes hard to start, and need servicing. But being self-sufficient, they afford excellent mobility and wide range. Most power mowers are gasoline-propelled. Manufacturers have introduced recoiling starter ropes, plug-in electric starters, wind-up self-starters, and similar innovations to end the tyranny of balky engines. Garden tractors and larger riding mowers have battery-powered self-starters much like an automobile.

Mower Propulsion

Mower wheels generally operate on bearings for easy forward movement. Some rotary mowers are so light and easy to push that self-propulsion has little advantage. In these, full motor power is devoted to the cutter. The operator can delay longer over tough, thick grass that might clog or stall a mower moving rapidly forward. In propelled models it is preferable to have adjustable forward speeds (the cutter speed remaining constant), to accommodate different grasses or seasonal growth. Zoysia, for example, needs more cutting activity in a given distance than a less tough grass; if a reel mower is used on this fibrous grass, extra blades are an advantage. In spring, Kentucky bluegrass may produce several times the volume of clippings as in August, and will stall a mower which would have no difficulty later.

Wheeled mowers predominate over skid or roller types, although most reels have a roller height control. At certain seasons, and especially on young turf, a one-piece roller tends to tear the lawn on turns. Obviously a roller that revolves at a single speed over its length can't accommodate both the reduced distance at the inner edge of the turn and the extended distance at the outer edge. Some mowers have a segmented roller, each part pivoting independently.

Skids, such as the "shoes" on garden tractor sickle-bar mountings, sometimes tear soft turf. Fortunately, with most sickle-bar cutters, the weight is balanced on large pneumatic tires, permitting an essentially frictionless glide of the shoes over grass.

There is a trend toward ridden rather than walk-behind mowers. Whether one rides or walks is a matter of preference and pocketbook; but see that riding mowers have sufficient power, ease of turning and maneuvering, the ability to reverse, and forward speed independent of mower speed. Most large riding mowers have "hydrostatic drive," a single handle controlling speed and forward or backward motion without influencing the mower's activity.

Planning Mowing

Even with the best planned lawns one must somewhere maneuver corners and boundaries. Mower wheels or bulges that extend beyond the cutting radius make it difficult to mow the extreme edge of the lawn. Light construction facilitates handling, both in storage and for turning. Because four-wheel rotaries are difficult to turn, some manufacturers use a pivoted handle by which the mower can be guided equally well forward or backward. A rotary cuts in either direction, but the very nature of reels permits cutting only during forward motion.

Grass that is repeatedly mowed in the same direction, especially with reel mowers that don't suck up the stems, may develop grain. That is, the grass leaves are pressed forward and remain pointing in the direction of mowing. As a result the lawn is streaked or banded.

This can be avoided by occasionally altering the pattern of mowing. Mowing against the grain, that is, opposite to the direction in which the grass blades lie, will help eliminate severe grain. Alternate mowings at right angles would be a more familiar way, not requiring intensive attention.

Most mowers throw clippings to the side, where they will be worked over again in a subsequent pass. It may be well to arrange the mowing system so that clippings are thrown into the path of the next swath. In that way they are twice cut and will sift more easily to the soil surface. Avoid models with wheels that press down the grass in front of the cutter, make deep tracks, or tear the sod in turning.

The wider the swath cut, the quicker the mowing job—and the more expensive the machine. The trend is away from 16-inch models to the 19-inch and bigger. Riding mowers sport multiple-bladed rotaries cutting a swath as wide as 60 inches. For large lawns, wing attachments for riding mowers are available that cut an even wider swath, but such units may prove cumbersome for home lawns. Comparing the area to be mowed with swath width will indicate an appropriate compromise between size and cost.

In purchasing any mower it is a mistake to skimp. Nothing puts more pleasure into keeping a lawn than an adequately powered mower capable of doing the job quickly. A well chosen mower eliminates much of the nuisance of hand-trimming, servicing hidden mechanisms, or repeated calls for help and spare parts.

Chemical Mowing

Chemical mowing may simply mean the elimination of coarse weeds so that the grass looks better unmowed. Along roadsides, for example, this is appropriate. For the lawn, chemical mowing involves the use of a growth inhibitor. The only chemical to have received a widespread trial for this is maleic hydrazide. Results have been less than satisfactory for home use. The effectiveness of the chemical varies with humidity and other environmental circumstances, and it is seldom possible to repress growth equally on all plants. Either inherent plant differences or uneven application may be the cause. Irregular growth necessitates mowing, even if there has been little added leaf. Then too, weeds may not be repressed so much as the grass, and actually gain an advantage as a result of the treatment. Field trials on bluegrass in California have given quite satisfactory retardation for several months, but without continuous new growth rust infection often becomes so severe as to kill

In America, almost all mowing is powered, even the edging operations.

the grass. And there is the risk of burning the grass by careless application, as well as the expense of treatment. It looks as though lawn mowing still has a long life ahead. Although some of the newer growth retardants (e.g., ethrel) may eventually find a place in lawn management.

Maleic hydrazide has proved useful for repressing seedhead production, an especial mowing nuisance on bahiagrass in the South. In combination with chloroflurenol it has suppressed grass growth up to 50 per cent of normal on northern roadsides, lessening the need for mowing (this combination, marketed as "Maintain," also exhibits some herbicidal activity, killing dandelions and clover, and retarding several other common turf weeds). In greenhouse and field trials another chemical, cycocel, has suppressed growth of several bermudagrass cultivars, and inhibited the onset of dormancy.

Edgers, Trimmers

Trimming, the handmaiden to mowing, has yielded to technological advancement. Today there are power trimmers that do an effective job, adjustable to vertical or horizontal cutting, and which can be wheeled close to barriers. For those willing to invest gusto rather than dollars, hand shears are still effective, and several edgers (such as the half-moon spade device) have back-saving long handles.

Modern garden centers supply grass barriers. These are usually corrugated plastic or metal strips sunk several inches into the soil in the hope of keeping rhizomes from sneaking under. When used to encircle trees or flower beds, the interior area may be filled with pebbles or mulch, the barrier protruding slightly above the soil as a mowing demarcation. Grasses that rhizome or stolonize vigorously seem to find ways to grow under or over such barriers, which should be checked from time to time.

Chemical trimming with a hand sprayer instead of an edger can save considerable labor. The same chemicals suggested for chemical knock-down in renovation (Chapter 9), such as paraquat or cacodylic acid, can be used. They will dry up any green foliage contacted, but will not bother stems covered with bark or toxify the soil. They are thus excellent for eliminating growing vegetation around the base of trees, for edging drives or walkways, and so on. Leave the scorched sod in place as a mulch to prevent weeds. Treatment may have to be repeated several times during the growing season, but this is still a lot easier than trimming mechanically each week or two.

Careful spraying of borders with a contact herbicide makes trimming unnecessary.

Lawn Thatch

From all the admonitions about thatch one might suppose that organic residues at the base of a sod are a novel and particular curse of lawn keeping. Thatching has, in fact, been intensified by modern practices and it has been more noticed because standards are higher, but there is no great mystery about thatch and its formation. Thatch is a natural response to the "bioenergetics of the ecosystem," to use an ecological phrase (Chapter 2).

Any planting experiences a crescendo of growth during which plant substance accumulates in excess of decomposition. Then, as time passes, much energy is tied up in residues—whether in litter on the forest floor or in its organic duff of prairie and lawn—at which point a level of decay is reached that roughly balances energy input (photosynthesis). This balance may be altered by changes in the season, the weather, or by disturbances such as fire and cultivation.

Most of the lawngrass varieties now used have been selected for heavy foliage and vigorous growth. Naturally, this intensifies thatch production. By the same token, some less dense, older varieties seem little bothered by thatch. There are natural bluegrass pastures in north central Kentucky and bluegrass fence rows in Iowa that have survived with no particular attention for scores if not hundreds of years. They have accumulated a humusy thatch layer about an inch thick but it does not seem to interfere with survival or general attractiveness. Yet such grass is not dense enough nor adapted to low enough mowing for modern urban and suburban tastes.

Differing habits, rapidity of growth, and chemical and structural discrepancies in the plant tissues cause species (even varieties within a species) to have differing tendencies toward the formation of thatch. Trailing grasses such as the creeping bentgrasses in the North and almost all of the southern lawngrasses, tend to build thatch more readily than those which spread underground by rhizomes, such as the bluegrasses and fescues. The stems or runners not only hold organic material away from the moist soil which would hasten decay, but the stems themselves are coarse and woody, slow to die and decompose.

The thatching tendency is further aggravated with the bermudagrasses by their rampant growth; with the zoysias because leaf and

Chemical trimming at the base of trees both protects the tree from bruising and facilitates mowing. (Photo courtesy of The Dow Chemical Company)

stem tissue is very resistant to decomposition; and with st. augustine because nearly year-round growth in its subtropical climate adds great volume. In almost all cases, the highly selected, elite cultivars thatch more than do the old-fashioned types. Thus, Tifgreen bermuda thatches more than common bermuda from seed, and Fylking, Merion, and Pennstar bluegrasses more than the natural type.

What are the disadvantages of thatch? Impeding the penetration of water, fertilizer, and pesticide to the root-zone is an obvious drawback. Thatch may become so thick that it blocks the emergence of new shoots. It may even insulate the soil from the warmth of the spring sun sufficiently to delay green-up of the lawn by a week or so. Many experts also feel that thatch harbors inoculum of insect pests and disease spores which attack living grass under appropriate conditions. In their protected thatch home these pests are harder to reach with pesticides, too. Indeed, the use of fungicides may intensify thatch accumulation by inhibiting the organisms responsible for decay as well as those which cause disease.

Thatch may prevent access of air to the soil, causing the grass roots to grow into the thatch rather than downward into the soil. Drought quickly affects such a sod. Likewise, heavily thatched turf often lifts like a carpet because it has relatively few roots anchoring the grass to the anoxious soil. Sometimes thatch shows as an undertone of unattractive brown, especially when it's so massive as to have thinned the grass.

But there are also some benefits from thatch. It serves as a mulch, preventing the germination of crabgrass and *Poa annua* seed which need light. To an extent, it preserves soil moisture, reducing direct evaporation and insulating the soil from the sun's heat. As decay progresses, nutrients are returned to the soil much as they might be from an organic fertilizer. The aggregating gums released by decaying vegetation have a beneficial effect upon soil structure making it crumbly and more porous. And thatch is sustenance for many helpful microorganisms contributing to the natural balance of sod and soil. Today's lawn equipment and products, however, provide most of these benefits without the disadvantages that thatch brings.

A certain amount of thatch is natural and not harmful. How much is acceptable depends upon the kind of turf and its maintenance. Kentucky bluegrass lawns generally have a half inch or so of thatch that causes no difficulty. But if thatch is allowed to get an inch or more thick, it can bring troubles such as we have discussed. What to do about this is the next question. There are two possible approaches—prevention and correction.

Preventing and Correcting Thatch

The usual suggestion for preventing thatch is to collect the clippings when mowing or to sweep them up afterwards. While this may help to a degree, close investigation of thatch shows that it does not consist primarily of clippings (which are little lignified and decompose readily). Rather, thatch is mostly a network of lignified roots and stems that are much more durable than leaf tips, plus the less-succulent basal leaf sheaths. These are untouched by the mower. The only way to get rid of them is to rip them out mechanically.

A wise choice of grass and lawn tending that encourages decay will aid in thatch prevention. Needs vary with the circumstances but keep in mind that, in general, decomposition of organic material is encouraged by humidity, air access (material not tightly packed), near-neutral pH, and nutrient balance (enough nitrogen to stimulate the organisms which decompose carbohydrates, but not so much that the grass is stimulated to make even more organic material). In some instances, perhaps, chemical applications might even be restrained lest decay be interfered with. There have even been attempts to add enzymes artificially to hasten decay.

Thus, fertilization, liming, watering, raking or sweeping, and application of pest controls influence thatch formation. Sometimes just the right combination of microorganisms and weather brings a boon. In one case, thatch built up to a tremendous thickness for 7 years on an experimental golf green and then suddenly, in one year, decomposed almost completely. No one knows just what triggered the sudden surge of decay.

Of course, biological methods can help reduce thatch as well as prevent it. A simple procedure like liming an acid lawn, or draining a wet one, may speed up thatch decomposition. Biological interactions are so complex, however, that results are seldom assured. A commonly used method on golf greens is to topdress with about a quarter inch of soil. The moist microclimate around the thatch is then ideal for decay.

Usually more practical is direct elimination of thatch. With grasses that have underground parts not easily injured, burning the thatch during the dormant season is sometimes practiced. This is appropriate for bermuda and zoysia lawns during winter but is not esthetically pleasing, leaving a dirty, charred area to contend with until the next growing season.

More widely utilized are mechanical turf thinners. Some thatch-removing machines have flexible tines on a rotating reel which comb out most of the thatch for subsequent sweeping. More commonly, the reel supports a series of toothed discs or knives a half inch or so apart which cut vertically. The reel can be set to slice to any depth (but a great deal of power is needed if it cuts much into the soil). The blades are like buzz saws, slicing into the sod as the machine moves forward. They cut the thatch to pieces, kicking most detritus to the surface. Much thatch is removed, and oxidative decomposition of that which remains is encouraged.

Such an operation rejuvenates the turf, stimulating it to fresh growth. It both prunes the live grass and stimulates it physiologically through mineralization of the humus and general microbiological speed-up. The lawn assumes a fresh, attractive appearance in just a few days. It is best to remove thatch when the permanent turf is growing actively to heal the scars quickly and prevent weeds from finding space.

A homeowner seldom needs to remove thatch even annually. Consider whether thatch is a serious problem before undertaking its removal. The cultivation that comes with thatch removal can give unwanted vegetation a chance, especially pesky annual bluegrass.

Unbelievable piles of fluffy thatch can be taken out of even a small lawn. But even after a thorough dethatching, don't be surprised if a year later there seems to be almost as much thatch again. Thatch removal is an aid toward a sparkling lawn mainly because it makes other care more effective. It is not a cure-all and not a substitute for other maintenance necessities.

REGIONAL FOCUS

Certain grasses present mowing peculiarities. When creeping forms of bent crop up in northern lawns, it may be desirable to use a mower that sucks up the trailing growth to help prevent clumping. A rotary mower with strong "lift" might prove preferable for such a grass, although a reel mower ordinarily is appropriate for bentgrass. This also applies to some extent to bermuda and most stoloniferous grasses. Research suggests that a vigorous thinning gives bluegrass some advantage over invading bent if done in autumn.

Thick-textured southern grasses, especially zoysias, but also some bermudas and centipede, need a many-bladed reel mower for precise cutting. Golf-green mowers have always had about eight blades; but the typical home mower, until recently, was only five-bladed. For easily mown bluegrass and fescue this sufficed; heavy-textured zoysia not only needs more blades to the reel, but more power in the motor.

Dichondra should be clipped fairly short, managed much like fine bermuda, but because of its slower growth it does not need quite such frequent mowing. Mowing is preferable every week during the growing season, at as low a mowing height as one-half inch in the cooler coastal areas, up to one-and-a-half inches in warmer areas and during the summer. Clippings are customarily removed to prevent formation of an organic mat which might encourage disease. The tight growth of dichondra clipped at these heights causes most weeds to grow upright and gradually succumb from constant mowing.

COMMON MISCONCEPTIONS

CLOSE MOWING IS MORE ATTRACTIVE. In general, it is the uniformity of a mowing, not height, that governs attractiveness. A newly clipped lawn, even at three inches, looks most attractive if weed-free and of good color. Clipping height will vary with the kind of grass, but with almost any species a sudden lowering of clipping height will expose brown leaves and stubble. Low clipping favors invasion by weeds, whose different texture then detracts from the lawn, even when newly mown.

VERY FREQUENT MOWING CONTRIBUTES TO LAWN HEALTH. Mowing every other day will probably improve the appearance of a lawn, but may actually restrict root growth compared to grass mowed only once a week. Root growth corresponds to leafage aboveground, and evidently the extra growth, even if present for only a few days, helps promote greater vigor in individual grass plants.

COLLECT CLIPPINGS TO AVOID THATCH. While clippings add a little to the vegetational load, they consist mostly of the soft leaf tips which decompose quickly. Thatch most often derives from lignified stems and the base of the grass plant not reached by mowing. Clippings left on the lawn may be undesirable for several reasons; but ordinarily they are only a minor contribution to thatch build-up.

LAWN MOWING, WHAT A CHORE! Unfortunately, this impression is common. But, if indeed true, it signifies undersized or poorly designed equipment combined with a negative psychology. In a crowded world, mowing the lawn should provide release from tension and something of a "back-to-nature" contact whereby the rhythm of natural events is appreciated. But a capable mower is necessary to get the job done quickly without disruptions. Actually, there can be a lot of healthy fun in being out on the lawn and satisfaction from seeing the neat stripes of mowing falling into place one by one.

12

watering lawns

WATERING IS PERHAPS the most debatable practice of lawn care. Next to mower scalping, it is perhaps the most abused lawn-keeping procedure. There is no question that irrigation is necessary if a lawn is to be kept green during dry weather or in arid locations, but many homeowners take it for granted that sprinkling—any sprinkling—is desirable. Even experts are guided more by presumptions in this regard than by thorough research. A prominent turfgrass research man with decades of experience has stated that lawns are watered improperly so frequently that he ceased to recommend watering at all. Backing him is the fact that well established turfgrass is usually able to live out desiccation during drought, though it may turn totally brown. When more favorable weather comes, it quickly perks up into an expanse of green.

The uncertainty and differences of opinion about watering reflects the great diversity in lawns and human expectations. Recommendations concerning the frequency and duration of watering *must* vary widely, depending upon whether or not a lawn is to be kept green all summer, whether it is of bluegrass or bentgrass, on a slope or level, in shade or sun, growing on light or heavy soils, even whether water is cheap or dear. Each lawn has to be judged individually. Blanket recommendations are seldom faultless.

Lawns irrigated frequently favor grasses that thrive on moisture.

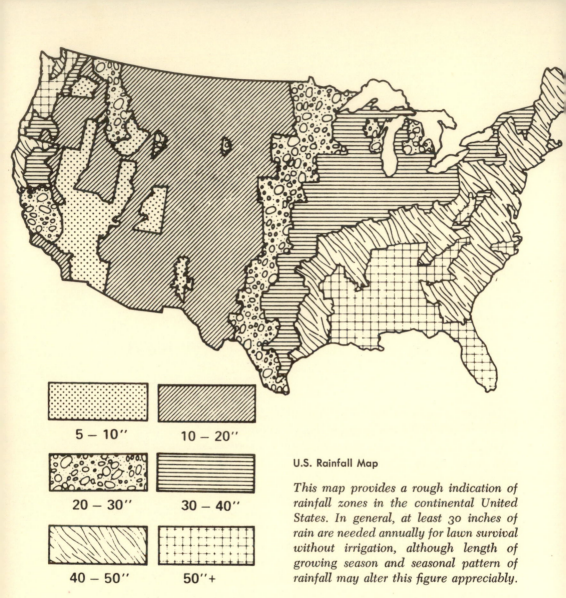

5 – 10" **10 – 20"**

20 – 30" **30 – 40"**

40 – 50" **50"+**

U.S. Rainfall Map

This map provides a rough indication of rainfall zones in the continental United States. In general, at least 30 inches of rain are needed annually for lawn survival without irrigation, although length of growing season and seasonal pattern of rainfall may alter this figure appreciably.

Bents, clover, annual bluegrass and a number of other weeds are encouraged by generous watering, while red fescue and buffalograss, for example, need very little. Bluegrass and most southern grasses are widely tolerant, but may suffer from invasion of rough bluegrass, bent, clover, and weeds in lawns that are kept saturated. If a lawn is watered only enough to keep the grass green, letting the soil moisture become almost exhausted between irrigations, the grass tends to develop deep roots without encouraging excessive growth of hydrophyllic weeds and grasses. This may prove especially important with lawns that can't be tended constantly, or where watering becomes seasonally restricted.

Water Is Vital for Life

Living tissue is largely water, and water enters into almost every life process. Cells must be bathed in moisture to keep from shriveling.

Grass picks up water mainly through the roots, although there is considerable benefit from dew or mist. Condensation on the grass blades during night and early morning substitutes to some extent for soil water. Some desert species, for example, exist almost entirely upon dew. In parts of the Midwest, where dew accumulations total as much as ten inches a year, condensation may furnish up to 20 per cent of the water utilized by crops.

In addition to being vital to living cells, water is a partner in nutrient utilization. Much of the fertility entering a root comes dissolved in water, and nutrient intake is commonly reduced during times of drought. The best utilization of fertilizer occurs only when water is ample. Conversely, abundant moisture needs high fertility to stimulate maximum growth. Even the vital carbon dioxide from the air is absorbed into a water film in the leaves.

Water in the Soil

Water often is recognized only for its direct utilization by the plant. For root development, however, it is one with the air which trails it into the soil pores. Wherever the soil remains continuously saturated, either from overwatering or from poor soil drainage, grass suffers because roots are stifled when air cannot reach them. Moreover, a perpetually soggy soil forces roots toward the surface, and the shallow grass is then in distress should the soil dry a few inches deep.

Intelligent irrigation attempts to match water volume with soil. In good soils the pore space fills readily; then the excess water drains by gravitation from the larger spaces, pulling air in behind. Where drainage is good this cycle is fairly rapid, a matter at most of but a few days. After water has drained by gravitation, moisture and air remain in about equal volume. The smaller pores and particle surfaces hold water tenaciously. The water molecules coat the soil-pore walls as a film, held by molecular attractions termed capillarity and surface tension. Most of this water is available to roots, but when it approaches exhaustion, replenishment by irrigation is needed to keep the grass from wilting. Watering may even be needed in the winter if the autumn was dry, especially in zones of doubtful hardiness.

Soils of fine texture—clays and silts—have many small pores that hold water for lengthy periods. These small-pore reservoirs may fill slowly, but once filled they provide a good moisture backlog for grass roots to draw upon. A clay loam may hold over 3 inches of water in the top foot of soil, some 300 tons of water to an acre of lawn. Sandy soils, with large pores, accept water quickly, but it drains away equally fast; there is not as large a reservoir of held moisture as in the fine-particle loams and clays. Sand holds only half as much water as loam, one-fourth as much as clay. Some comparisons are given in the chart below.

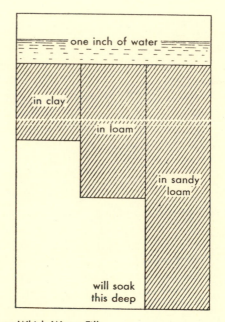

Approximate Depth to Which Water Fills
Pores in Three Types of Soil. Generally,
"insoak" is fastest in sand, slowest in clay.

When to Water

It is difficult to suggest an irrigation schedule more definite than "when needed." As we have seen, some grasses are favored by abundant watering, others survive with little. The faster-growing grasses, such as bents and bermuda, generally use the most water. Some soils should be irrigated frequently, others less often but longer at a time. The growth rate of most lawngrasses slows as moisture becomes scarce. Then the grass turns bluish, loses resiliency, and in the heat of day, shows footprints readily. It may recover at night when roots garner enough moisture to match the reduced loss from evaporation and transpiration (water loss through the leaf). If the shortage lasts, the grass wilts and curls; if drought is not then relieved, it turns brown.

Even complete browning, however, need not be disastrous. A few pampered and shallow-rooted lawns might be killed, but drought is a natural occurrence on grasslands. Unlike trees and shrubs, grasses are flexible enough to withstand seasons of desiccation, sprouting vigorously when the rains return. This is why constant give-and-take occurs where woodland meets prairie, the grasslands advancing during eras of drought, the woodlands invading when rain is plentiful.

But if the lawn is to be kept green for the sake of appearance during drought, irrigation should be practiced as soon as slowed growth and bluish cast suggest that water is limited. Even at the wilting state, water revives shrunken grass almost immediately. If desiccation proceeds beyond this, there is no recovery until new leaves sprout, perhaps a matter of many days.

Testing devices can be installed in the soil to measure moisture. Intended for professional use, they seldom are needed by the homeowner. The most accurate devices operate on the principle that the greater the moisture in the soil, the greater its electrical conductivity. A current running between two electrodes measures highest if the soil is moist.

Amount of Water Lost (evapotranspiration) from a
Perennial Ryegrass Turf Grown at Davis, California.

Jan.	0.94	Apr.	4.84	July	8.37	Oct.	3.35
Feb.	1.91	May	6.07	Aug.	6.64	Nov.	1.67
Mar.	3.01	June	8.35	Sept.	5.04	Dec.	0.91
Quarter	5.86		19.26		20.05		5.93

The figures are in inches of water per month, with well-irrigated turf. Grass watered less liberally would not transpire quite so much, but these figures serve to indicate lawn needs in a semiarid climate.

A satisfactory moisture indicator for average home use is a soil probe. The hollow-tube type removes a core of soil, one side of which is exposed by a cut-away section of the probe. It is fairly obvious from color and feel whether or not the soil is damp, for damp soil usually is darker in color, and feels cooler and stickier than dry soil. Lacking a probe, a small trowel or even a plug cut out with a knife may be sufficient to indicate soil moisture and the depth to which water has penetrated. Six-inch penetration is usually ample to merge with well-moistened subsoil; soil at a depth of one foot seldom dries out. The aim in watering, of course, is to wet the entire root zone. Moistening only the surface, leaving the deeper soil undampened, is the road to weak perennial grass with flourishing annuals.

Moisture in the soil is not the only critical factor. Where bright sun heats the grass, and where dry winds blow, vapor loss is rapid and wilting occurs quickly. Average evaporation from an exposed water surface in the Midwest runs about 30 inches per year, and in the arid Southwest may reach 120 inches. Evaporation and plant transpiration from a well-watered lawn may not be much less.

Applying the Water

There are many methods for irrigating lawns. In the West, where gravity-flow irrigation is familiar, lawns may be flooded periodically to supply needed moisture. More often sprinkling devices of one kind or another are used.

The hose-with-nozzle, fortunately, is largely a thing of the past. Seldom does a hand-regulated application place sufficient water uniformly over a lawn to be worthwhile. More often than not, a quick

Surface sprinklers that plug into underground outlets are often used for larger properties.

Small sprinklers attached to the hose can be set for part-circle coverage as well as for full circle.

summer sprinkling is an aid to crabgrass, while scarcely benefiting the deeper-rooted lawn species.

The ultimate in sprinkling comes from underground systems with pop-up sprinkler heads. These may be turned on automatically by timers, or when moisture meters show the soil has become dry. A well-designed system will give uniform spray coverage to all corners of the lawn. The installation, however, requires skill and is expensive.

Lay-it-yourself kits, with plastic pipe and fixed sprinkler heads, have been widely advertised. Those having plastic pipe which can be cut with a knife are not difficult to install. Check the layout on the lawn surface before burying it. Water pressure may be too low to achieve expected coverage, or the pipe size may be insufficient to supply several sprinkler heads with the needed volume of water. Spacings may be miscalculated, too, in amateur installations, resulting in uneven application. And sprinkler heads do develop spray eccentricities, perhaps due to dirt clogging the retractable shafts or to unforeseen buffeting by mower or lawn traffic. Frequently turf grows around the heads, disrupting the spray pattern. Unless resources are sufficient for a carefully engineered installation, with sprinklers providing assured uniform coverage, underground irrigation systems are less satisfactory than surface applications.

For surface irrigation there are many kinds of sprinklers. Most screw onto the conventional ½- to ¾-inch garden hose, although for major turf areas, such as athletic fields, higher capacity piping may be installed to provide 1- or 1½-inch flow. The greater the pipe and hose size, the quicker will be the application of a given amount of water. With a 5-gallon-per-minute flow, about 1 hour is needed to apply 1 inch of water to a 25-foot-diameter circle. At 2 gallons per minute, 2½ hours are needed. Most home water hydrants deliver up to 10 gallons per minute, or more. A half-gallon of water will supply nearly an inch of water to a square foot of lawn.

Some sprinklers rotate, some swivel back and forth, and others are a combination of a distant heavy spray with a close-up mist. Any such device is satisfactory as long as it applies water uniformly at a rate acceptable by the soil in question. A sprinkler can be tested by placing tin cans or other vessels at random within the spray area, and noting if all accumulate approximately the same depth of water in a given time. If the amount received is markedly different in one place when compared with another, the sprinkler is not distributing water uniformly.

Sprinklers that can be set to spray only part of a circle are especially useful, as one is able to approach them without getting soaked. On a new seedbed they can be handled from the firm footing around the edge. On both new and established lawns they can be adjusted to fit corners and lawn layout. Sprinklers having a rectangular spray pattern may prove preferable to circular types on some lawns.

Other sprinkling devices include long plastic ribbons with regularly spaced perforations to emit a fine spray; or canvas seepage sacks (soil soakers) which allow the water to ooze through to the soil (usually these are for shrub beds rather than lawns). Still other, more elaborate sprinklers wind up on a cable starting at one end of the lawn and traveling slowly across to the cable fix; some shut off automatically upon reaching the terminus.

In the heat of summer, searing winds make adequate sprinkling difficult. More water may evaporate than soaks into the soil. Then heavier sprays of large drop size would be more economical than fine mists that evaporate almost before hitting the lawn. Seepage directly at the lawn surface, as with a soil-soaker hose, might be even better.

Although big drops beat down a newly worked soil surface, on an established turf droplet size is relatively unimportant. Because the grass breaks the force of the water, the soil is not pounded. Then the chief concern becomes how much water can be applied at a rate that will let it soak in rather than run off.

Water Penetration

Applying water is only half the job. The other half is getting it into the root zone. A receptive soil, its surface not sealed, will absorb moisture rapidly. Soil stays aggregated and resistant to slaking if it is well structured, with ample organic content. We have seen also that clippings left on the lawn improve surface aggregation. But even where clippings are removed, the fine grass roots of established turf improve soil structure and aid in water capture.

If water penetration is slow on heavy soils, or precarious because of slope, aerification—the punching of holes into the soil—may aid infiltration. Motorized hole-punching machines are regularly used on most golf greens, where the wet soil is packed by constant trampling. Aerification has proved less advantageous on lawns than on heavily used turfs. Ordinarily, water soaks in well enough on a lawn without aerification if it is applied at the proper rate. If penetration is slow, as on heavier soils, a gentle spray for a prolonged period is called for.

When a lawn is irrigated, most water sinks straight downward. If the soil is layered, that is, changes abruptly in particle size (as from loam to sand), water may spread laterally rather than bridge the large pore gaps. Nor will water pass readily through an organic layer (as a buried mat of tree leaves) or a tight clay (hardpan). In the same way, capillary action cannot move water upward through such strata to replenish surface moisture.

Sprinklers thus should apply the water directly where it is needed. Grass plants a little out of range of the spray will not receive the benefit of horizontal seepage from an adjacent zone of saturation. Uniform and complete coverage is the only solution for satisfactory lawn irrigation.

Sandy soils merit sprinklers that release a large volume of water quickly. This is because they are quite receptive to "insoak." They become saturated quickly, the pore spaces filled. Further watering is wasteful, since it simply drains away. Such soils are best sprinkled frequently but briefly. A high-capacity sprinkler will do the job efficiently. Keeping the spray in one location for twenty minutes may suffice to saturate a sandy soil; an inch of water will soak more than a foot deep.

Clay soil is best served by a fine spray applied slowly. This allows time for penetration without run-off. Two or three hours may be needed at a given position on many heavy soils for the water to soak to the subsoil. Some clays swell, narrowing their pores and further slowing water movement. The sprinkler should be left in position until the soil receives moisture to the full depth of the roots. Two or three inches of water will be needed to saturate clay loams a foot deep.

Certain wetting agents or surfactants have been recommended to "make water wetter." It is theorized that with surface tension lessened, water sinks more quickly into the ground and into soil pores. In some instances this may be true, but in general there seems little advantage for lawns to the use of wetting agents in water, or to spraying the turf with them before watering.

Problems in Watering

Some of the problems that may arise with lawn irrigation have already been mentioned. Waterlogging from too much irrigation, causing shallow rooting and physiological upset, is one. Another is the selective encouragement of water-loving species (bentgrass, *Poa trivialis*, *Poa annua*; even nimblewill) with consequent inroads on the lawngrasses that are less benefited. And of course there is the expense and difficulty where water is scarce.

One of the more subtle side effects of watering relates to weeds. Certain weeds, such as *Poa annua*, crowfoot, and pennywort, thrive in moist soils. Watering too often during their peak season may benefit such plants at the expense of the grass.

Frequent light sprinkling caters especially to crabgrass, and might generally favor annuals over perennials. Annual weeds sprout whenever moisture is sufficient and the temperature warm. If conditions remain favorable for the new seedlings, growth continues on to maturity. If, on the other hand, initial sprouting is followed by drying of the upper soil, the seedling weeds might die while the more deeply rooted perennial turf is unaffected. Seasons when young crabgrass is killed by unexpected cold or drought are not uncommon.

Watering during a dormant season brought on by heat and drought may weaken the grass. It may encourage exhaustion of food reserves more rapidly than they can be accumulated. Watering in itself is hardly injurious, and many of its accompanying effects are beneficial.

However, just enough water to break dormancy might prove exhausting if the grass is repeatedly started only to be stopped short again by heat and drought.

The combination of humidity and high nitrogen fertility during the heat of summer often spells disaster for northern grasses. Their demise is usually blamed on disease, but general imbalance in the grass enables the disease to take hold.

Anti-transpirants

Certain chemicals, such as phenyl mercuric acetate, may be sprayed on grass causing it to transpire ("evaporate") water less abundantly. The chemicals seem to operate chiefly by stimulating the stomata (leaf pores) to close. The net result should be less water lost and reduced wilting, and also less gas exchange that might encourage maximum food production (photosynthesis). The technique has little applicability to the average home lawn, but is employed by some golf course superintendents.

Dyeing Grass: Lawn Colorants

The painting or dyeing of off-color grass to make it green is frequently practiced, especially in the South on dormant zoysia or bermuda. Dyes can also be used on northern grasses that have browned from summer drought, or on any turf suffering discoloration. Athletic fields and golf courses are frequently brightened with a green colorant before exhibitions that are to be televised. The colorant is best sprayed on the grass when it is dry.

Turf colorants are available at most garden centers and can be applied with the usual sprayers. The practice is not entirely without its headaches. Coverage may be so poor that two or more applications must be made, and seldom is the artificial green attractive for more than a few weeks. The dye discolors sidewalks, buildings, and shoes as readily as it tints the grass. Sometimes the painted masterpiece is a giddy green, unnatural against adjacent vegetation, which changes its shade of color seasonally. A test made in California indicated only two out of ten products tested gave good intensity of color when used at recommended rates on bermudagrass. Even at twice the recommended rate all products began to fade after five to seven weeks. "Stayz-Green" and "Greenstuff" had the best ratings.

Trees Compete for Water

The demands for soil moisture by a large tree are phenomenal. A mature tree in warm and windy weather may transpire as much as one thousand gallons per day. Tree roots range deeper than grass, extracting moisture from the lower soil layers. Where grass and tree compete for water in the lawn, grass usually sits at the second table.

Since both trees and green grass are desirable, an attempt should be made to provide enough moisture for both. To do so, increase irrigation and fertilization of that portion of lawn situated under trees.

REGIONAL FOCUS

The map on page 23 indicates zones of grass adaptability. Most of eastern North America has an average annual rainfall in excess of thirty inches, the approximate breaking point for maintaining conventional lawngrasses without supplementary irrigation. Of course, this is not an absolute figure, since less water is lost by evaporation and transpiration in northern climates than in the South. Twenty-five inches of rainfall in the North may keep grass as green as forty inches in the South; so annual rainfall maps are not entirely indicative of where lawngrass might flourish without irrigation. Similarly, local influences, such as shade, slope, seepage, and a tendency for downpours rather than frequent, gentle rains, can have a marked effect.

As one moves westward, availability of water becomes increasingly critical. A minor consideration in much of the East, water becomes the major limitation to fine lawns in the High Plains. Almost all lawns from the longitude of Wichita, Kansas, to the Pacific coastal ranges, mountain elevations excepted, require regular watering. In such arid and semiarid sections, good lawns are not possible without approximately one inch of supplementary irrigation per week during the growing season. Five inches per month of combined rain and irrigation should keep a lawn attractively green. More may further spruce up the lawn, but this hardly justifies the cost of irrigation. If an inch of water per week can be supplied, lawn tending in arid climates may be even simpler than in humid regions. Diseases are seldom much of a problem in arid areas, and many of the troublesome weeds are absent.

Across the country the demand for water is increasing. During drought periods lack of water may become so critical, even in humid areas, that lawn irrigation must be prohibited or restricted. Elsewhere, the drain so exceeds supply that insufficient pressure exists in the mains for volume irrigation. In some locations the cost of water becomes almost prohibitive for lawn use. Very likely the years ahead will witness even less availability of ready water. This is a good argument for developing the kind of lawn that can exist with a minimum of irrigation.

When water is not sufficient, grass gradually wilts, turns brown, and becomes dormant. With prolonged drought, death may ensue. Unfortunately, severe drought is usually accompanied by watering restrictions. Where water is available but expensive, turf can sometimes be replanted for less than might have been the cost of the necessary voluminous irrigation during drought.

Where water is consistently in short supply, choose grasses needing very little. Seldom are these the most attractive lawn species. Nevertheless, some prairie grasses that are naturally tolerant of low rainfall —buffalo, wheatgrass, various bluestems, gramas, and lovegrass— make an acceptable cover where rainfall is limited and irrigation impossible. This is often the situation in High Plains locations divorced from city water supplies, as from western Texas north into Montana.

COMMON MISCONCEPTIONS

WATERING IN ONE SPOT HELPS ALL THE GRASS. Water seldom spreads horizontally through the soil until a zone of saturation (water table) is reached. Moisture applied to a lawn is of primary benefit to those grass roots in the area of vertical movement where it is applied.

DON'T WATER IN THE SUN. Somehow the idea got around that drops of water act as small magnifying lenses that burn vegetation. Mechanically this is next to impossible, and actually never occurs. Watering in the sun is, if anything, beneficial to the grass, because it cools the plants through contact and evaporation. A more valid objection is that a good deal of the moisture is wasted through evaporation.

WATER AT NIGHT. A corollary to the above has a little more logic, since evening sprinkling would save water because of reduced evaporation. However, disease thrives under high humidity, and it is best to put the lawn to bed as dry as practicable. Even a light evening sprinkling will promote heavy dew, while morning watering has disappeared from the foliage before the day is far along.

TAP WATER IS BAD FOR THE GRASS. There are some misconceptions that the treatment given tap water may be harmful to the lawn. Actually, turfgrasses are more tolerant of chemical additions than animals would be; anything fit for human use, pets, or livestock, would certainly be fit for the lawn. Some water supplies are alkaline and carry calcium. If soils are already alkaline this could build up pH a little, but most fertilizers have a compensatory acidifying influence. Nor is there any harm from cold tap water. In summer, cold water might help improve soil temperatures.

MY LAWN IS POOR BECAUSE I CAN'T WATER. Many use this excuse as a crutch; chances are the lawn would be equally poor for other reasons even if irrigated, probably full of crabgrass and water-loving weeds. True, severely wilted turf thins enough to give some existing weeds the chance to expand or get a seasonal start, but many others are restricted by virtue of the drought. If drought is not too prolonged a good lawn snaps back quickly when rain comes, and comparisons often show such lawns to rate more highly then than companion turf that was watered. While it is nice to have control of water, a vital factor for plant growth and essential for the sprouting of seedings, few mature lawns in humid climates are consistently poor for lack of irrigation.

13

fertilizing lawns

A SOIL CANNOT be productive, regardless of its nutrient content, if its structure is not reasonably good. Conversely, perfect soil structure means very little unless sufficient nutrients are present. This chapter will deal largely with the nutrient aspects of fertility, and the addition of those elements through fertilization. Soil structure is more fully discussed in Chapter 5.

With experience one learns to keep major nutrients in balance for the particular soil, climate, and level of lawn care. Use the smallest quantity of nutrients needed for consistent good results. Keep in mind that too much of one mineral can bring on a deficiency in others; for example, excessive ammonium may lead to an undersupply of potassium; too much potassium, to a deficiency of magnesium; excessive phosphorus to too little iron; and so on.

Fertilization Needs

Fertilization has been repeatedly referred to as a major lawn management procedure. Its influence is striking and quick, its results easily appreciated by the purchaser of the fertilizer. In fact, per dollar spent, nothing shows up more emphatically on the lawn than fertilization. Yet a fertilizer institute survey showed that only about half the nation's homeowners use fertilizer.

Lawngrass, unlike flowers and fruits, is valued almost alone for the green foliage that it produces. Fertilizer for a lawn should be the kind that encourages leaf growth, not flower and seed. This means high nitrogen content, nitrogen being the element primarily responsible for deep-green color and leafiness. Turfgrass fertilizers almost invariably carry at least twice as much nitrogen as phosphorus or potassium.

Analyses of clippings show the major nutrients in grass foliage to run approximately four parts nitrogen to one part phosphorus to two parts potassium. When clippings are left on the lawn these elements are returned as the clippings decay. Clippings are generally at least three per cent nitrogen, half of which is converted to a form available to the grass within a month during decomposition. Some of the nitrogen may be lost through volatilization, and some of the potassium through leaching. The phosphorus is normally fixed in the soil immediately and hence is not lost.

Nitrogen Fertilizer Recommendations

Grass	Lbs. Nitrogen Per 1,000 sq. ft.
Bentgrass, Creeping	8–20
Bermudagrass, Improved	6–12
Kentucky Bluegrass, Improved	6–12
Perennial Ryegrass, Improved	3–12
St. Augustine	3–10
Bermudagrass, Common	3–9
Kentucky Bluegrass, Common	3–8
Dichondra	4–8
Tall Fescue	3–8
Zoysiagrass	2–8
Bentgrass, Colonial	2–6
Fine Fescue	2–6

Amount of nitrogen fertilizer recommended annually for turfgrasses grown in California (slightly less might suffice in more northerly locations with a shorter growing season). The lower figure is a minimum for good performance, the higher one is for intensively managed lawns only (receiving especially frequent mowing, irrigation, etc.).

If the amounts of these major elements in green leaves are used as a guide, with adjustment for the needs, losses, and availabilities in the soil, a complete fertilizer might well be proportioned 3-1-1; or where phosphatic fertilizers have been used much in the past, a 5-1-2 ratio might suffice. Of course, ample phosphorus should have been applied to the seedbed at the time the soil was tilled because this element is

The difference fertilizer makes. The area on the right received none, while the turf on the left, of the same age, received regular feeding.

difficult to move down into the soil. Where complete fertilizers low in nitrogen are customarily used, these may be alternated with feedings of straight nitrogen.

It is apparent that lawn handling varies markedly from region to region. Chapter 5 discussed soils as they correspond to climate. Fertility requirements must take into consideration local characteristics. Agricultural experience in the area may suggest the major needs, and of course soil tests can pinpoint deficiencies. But grass growth is the final payoff and should be the major criterion—not a soil test or some theoretical consideration. Soil tests by different methods are often inconclusive if not contradictory. Certainly grass requirements differ: bluegrass, for example, thrives on phosphorus more than fescue or bent. And nitrogen, the main need for attractive turfgrass, does not yield a meaningful soil test. Turf quality ratings invariably show that three or four pounds of elemental nitrogen per 1,000 square feet per year are the minimum for top performance. This means that if you are using a 30-3-6, at least ten pounds would be needed for 1,000 square feet of turf.

Complete fertilizers—those containing nitrogen, phosphorus, and potassium—have been recommended as the safest bet. Even if one of these elements is not badly needed, it is good insurance to include it from time to time. It would probably be more expensive to design a custom fertilizer leaving the unneeded element out, than to use a mass-marketed complete plant food. The majority of lawn soils are under-fertilized, and would benefit from many years of complete fertilization without becoming out of balance. Only on intensively managed turfs, such as putting greens, have certain elements, especially phosphorus, built up enough to have significant influence on soil reactions (such as making arsenical herbicides less effective).

Acidity, indicating a need for lime, corresponds roughly to the zones of rainfall. The map on page 53 shows general lime needs. A soil test to indicate pH is a good indicator of need for lime. As mentioned, 50 to 100 pounds of ground limestone should be applied per 1,000 square feet of lawn for each pH unit less than 6 or thereabouts. Don't use more lime than this in a single application. Instead, for very acid soils, repeat treatments in subsequent seasons until pH reaches an acceptable level.

Percentage of Deficiency in 20,000 Wisconsin Soil Samples,
and 121 New Lawns in Indiana (adapted from
Better Crops with Plant Food)

	Wisconsin	Indiana
Acid, needing lime	64%	40%
Low in phosphorus	49%	44%
Low in potassium	65%	76%

Kinds of Fertilizers

There are two general categories of fertilizer: the organic and the inorganic. When chemical fertilizers were first suggested by Justus von Liebig in Germany over a century ago, the distinction between organic (carbon-linked molecule, derived from life) and inorganic (simple chemical salts) was clear-cut. Gradually this distinction faded, as many of the organic substances were synthesized by man. Urea, one of the main nitrogenous ingredients of fertilizers, is technically organic, although production and handling follow the inorganic pattern. Usually urea is treated as a soluble chemical (inorganic) fertilizer. More recently, the combination of urea with formaldehyde, to make ureaforms or methylene ureas, has further complicated the designation. This group is generally separated as a third type, the synthetic organic fertilizer.

The natural organics are obtained from animal or vegetable sources. Coming from living cells, they contain a great many complex molecules. Theoretically, the various trace elements, vitamins, growth factors, and other obscure constituents may be beneficial to lawn grass. But because they are not so rapidly exhausted in most lawn soils as they might be in a continuously cropped agricultural soil, the lack is seldom serious. Rarely does a lawn suffer from trace-element deficiencies, especially if clippings are left on the lawn.

While the completeness of natural organic fertilizers may be an advantage, the comparatively low quantity of major nutrients is a disadvantage. Without fortification from inorganics, the nutrient content seldom runs more than a small per cent. And because the materials from which these organics are derived are comparatively dear, with tremendous bulk needed to achieve the recommended nutrient concentration, they become expensive for general use. Also, some fear has been expressed that those organic fertilizers processed from urban wastes may contain rather high quantities of unwanted industrial materials such as heavy metals like lead or mercury.

Since most of the nutrients of the natural organics are tied up in large molecules, insoluble until decomposition occurs, these fertilizers do not burn the foliage. They are therefore safest for use by the amateur, with whom there may be some likelihood of misapplication. This is in contrast to the inorganic types, whose soluble salts will desiccate leaves to which they may stick, causing "burn." Chance of this type of injury varies with formulation, condition of grass, and season.

The release of nutrients from organic fertilizers of all types, dependent as it is upon the activity of soil organisms, will be favored by warmth and humidity, repressed by coolness or aridity.

Organic fertilizers are usually made from tankage, fish scraps, manures, slaughterhouse wastes, processed sewage, cottonseed meal, soybean meal, castor pomace, seaweed, or other by-products of low commercial value. In some instances these organic ingredients are blended with inorganic elements to make a higher-analysis fertilizer that has some of the broad nutritional advantages of the organics.

Inorganic fertilizers are usually based upon soluble salts of nitrogen and potassium and a complex of phosphorus compounds known as superphosphate (derived from acid treatment of phosphate rock). The nitrogen source may be ammonium sulfate, ammonium nitrate, some of the ammonium phosphates, urea, sodium nitrate (not much used), or occasionally, other readily procurable compounds. Potassium usually comes from potassium chloride (muriate of potash) although there have been some attempts to introduce potassium nitrate and especially sulfate (of greater fertility value but more costly).

When these ingredients are merely mixed, interactions occur that cause caking and poor handling characteristics. Consequently, most inorganic fertilizers are blended with a carrier that prevents caking, and facilitates storage and use. Both superphosphate and the carrier may contain some sulfur and calcium, and perhaps other ingredients of minor fertility value. The supplementary elements are not listed in the fertilizer analysis.

Synthetic organic fertilizers are a fairly recent development. They resulted from a search for the potency of the inorganic combined with the non-burning features of the organic. They are precisely tailored, clean and pleasant to handle, free of hazardous contaminants. The polymerizing of formaldehyde with urea yields a big "ureaform" (UF) molecule that breaks down slowly in the soil, releasing the nitrogen over a prolonged span. Dr. J. T. Hays of Hercules estimates that about one-third of the nitrogen is "quickly" released (during the first week or two after application), another third after the second week (about 10 per cent weekly, tapering off until exhausted), and the remaining third as much as 6 months later. Presumably about 65 per cent of the nitrogen is retrieved the first growing season, 25 per cent the second, and 10 per cent the third. Persistently used for 3 or more years, 100 per cent feedback will result. This gradual feed-out of nitrogen is responsible for the "slow release" appellation accorded UF and other synthetic fertilizers of this type (IBDU, isobutylene diurea, is another having some commercial sale). UF nitrogen is neither as quickly available nor as quickly exhausted as are the inorganics. For this reason, ureaform has received wide favor in turfgrass fertilizers. But the cost of the ureaforms, like organics, is such that

On the left, the lawn received slow-release ureaform fertilization resulting in reasonable clippings; on the right, the same rate of soluble nitrogen was used, giving excessive clippings in a short-lived surge of growth.

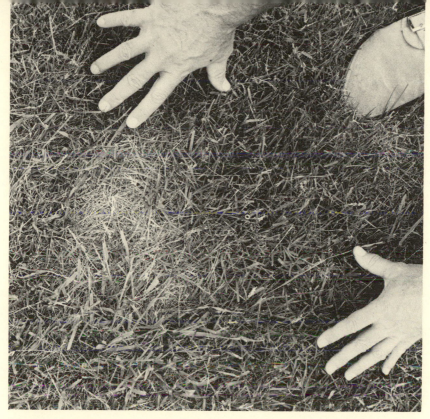

Burn in turf from two pounds per thousand square feet of a fertilizer compounded with soluble nitrogen (above). Contrast this with a turf on which
no burn is shown from summer application of two pounds per thousand
square feet of ureaform nitrogen (below).

Here an early spring feeding while light snow is on the ground will help with quick spring green-up (especially accompanied by a lawn scalping). The turf is bluegrass.

nitrogen derived from them is not as economical, on a nutrient basis, as is nitrogen from soluble sources. There are also indications that heavier rates of the ureaforms may be required to get the same grass response as is produced by most inorganics, especially on alkaline soils. Possibly, as in the breakdown of clippings, a portion of the nitrogen may be volatilized or mechanically lost.

Quantity of Nitrogen, from Differing Fertilizer Sources,
Needed During a Year to Keep Turf Looking Well
at Purdue University (based on a three-year average)

Nitrogen Source	Total lbs. N for Each 1,000 Square Feet	Divided into this Many Applications
Soluble—urea	6.4	4
Natural organic—corn gluten	6.6	4
Natural organic—processed sewage	7.3	5
Synthetic organic—ureaform A	9.8	2
Synthetic organic—ureaform B	8.3	2

Still another approach toward long-lasting lawn fertilizers is to coat the particles ("prills") of economical inorganic fertilizer with resinous or waxy materials that restrict rate of solution. Nutrients escape only slowly, and the pace can be regulated by using differing kinds or thicknesses of coating. Mixing complete fertilizers from lots having harder-to-break-down or different-thickness coatings could conceivably produce a plant food that would become available to the grass a portion at a time over a series of many months.

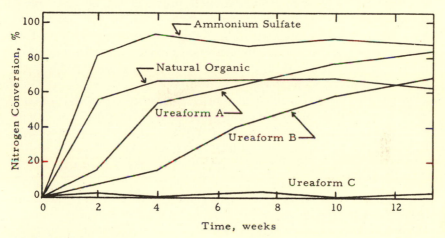

Nitrification of Ureaforms

The graph above shows the rate of nitrogen mineralization from different sources. Note that there is nearly complete availability of soluble nitrogen (ammonium sulfate) within two weeks, but there is slow feed-out from ureaforms "A" and "B" over a period of months. (Data courtesy of Hercules)

The kind of fertilizer makes little difference as long as it is applied at intervals appropriate for its type, and in amounts that give the grass the necessary nutrients at moderate, sustained rates. How fertilizer is used is just as important as the kind chosen.

Application of Fertilizer

Fertilizer burn has been one of the biggest bugaboos in lawn tending. No matter how clearly instructions indicate rates and method of application, it is easy for an inexperienced person to put on too much, in the wrong way, or at the wrong time. The resulting discoloration is a frequent source of complaint. Such a burn is seldom permanently damaging. If an overdose is flushed away, the grass will recover within a few weeks, and be greener and more vigorous in the over-applied area than elsewhere in the lawn.

Burning comes from salts drawing water from the tissue, thus drying out and killing the cells (contact burn), or salts becoming so concentrated in the soil that its "salt index" is raised to levels where grass physiology is impaired. If contact burn is severe enough there is no recovery for the leaf, and new foliage will have to grow from the base before the blemish is corrected. Consequently, manufacturers of soluble fertilizers recommend that their products not be used when the grass is damp (when fertilizer particles stick to the leaves), or that the lawn be immediately watered after application. Both contact and physiological burn are more apt to occur when the weather is hot than in cool weather. If there is any doubt about safety, the lawn should be watered soon after application.

Ordinarily, there is little chance of fertilizer burn, especially if the grass is dry and the rates are about as recommended (not over one to two pounds of each major nutrient per 1,000 square feet). The fertilizer will sift off the dry foliage to the ground. This is especially true with granular or pelleted types, or those impregnated upon granular carriers, that roll off the foliage. With dusty fertilizers it is a good safety precaution to water the grass after application to wash adhering fertilizer off the foliage.

Application is most effective with mechanical distributors such as those recommended for seeding. Mechanical spreaders give uniform application with little likelihood of overdosage. In using the drop-from-hopper spreaders be certain to overlap the wheel tracks. Missed bands will stand out sharply a few weeks later when the grass in the treated portions has responded to the feeding. In using the whirlwind type, overlap applications enough for the edges from successive bands to feather one into the other, without the humps and hollows resulting from heavy banding.

Timing of Fertilization

In reviewing the seasonal needs of lawngrasses in earlier chapters it was evident that heavier fertilization is appropriate to certain seasons. In general, soil minerals are more abundant in spring than in summer and autumn. This is because the soil has mineralized and released these nutrients throughout the winter, a time when vegetation draws upon them very little. As a result, lawns typically green-up nicely in early spring even though they have not been fertilized.

For the bluegrass lawn in the North it is hard to imagine too much fertilization in autumn, even at double normal rates. Similarly, for southern lawns, spring and summer fertilization can be heavy. Ten pounds per thousand square feet of modern high-analysis fertilizer such as 24-6-6 is ample (follow rates suggested on the bag). In general, three or four pounds of actual nitrogen per year are required to keep lawns in all climates looking reasonably well. As noted in Chapter 3, grass populations strong in the fescues or centipede require less fertilizer, while bermuda and highly managed bents need considerably more, with other grasses somewhere in between. Phosphorus and potassium needs vary, but nitrogen is always essential for good turf growth.

If organics or ureaform fertilizers are used, their application need not be as frequent as that of the more quickly exhausted soluble inorganics. Since they do not burn, high rates can be used at a single application; then lawn feeding can be forgotten for a while. But even with slow-release products, at least two feedings a year are suggested: a generous one in autumn for bluegrass lawns, and another perhaps in the spring. Depending upon hot weather handling, there may be additional lighter requirements through summer, a time of year when slow-release nitrogen is more suitable than soluble nitrogen. On southern lawns there should be heavy application in spring, with at least one more in summer; autumn and winter feeding may encourage henbit and other winter weeds while bermuda is dormant, but if a "winter grass" overseeding of northern species is made fertilization will be helpful in autumn, too.

To lessen the risk of burning with the inorganics, and to be most effective throughout the year, frequent light applications are advantageous. Plant foods based on urea (44 per cent nitrogen) or ammonium nitrate (33 per cent nitrogen) might be spread every five or six weeks, at about ½ pound of actual nitrogen per 1,000 square feet. A heavier schedule might be recommended for the bluegrass lawn in autumn, a heavier summer schedule for the southern lawns. Don't overstimulate middle-latitude lawns during the heat of summer. Heat and heavy feeding risk loss of grass, especially with the traditional cultivars.

It is not necessarily wasteful to fertilize during cooler seasons when low temperatures restrict grass growth. The fertilizer is quickly trapped by soil organisms and plant roots, or by ion exchange with the soil particles, where it remains as a fertility reservoir for future root absorption. Any time soil temperatures drop to around 55 degrees, fertility will be retained. When temperatures are much warmer than this, some of the nitrogen unused by grass may be lost through volatilization. For northern lawns, it is wasteful to fertilize grass browned during summer drought; but in October, plant food is needed, even though grass growth is slowing at that season. Next spring the carryover from autumn fertilization will become apparent.

Plant foods are so readily fixed in the soil and by vegetation that little loss occurs from surface washing, unless by chance a downpour strikes very soon after the application, washing the fertilizer particles away before they have even dissolved. In general, the humus and clay of the soil behave as a savings bank into which fertility ions can be deposited for later use. K^+ or NH_4^+ (ammonium) may be transferred from fertilizer to soil particle, then be withdrawn later for the exchange of an H^+ (hydrogen or acid ion, which grass roots release).

Dissolved Fertilizers

There has been some fanfare about fertilizers applied in solution, with sprinkling can, spray apparatus or, more commonly, suction devices attached to the garden hose. High-powered concentrates are sold for diluting at home. In some areas oil delivery tank trucks have developed an off-season business by offering custom application for lawns.

There is nothing wrong or basically different about fertilizer solutions if they carry sufficient potency. Even when dry fertilizers are spread, they ordinarily go into solution before becoming utilized. Of course, very concentrated solutions can burn foliage just as dry fertilizer can. And a soluble fertilizer will certainly be of the inorganic type, not long-lasting (although hydraulic seeders such as those used to plant roadsides can spray a slurry of either seed, fertilizer, or mulch, or a combination of any of these items).

The chief complaint about soluble fertilizers is that, as commonly marketed, they do not supply sufficient fertility for the prices asked. By the time a concentrate is diluted, it may be so weak that it supplies relatively little stimulus to a lawn. Leaf-feeding of house plants or rose beds is one thing; being able to supply enough concentrate for a whole lawn is another. By and large, liquid feeding has no advantage for the lawn over a conventional dry fertilizer, and is apt to be more inconvenient for most people.

One advantage of soluble fertilizers, however, is their readily available nutrient supply. A lawn can be "spruced up" for a special occasion without waiting the several days required for action through the soil and root system. Or minor elements needed by the grass in very small quantities can be supplied through an occasional spray. Iron chlorosis under alkaline conditions, for example, yields to iron sulfate or iron chelate sprayed directly on the foliage. Grass that is blanched (chlorotic) because of such a nutrient deficiency responds within a matter of hours to the application. If the iron were applied to the soil it might well become tied up, unavailable to the grass.

It is interesting that rainfall provides a very weak fertilizer solution. A trace of nitrogen may be picked up, especially where lightning changes gaseous nitrogen to soluble and reactive compounds. More significantly, rainfall provides appreciable additions of sulfur, especially near industrial areas. The approximately 40 inches of annual rainfall in Kentucky has been shown to yield 7 to 16 pounds of sulfur per acre in recent years; back when coal was the usual winter fuel (1921), the yield was 30 pounds.

Special Fertilizing Problems

In shaded lawns both grass and trees must be satisfied. As with irrigation, apply enough plant food for both. Remember, however, that if shade is appreciable, grass growth may be limited by lack of light and the lawn will be unable to take advantage of extravagant fertilization. More generous or more frequent feeding usually provides enough fertility for both the grass and the trees. Some arborists feel that surface feeding encourages tree roots to come to the surface, and they suggest punching holes into the soil around the overhang of the tree, filling these with fertilizer to feed the tree separately. However, most of the time tree roots will be near the surface whether the lawn is fed or not. Since trees have a way of taking their share, more fertilizer is required for grass under trees.

Another minor problem is supplying sufficient nitrogen for the breakdown of carbohydrates. Energy-rich sugars, starches, and cellulose, such as may be found in straw, chopped corncobs, or the mat that develops in a turf, lack sufficient nitrogen to stimulate decomposition. Research has shown that for every ten parts of carbon one part of nitrogen is needed. Frequently, it is necessary to supply nitrogen. When mulches are left in place, or where there is a scattering of old dead leaves, the application of a nitrogenous fertilizer may hasten decay.

REGIONAL FOCUS

Humid eastern areas are leached not only of their calcium (lime), but ordinarily of the major nutrients too. Thus most eastern soils benefit greatly from regular additions of fertilizer. There are special cases;

such as the high-phosphate soils running approximately from Lexington, Kentucky, to Nashville, Tennessee, where additional phosphorus is seldom needed. But practically everywhere nitrogen and usually potash are badly needed.

One Manufacturer's Suggestion for Nitrogen Fertilization Rates
According to Region and Type of Turf. (Data courtesy of Du Pont.)

	Seasonal Nitrogen Requirements by Regions	
Intended Use	Northern Cool Humid	Southern Warm and Humid
	West Central	Southwest Irrigated
Golf Greens		
Bowling Greens	6–10 lbs./1,000 sq. ft.	12–20 lbs./1,000 sq. ft.
Tennis Courts		
Golf Tees and Athletic Fields	4–6 lbs./1,000 sq. ft.	8–12 lbs./1,000 sq. ft.
Home Lawns	3–6 lbs./1,000 sq. ft.	4–12 lbs./1,000 sq. ft.
Large General Turf Areas (Fairways, parks, cemeteries, estate lawns, industrial grounds, playgrounds)	80–160 lbs./acre	120–240 lbs./acre

From Wichita, Kansas, westward fertility needs differ markedly from the East. This is the area of original prairie, in which nutrients accumulated rather than leached away as they did under the heavier rainfall of the East. Unless the soil has been long under cultivation, or has been maintained as a lawn with irrigation, the need will be mainly for nitrogen. Again there will be local differences, but a straight nitrogen source may sometimes be appropriate here where a complete fertilizer was preferable in the East. Usually there is no need for lime; in fact, many western soils become so alkaline that they must be acidified by the addition of gypsum or sulfur.

In some highly alkaline soils, such as are found in deserts, the prevalent sodium destroys aggregation, compacting the soil sufficiently to make plant growth almost impossible. Here, the addition of gypsum supplies both the acidifying sulfur and the aggregating calcium (which substitutes for sodium by soil ion exchange). From western Kansas to southern California, many lawn soils must be treated for high alkalinity. Dichondra benefits from acidification, and because of its thick growth profits more from frequent light fertilization with inorganics than it would from organic additions that increase its "mat."

On sandy soils, such as generally occur in the southeastern Coastal Plain, and spottily in the Great Lakes region, the use of some organic fertilizer might have especial advantage. Unless soil contains ample clay particles or humus, ion-exchange capacity for trapping soluble nutrients is very much diminished.

COMMON MISCONCEPTIONS

ROOTS ABSORB NUTRIENTS ONLY IN WATER. Roots can take ions (charged nutrient units) directly from clay particles. Nutrients in solution may ordinarily be more voluminous, more readily available, than ions stuck on clay. But it is likely that even large molecules can be transferred directly from soil to growing plant.

IF A LITTLE IS GOOD, A LOT IS BETTER. Fertilizers, herbicides, and water are frequently applied too generously for lawn health, particularly if used during seasons of lessened requirement.

MOSS INDICATES A NEED FOR LIME. Moss appears on compact, poorly drained, or sterile soils where grass languishes. Soil acidity has little to do with the problem. Fertilizer and aerification usually are a better cure than lime.

LAWNS SHOULD BE TOPDRESSED REGULARLY. Topdressing, with a mixture of topsoil, organic material, and at least some fertilizer, is used on golf greens to cover surface stolons and level the putting surface. While such topdressing might help level minor indentations in lawns, it is not necessary for the grass. Fertilizer alone will accomplish more at less expense. If the soil used in topdressing contains weeds, or if the mixture does not match the native soil (thus causing layer formation), it can do more harm than good.

LAWNS NEED FERTILIZATION MOST IN SPRING. That's when grass growth is most apparent, but with northern lawngrasses the basis for good spring performance was established the autumn before. Soils naturally release mineral nutrients more abundantly in spring than in autumn, after winter weathering, with little use by vegetation. Autumn should receive first call when fertilizing northern lawns.

LAWN FERTILIZATION CONTRIBUTES TO ENVIRONMENTAL POLLUTION. Very little fertilizer applied to the lawn ever reaches drainage streams. Indeed, the plant growth that is enhanced by fertilization may diminish pollution, by making a better soil cover and absorbing free nutrients. Most stream pollution comes from industrial wastes, and even in rural areas about 98 per cent of stream pollution is due to erosion, not leaching of nutrients or surface wash of fertilizer.

ORGANIC FERTILIZERS ARE BEST FOR LAWNS. Organic fertilizers are fine, but perhaps less beneficial in the lawn than in the garden (where they contribute to soil tilth and chemical balance as well as supplying nutrients). The main requirement of grass is nutrients. The grass is continually improving the soil through fine root growth and clippings, and surface additions of organic materials essentially add to the thatch layer. On the whole, organic fertilizers are weaker in nutrients than either soluble or synthetic organic (ureaform) types, and the latter are probably more efficient for feeding established lawns.

14

lawn weeds

If it can be said that there's a grass for every location, so is there a weed. Lurking in every soil, with compatriots for every season, weeds await any turn of events that gains them a chink of bare ground. A foothold achieved, rampant weeds slither among grass shoots, thinning the turf; or they pockmark the lawn as with the tight rosettes of dandelions and plantains. Ironically, they profit from the same attentions that are bestowed upon the grass.

Any plant growing where it is not wanted is a weed. To cite a familiar example: you may encourage clover, while your neighbor thinks it a pest. Dichondra may be cherished in Los Angeles, yet be stamped out of a Florida lawn. Creeping bentgrass may make a velvet golfing green, but form a disruptive patch in a lawn that receives average care. In a fine bluegrass lawn, neither tall fescue nor ryegrass has a place. Yet both are often components of inexpensive seed mixtures.

There is no need to agree with every entry in the rogues' gallery of this chapter. In certain locations, weeds, such as *Nepeta* or *Phyla*, make an attractive ground cover. In other cases, commercial grasses might justifiably be listed as weeds.

More serious than crabgrass are the perennial grass weeds, such as this coarse tall fescue making an unsightly and hard-to-get-rid-of clump in fine-textured turf.

Troublesome Lawn Weeds

As with the better lawngrasses, where relatively few species "have what it takes," only a handful of weeds are universally successful. These weeds, like the grasses with which they compete, are the attendants of mankind, appearing worldwide wherever he turns the soil and upsets the primeval balance. Most familiar, found North and South, East and West, are the perennial dandelions *(Taraxacum)* and plantains *(Plantago)*; the annual knotweed *(Polygonum)*, spurge *(Euphorbia)*, and purslane *(Portulaca)*. Notorious crabgrass *(Digitaria)* is almost as far-ranging.

In the tables that follow, it will be noted that there is a greater diversity of weeds in the more southerly locations. Whereas only a few weeds are abundant in the North, in the South many kinds are likely to be represented, but these are individually less important. This suggests emphasis on selective weeding in the North, with general broad controls for the South.

The following tables describe the species that most often invade lawns. State universities and some commercial organizations will make or confirm identification if a specimen is sent to them, preferably in flower. Specimens are best pressed flat and dried, as between pages of a telephone book, before mailing. Fresh specimens usually mold and deteriorate before identification can be made.

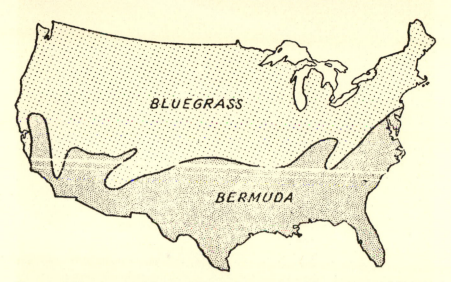

Extent of bluegrass and bermudagrass dominance in the Continental U.S.A.

The chief northern lawn weeds of bluegrass country are listed, first. Those most frequent in the South in bermudagrass country are listed on page 200. In both regions the most troublesome species are apt to be perennial grasses with habits similar to the lawngrasses, making them difficult to control selectively without also injuring the turf.

Northern Lawn Weeds (Bluegrass Zone)

Common name	Botanical name	Life span*	Comments
(a) Dicotyledons: not grass-like, the leaf veins forming a network:			
black medic	Medicago lupulina	A B P	yellow flowers, clover-like leaves
carpetweed	Mollugo verticillata	A	whorls of leaves on prostrate stems; hot, bare soils
chickweed, common	Stellaria media	A	smooth leaves, small white flowers†
chickweed, mouse-ear	Cerastium vulgatum	A P	hairy leaves, small white flowers†
dandelion	Taraxacum officinale	P	rosette with deep taproot; yellow flowers and feathery seedheads
dock	Rumex crispus	P	broad rhubarb-like leaves; deep taproot
ground-ivy	Nepeta hederacea	P	trailing; minty fragrance; blue flowers; likes shade

Common name	Botanical name	Life span*	Comments
hawkweeds	Hieracium species	P	rosettes of hairy leaves, spreading by runners; likes poor soil
heal-all or self-heal	Prunella vulgaris	P	purple flowers; square stem; needs moisture
henbit or dead-nettle	Lamium amplexicaule	A	trailing square stems; purple flowers†
knawel	Scleranthus annuus	A	harsh, spiny; dry situations†
knotweed	Polygonum aviculare	A P	silvery sheath where leaf joins stem; hugs ground
kochia or summer-cypress	Kochia scoparia	A	bushy-branched, narrow leaves; common in plains states
lambsquarters	Chenopodium album	A	white mealiness; in new lawns, disappears with mowing
mallow or cheeses	Malva rotundifolia	B P	trailing stems, umbrella-like leaves; new lawns, disappears as sod improves
peppergrass	Lepidium virginicum	A	rosette; round pods; new lawns†
pigweed or amaranth	Amaranthus species	A	spiny; new lawns, disappears with mowing
plantain, broadleaf	Plantago major	P	rosette with deep taproot; often in shade
plantain, narrow-leaf or buckhorn	Plantago lanceolata	P	narrower leaves and more condensed seedheads than P. major
purslane	Portulaca oleracea	A	smooth, fleshy, watery leaves and stems
Russian thistle	Salsola kali	A	much branched; spiny leaves; mostly in plains, especially in dry years
sheep sorrel	Rumex acetosella	P	persistent, hard-to-reach rhizomes; characteristic of poor acid soils
shepherd's-purse	Capsella bursa-pastoris	A	heart-shaped pods; rosettes in new lawns†

Common name	Botanical name	Life span*	Comments
speedwell or veronica	*Veronica persica*	A P	mostly trailing; small blue flowers†
spurge, milky or spotted	*Euphorbia maculata,* other species	A	milky juice; trailing; often on poor, compact soils in hot locations
thistles	*Cirsium* species	B P	spiny leaves in rosette
winter cress or yellow-rocket	*Barbarea vulgaris*	B P	yellow-flowered mustard of new lawns; disappears with mowing
yarrow or milfoil	*Achillea millefolium*	P	feathery, fragrant foliage
yellow woods sorrel	*Oxalis stricta*	A P	yellow flowers; shamrock-like leaf with sour taste

(b) Monocotyledons: grass-like leaves, the veins running parallel:

Common name	Botanical name	Life span*	Comments
barnyard grass	*Echinochloa crus-galli*	A	coarse clumps, spiny seeds; usually disappears with good lawn care
crabgrasses	*Digitaria* species	A	several species; rooting at joints; "birdfoot" seedheads
foxtail or bristlegrass	*Setaria* species	A	tends to disappear as sod develops; "bushy" seedheads
goosegrass or silver-crab	*Eleusine indica*	A	tough, flat-stemmed; resembles crabgrass, but not rooting at joints
nimblewill	*Muhlenbergia schreberi*	P	often in shade; trailing stems with prominent knobby joints, slender seedheads in autumn
nutgrass (a sedge)	*Cyperus esculentus*	P	deep tubers make it hard to eradicate; sedges have three ranks of leaves, not two as do grasses
orchardgrass	*Dactylis glomerata*	P	clumpy, leaves folded
panicgrass, witchgrass	*Panicum* species	A	coarse, clumpy; disappears under good lawn conditions

Common name	Botanical name	Life span*	Comments
quackgrass	Agropyron repens	P	difficult to eradicate because of deep rhizomes; prevalent in North
rushes	Juncus species	P	usually on compact soil, as along pathways; wiry, tough
sedges	various species of Cyperaceae	P	three rows of leaves, seldom trailing or rooting stems
stinkgrass	Eragrostis cilianensis	A	temporary in cared-for lawn; dense silvery seedheads
timothy	Phleum pratense	P	clumpy, pasture grass
velvetgrass	Holcus lanatus	P	soft gray foliage, trailing; low, dense seedheads
wild onion or garlic	Allium species	P	ill-smelling clumps, making tufts in lawn; Ohio Valley southward, most noticeable in spring

* A = annual; B = biennial; P = perennial.
† Winter weed, prominent in early spring.

Most of the weeds in the preceding chart also occur in the South, at least the upper South or Piedmont down as far as middle Georgia. Generally, they are less dominating there, sharing laws with the species in the following list. A few, such as wild onion, are at their wicked best in central-latitude states such as Tennessee. A few others, quackgrass for example, prefer the North; others, such as kochia and Russian thistle, a drier plains habitat.

By the same token, some of the southern weeds crop up in Yankee country. They are seldom disastrous there, so I prefer to include them with the bermuda-zone weeds. The listing is divided into sections on the basis of whether the climate is humid or dry.

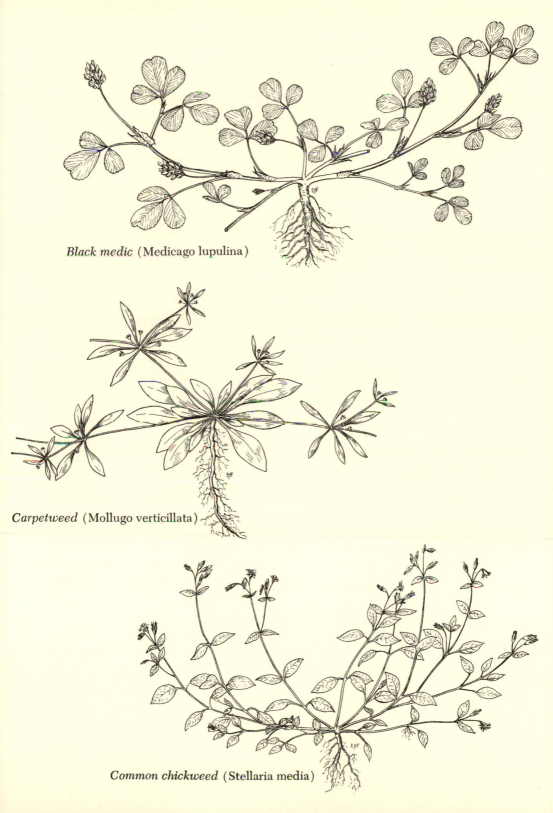

Black medic (Medicago lupulina)

Carpetweed (Mollugo verticillata)

Common chickweed (Stellaria media)

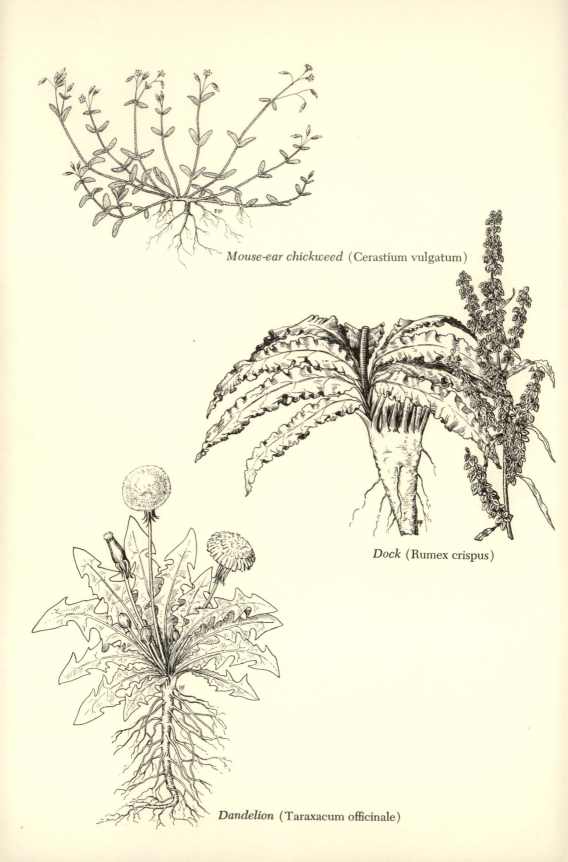

Mouse-ear chickweed (Cerastium vulgatum)

Dock (Rumex crispus)

Dandelion (Taraxacum officinale)

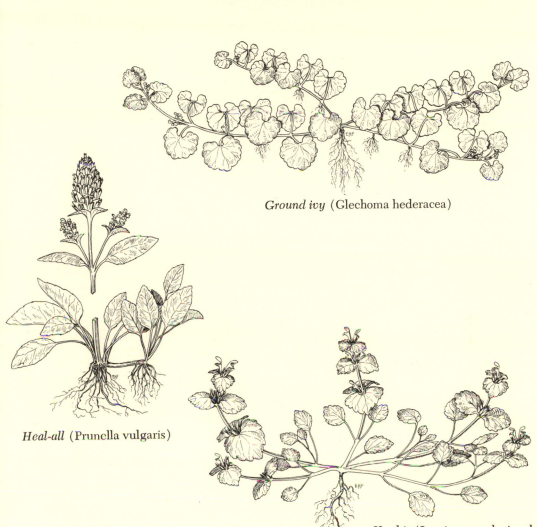

Ground ivy (Glechoma hederacea)

Heal-all (Prunella vulgaris)

Henbit (Lamium amplexicaule)

Knawel (Scleranthus annuus)

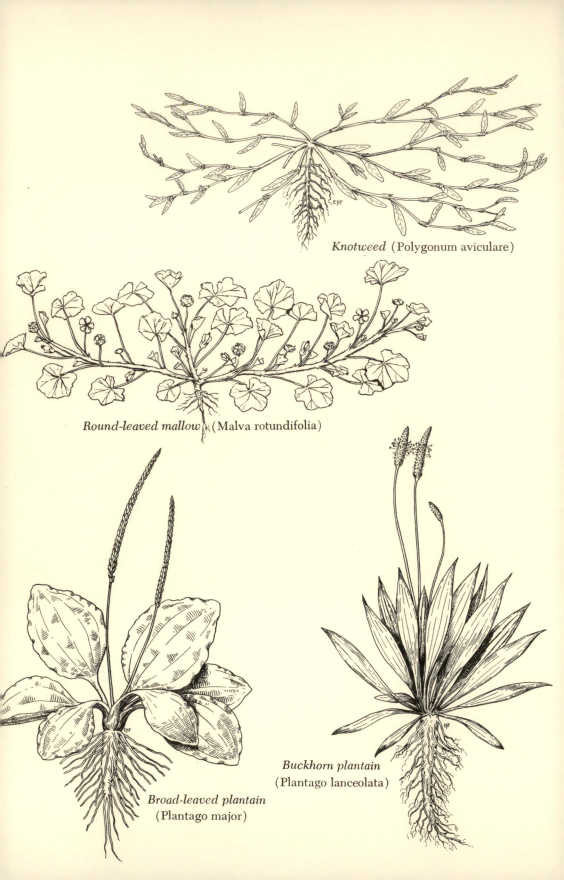

Knotweed (Polygonum aviculare)

Round-leaved mallow (Malva rotundifolia)

Buckhorn plantain
(Plantago lanceolata)

Broad-leaved plantain
(Plantago major)

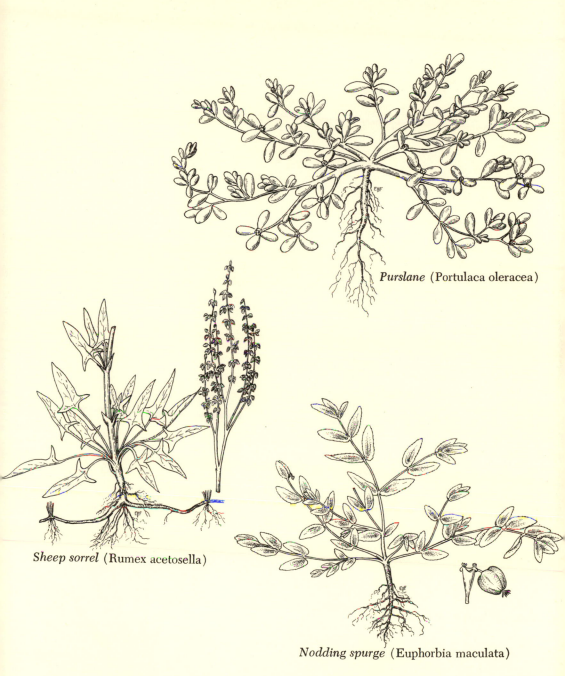

Purslane (Portulaca oleracea)

Sheep sorrel (Rumex acetosella)

Nodding spurge (Euphorbia maculata)

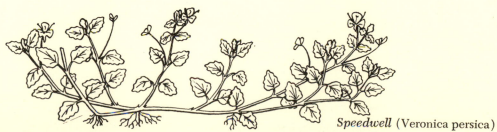

Speedwell (Veronica persica)

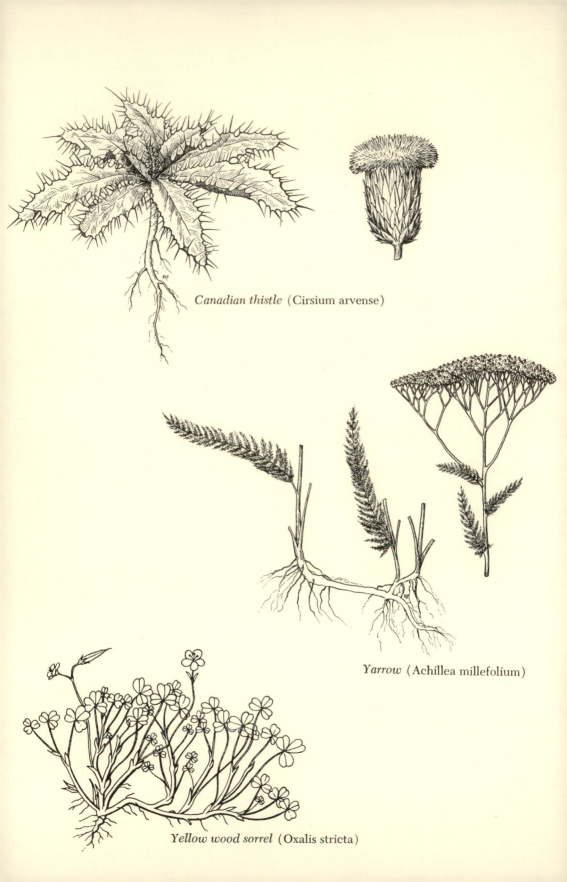

Canadian thistle (Cirsium arvense)

Yarrow (Achillea millefolium)

Yellow wood sorrel (Oxalis stricta)

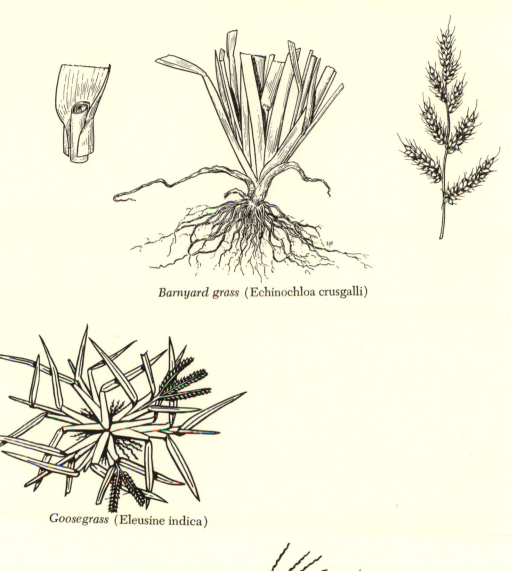

Barnyard grass (Echinochloa crusgalli)

Goosegrass (Eleusine indica)

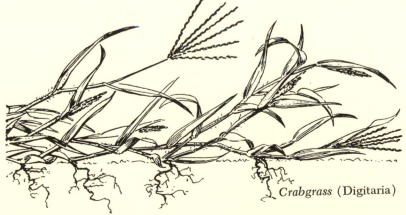

Crabgrass (Digitaria)

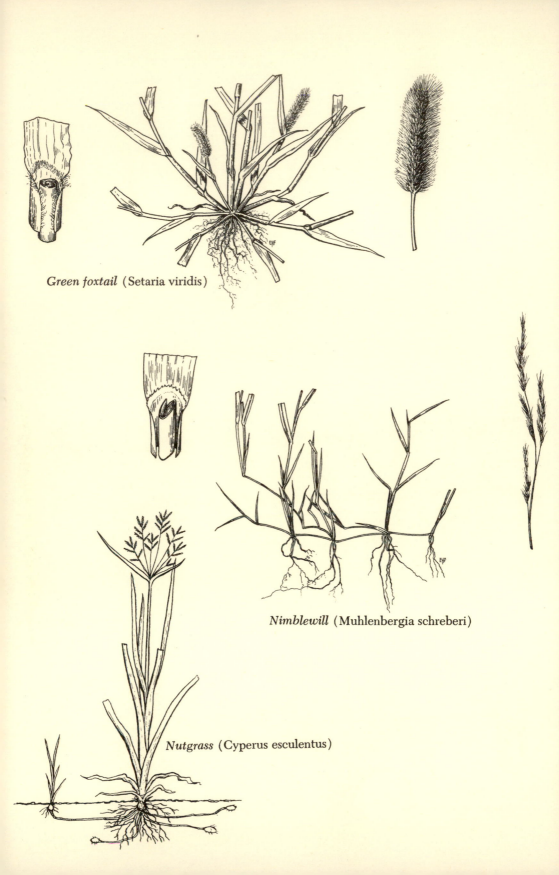

Green foxtail (Setaria viridis)

Nimblewill (Muhlenbergia schreberi)

Nutgrass (Cyperus esculentus)

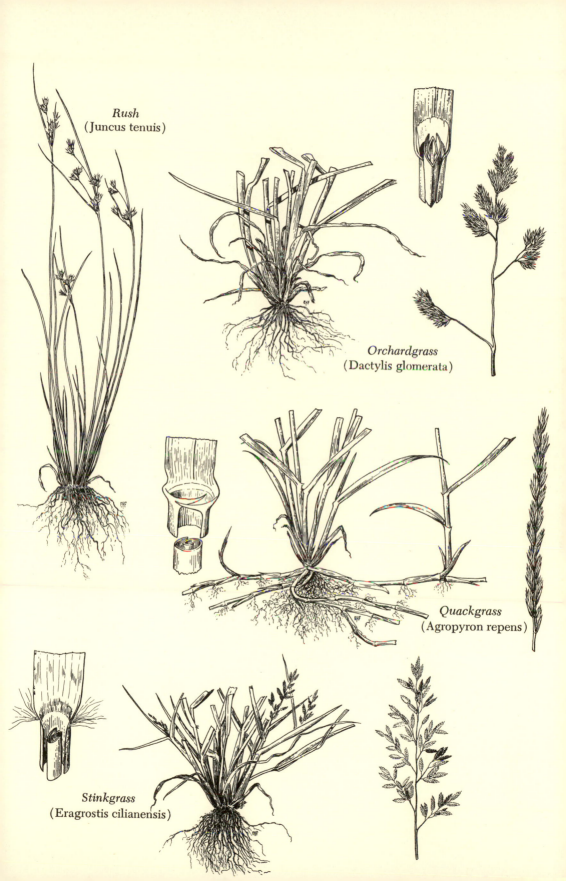

Rush
(Juncus tenuis)

Orchardgrass
(Dactylis glomerata)

Quackgrass
(Agropyron repens)

Stinkgrass
(Eragrostis cilianensis)

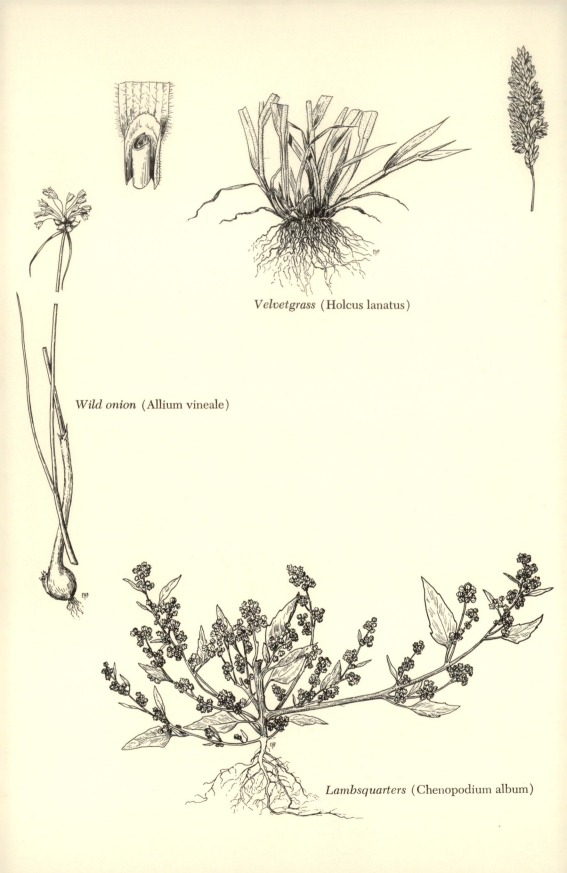

Velvetgrass (Holcus lanatus)

Wild onion (Allium vineale)

Lambsquarters (Chenopodium album)

Southern Lawn Weeds (Bermudagrass Zone)
The Humid Southeast

Common name	Botanical name	Life span*	Comments
(a) Dicotyledons: not grass-like, the leaf veins forming a network:			
beggarweed or sticktight	*Desmodium* species	P	some Florida species persist in lawn; flat pods stick to clothing
buttonweed	*Diodea teres*	A	whiskers where leaves join
cresses, various	*Cruciferae* (Mustard family)	A	rosettes like peppergrass†
cudweed, or cotton-batting plant	*Gnaphalium* species	A P	silvery-haired leaves
dichondra	*Dichondra repens*	P	heart-shaped leaf; planted in southern California
fogfruit	*Phyla (Lippia)* species	P	trailing, wedge-shaped opposite leaves; button heads of purplish flowers
hedge-nettle	*Stachys floridana*	P	spreads by underground stems; deep South
lespedeza	*Lespedeza stipulacea* and other species	A	clover-like leaves; likes poor soil
pennywort	*Hydrocotyle rotundifolia*	P	umbrella-like leaves on trailing stems; likes moisture
richardia	*Richardia* species	P	mostly Florida; similar to buttonweed
sida	*Sida spinosa*	A	mostly deep South; tends to disappear under good lawn conditions
Spanish needles or bur-marigold	*Bidens* species	A	white, daisy-like flowers; deep South
vetch, hairy	*Vicia villosa*	A B	trailing vine, purple flowers; temporary in lawn

Common name	Botanical name	Life span*	Comments
(b) Monocotyledons: grass-like leaves, the veins running parallel:			
bahia and bullgrass	*Paspalum* species	A P	broad, coarse blades
carpetgrass	*Axonopus* species	P	trailing; hard-to-cut seedheads resembling crabgrass
dallisgrass	*Paspalum dilatatum*	P	coarse, clumpy
dayflower	*Commelina* species	P	deep South; blue flowers
sandbur	*Cenchrus* species	A	low bunchgrass; spiny seeds are painful

* A = annual; B = biennial; P = perennial.
† Winter weed, prominent in early spring.

The arid Southwest offers less variety in weeds than the humid zone, but it has outstanding pests of its own. A few are listed below. Many of the humid-zone species, even northern types, are also serious pests in this zone. Among them are black medic, bur clover, carpetweed, chickweeds, dichondra, dock, fogfruit, ground-ivy, heal-all, henbit, knawel, knotweed, mallow, mustards, oxalis, pennywort, peppergrass, pigweed, plantains, purslane, Russian thistle, sheep sorrel, shepherd's-purse, sida, speedwell, spurge, among the dicotyledons; and such monocotyledons as barnyardgrass, bermudagrass, crabgrass, dallisgrass, goosegrass, nutgrass, orchardgrass, sandbur, and velvetgrass.

Southern Lawn Weeds (Bermudagrass Zone)

Common name	Botanical name	Life span*	Comments
(a) Dicotyledons: not grass-like, the leaf veins forming a network:			
baby tears	*Helxine soleirolii*	P	matted, moss-like; escaped from cultivation
bur clover	*Medicago hispida*	A	yellow flowers, spiny fruit
buttercup	*Ranunculus muricatus*	A	damp areas, yellow flowers
cat's-ear	*Hypochoeris* species	P	often in poor soils; stiff, wiry stems

Common name	Botanical name	Life span*	Comments
drymaria	Drymaria cordata	P	Hawaii; like large chickweed†
English daisy	Bellis perennis	P	rosette of hairy leaves; escaped from cultivation†
field madder	Sherardia arvensis	A	forms mat; whorled leaves, square stem
filaree	Erodium cicutarium	A B	prostrate; dissected leaves†
geranium, wild or cranesbill	Geranium dissectum	A	much-divided leaves, purplish flowers
petty spurge	Euphorbia peplus	A	leaves rounded, smooth; not lasting in lawn
pineapple-weed	Matricaria suaveolens	A	crushed leaves fragrant; daisy-like flowers
puncture vine or goat-head	Tribulus terrestris	A	injurious spiny fruits
red chickweed or scarlet pimpernel	Anagallis arvensis	A	low, matting; flowers red; S. California, especially
sandwort	Arenaria serpyllifolia	A	oval leaves, stems with reversed hairs
spurry	Spergula arvensis	A	dense leaves, glandular hairs
verbena	Verbena bracteosa	A	much branched; flowers blue

(b) Monocotyledons: grass-like leaves, the veins running parallel:

Common name	Botanical name	Life span*	Comments
annual bluegrass	Poa annua	A	low clumps; seedheads escape mower†
barley, little, Mediterranean, and mouse	Hordeum pusillum, H. hystrix, and other species	A	bushy seedheads; brown in summer, becoming a fire hazard†
kikuyugrass	Pennisetum clandestinum	P	hard to eradicate; trailing
knotgrass	Paspalum distichum	P	creeping; hairy joints; prefers moist soils

Common name	Botanical name	Life span*	Comments
ripgut grass	*Bromus rigidus*	A	sharp, pointed seeds injurious to stock†
soft cheese	*Bromus mollis*	A	velvety hairs†

* A = annual; B = biennial; P = perennial.
† Winter weed, prominent in early spring.

FAMILIAR WEEDS OF BERMUDAGRASS COUNTRY

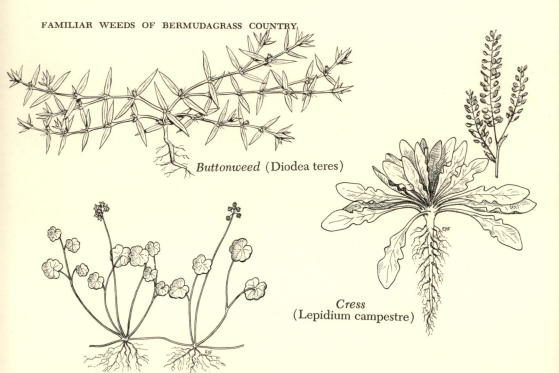

Buttonweed (Diodea teres)

Cress
(Lepidium campestre)

Pennywort (Hydrocotyle sibthorpioides)

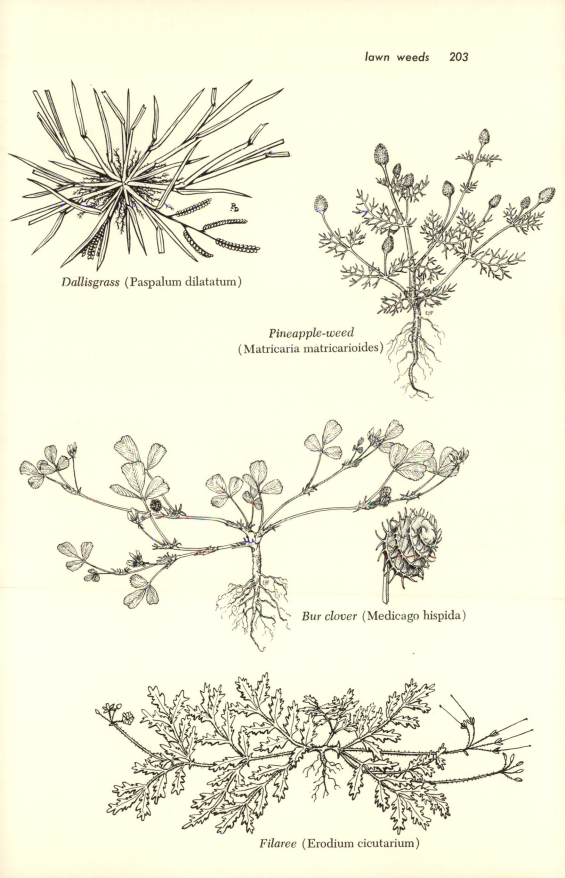

Dallisgrass (Paspalum dilatatum)

Pineapple-weed
(Matricaria matricarioides)

Bur clover (Medicago hispida)

Filaree (Erodium cicutarium)

15

how to control
lawn weeds

IF WE DIDN'T demand such perfection in a lawn, and if we were not so impatient to achieve it, we might wait for the grass to crowd out most of the weeds. With correct feeding and mowing, this is usually possible. The most effective weed control is a thriving turf. Without it, weed elimination can at best be ephemeral. Any maintenance mistakes should be rectified along with the killing of the weeds.

When a lawn is new, weeds are to be expected. Even where soil has been sterilized—perhaps the newest frontier in lawn making—some weed seeds are spared or are tracked in from elsewhere. A scattering of early weeds is not alarming, since the gradually strengthening turf has not matured enough to be fully resistant. Many of the taller weeds disappear as mowing begins. Others defer to the oncoming surge of grass.

This semi-automatic weed control by the lawn itself is not to be deprecated. But it is slow-moving, and a helping hand from the lawnsman is worth the effort. Weeds, in addition to being unattractive in a lawn, compete strongly with grass for space, water, and nourishment.

Lawn weeding once meant hours on hands and knees, grubbing dandelions or other weeds with a paring knife or cleft-tip weeding blade.

Some veterans, and some who fear chemicals, still do it this way. It's sure and it's safe and not too tedious on good lawns with few weeds. But the modern arsenal of chemical weed killers generally cleans up the lawn as effectively, and much more easily.

When Weed Seeds Sprout

Seldom do seeds of any two weeds exhibit identical requirements for germination. They vary in day and night temperature preferences, amounts of light and air necessary, and in dormancy or aging periods. Alternating periods of cold and warmth, perhaps seasonally or even just day to night, generally foster sprouting. Abundant moisture encourages the weeds, although continuously standing water usually stalls germination. The intensified crabgrass problem under a regimen of frequent sprinkling, or in unusually rainy summers, is familiar to most lawnsmen. Chalk up one drawback to irrigation!

Some seeds require light, too, for sprouting and seedling growth; crabgrass and bermudagrass need sunlight, although part of the response may be due to warmth from the sun. These influences explain why a high-cut lawn has fewer weeds, while a scalped lawn with weak grass and bare spots shows heavy infestation. Close mowing is an invitation to weeds (Chapter 11).

Chemical Weed Killers

Research has produced many excellent products for chemical weed control. These include granular herbicides applied by spreader, as well as the now familiar spray concentrates. Clear instructions accompany reliable brands. These are carefully worked out from widespread testing. If directions are heeded, not much can go wrong, although weather and local growing conditions may enhance or lessen effectiveness.

HERBICIDES AND THE ENVIRONMENT. In recent years great concern has been voiced about the effect of pesticides on the environment, causing many people to be unduly fearful of herbicides. Actually, almost none of the herbicides available to the homeowner are any more toxic than aspirin, salt, or gasoline. But of course every material used carelessly can be dangerous, and users should read product instructions carefully and follow them faithfully. When handling pesticide concentrates use gloves and protective clothing, avoid breathing fumes or spray, and bathe following a session of active spraying or spreading.

The effect of one treatment with a phenoxy weed killer is graphically shown.

Short of something like a child eating or drinking a pesticide, there should be no hazard from familiar weed killers, but the precautions just mentioned constitute added insurance.

The trend toward consumer protectionism has its drawbacks. Many useful products for the lawn are being denied the homeowner because legislation dictates they can be applied only by a licensed professional. Most people want to kill weeds in their lawn at odd moments, without great expense, and it is to be hoped that restrictions won't extend too far in presuming the homeowner to be completely irresponsible in his ability to handle weed killers judiciously. Already a dearth of new herbicides is beginning, because development costs and proving safety to government satisfaction has become so costly that the search for new products and their preparation for market is unprofitable. Recommendations in this chapter are somewhat uncertain, to the extent that many useful chemicals may not be available, at least in certain states, by the time of publication.

SELECTING A HERBICIDE: Even experts have been unable to keep up with the wide array of herbicidal chemicals developed since World War II. Many are quite specific, that is, designed to eliminate a certain weed in a certain crop without injury to the crop. Others are less specific, selectively eliminating whole groups of related plants without appreciable injury to others. Some chemicals kill back all living vegetation, and others sterilize the seedbed, at least temporarily.

All of these find a place in lawn maintenance. Each chemical is widely tested by the company manufacturing it, and instructions accompanying the retail product should be followed exactly. Because products and compoundings differ, no one rate or application method applies to all.

In deciding which chemical to use, the kind of weeds as well as any special requirements for the grass must be considered. Most product directions carry necessary precautions, noting such things as the

Incipient demise of a dandelion treated a few days earlier with 2,4-D spray. Note the typical twisting and curl of the stalks.

greater chance of injury to some grasses than to others. In the North, as a rule, bentgrasses or red fescues are more easily injured by herbicides in hot weather than is Kentucky bluegrass. In the South, most turfgrasses tolerate chemicals used in the North rather poorly (although bermuda and zoysia are quite tolerant). Yet st. augustine, even centipede and zoysia, tolerate triazine herbicides (simazine, atrazine) which are lethal to northern lawngrasses.

The chief distinction to be made in selecting a weed killer is whether the weeds to be eliminated are the broadleaf type (dicotyledons) such as dandelion, chickweed, and all the other non-grass kinds listed in the preceding chapter, or whether they are grasslike species known botanically as monocotyledons. A second distinction of importance is whether the weed is annual (can be attacked in the more vulnerable seedling stage), or perennial.

Lawn Weeds and Their Response to Phenoxy Herbicides

	Growth habit			Susceptibility	
	Rosette	Trailing	Upright	Susceptible*	Resistant**
I. Most evident in cool seasons (autumn-spring)					
buttercup, *Ranunculus sp.*			x		x
chickweeds					
common, *Stellaria sp.*		x			x
mouse-ear, *Cerastium sp.*		x			x
clover, *Trifolium repens*		x			x
cresses, several members of Cruciferae	x			x	
dandelion, *Taraxacum sp.*	x			x	
ground-ivy, *Nepeta hederacea*		x			x
henbit, *Lamium amplexicaule*		x		x	
knawel, *Scleranthus annuus*			x		x
mustards, several members of Cruciferae			x	x	
onion or garlic, wild, *Allium sp.*	x				x
peppergrass, *Lepidium sp.*	x			x	
sheep sorrel, *Rumex acetosella*			x		x
shepherd's-purse, *Capsella bursa-pastoris*	x			x	

* An "x" in this column indicates that 2,4-D or MCPP alone will generally eliminate the weed, at least in younger stages and when actively growing.

** An "x" in this column indicates a degree of resistance to 2,4-D or MCPP alone, although usually the species is controllable with combinations of 2,4-D and silvex or dicamba.

Lawn Weeds and Their Response to Phenoxy Herbicides (continued)

	Growth habit			Susceptibility	
	Rosette	Trailing	Upright	Susceptible*	Resistant**
II. Most evident from late spring through summer					
bedstraw, Galium spp.		x			x
bindweed, Convolvulus arvensis		x		x	
blackmedic, Medicago lupulina		x			x
buckhorn plantain, Plantago lanceolata		x		x	
bur clover, Medicago hispida			x	x	
buttonweed, Diodea sp.		x		x	
carpetweed, Mollugo verticillata		x		x	
cat's-ear, Hypochoeris sp.			x	x	
chicory, Cichorium intybus	x			x	
cinquefoil, Potentilla spp.		x		x	
daisy, ox-eye, Chrysanthemum leucanthemum			x		x
docks, Rumex spp.	x			x	
dog fennel, Anthemis cotula			x		x
fleabane, Erigeron spp.			x	x	
galinsoga, Galinsoga parviflora			x	x	
geranium, wild or cranesbill, Geranium dissectum			x	x	
hawkweed, Hieracium spp.	x				x
heal-all, Prunella vulgaris		x		x	
knapweed, Centauria nigra	x				x
knotweed, Polygonum aviculare		x			x
lamb's-quarters, Chenopodium album			x	x	
lespedeza, Korean, Lespedeza stipulacea			x		x
lettuce, wild, Lactuca spp.	x				x
mallow or cheeses, Malva neglecta		x			x
mugwort, Artemesia vulgaris		x			x
nutsedge, Cyperus spp.	x				x
pennywort, Hydrocotyle sp.		x		x	
pigweed, Amaranthus spp.			x	x	
plantain, Plantago major	x			x	
puncture vine, Tribulus terrestris		x		x	
purslane, Portulaca sp.		x			x
sedges, members of Cyperaceae	x				x
smartweeds, Polygonum spp.			x		x

| | Growth habit | | | Susceptibility | |
	Rosette	Trailing	Upright	Sus-ceptible*	Resist-ant**
speedwell, Veronica spp.		x			x
spurges, Euphorbia spp.		x			x
thistle, esp. Canada, Cirsium spp.			x		x
violet, Viola spp.			x		x
wild carrot, Daucus carota			x	x	
wood sorrel, Oxalis spp.			x		x
yarrow, Achillea millefolium	x				x

* An "x" in this column indicates that 2,4-D or MCPP alone will generally eliminate the weed, at least in younger stages and when actively growing.

** An "x" in this column indicates a degree of resistance to 2,4-D or MCPP alone, although usually the species is controllable with combinations of 2,4-D and silvex or dicamba.

In general, monocotyledons succumb less easily to the phenoxy (2,4-D) group of weed killers than do most broadleaf weeds. This distinction constitutes the basis for major weed control in the lawn. Science has now provided an almost miraculous way of separating the broadleaf pests such as dandelions, buckhorn, and henbit from the desired grasses. The grasses can withstand rates of phenoxy chemicals that are lethal to most broadleaf species.

CHEMICAL CONTROL OF BROADLEAVED WEEDS. The 2,4-D family of chemicals ushered in a new concept of weed control. Small quantities of growth-regulating substances (hormones) have been found to make the plant so unbalanced internally that it "gradually dies of confusion." Rates of less than one pound of active ingredient (a.i.) to the acre can wipe out all susceptible vegetation. Labels list the strength or percentage of the 2,4-D salt, amine, or ester, according to its actual weight and as if it were in the acid form (acid equivalent, or a.e.). The latter more accurately reflects the number of effective molecules contributing to the chemical's weed-killing potency. Only a few parts of chemical in a million parts of water make effective sprays. This is in contrast to older methods of "burning out" the vegetation with heavy rates of strong chemicals. Even then, underground parts might survive and sprout again.

The exquisite selectivity of 2,4-D, which enables elimination of certain species without injury to others, has been further refined by slight modification of the 2,4-D molecule. Thus the original 2,4-dichloro-phenoxy acetic acid has spawned a whole family of salts, amines, low-volatile and high-volatile esters, and other compounds of slightly different chemical structure. For example, 2,4,5-T (having an extra

An inexpensive spray device is the hose-end siphon proportioner. Herbicide is injected into the stream of water. Be careful with hazardous chemicals to avoid drift or damage to valued plants.

chlorine atom at the 5 position) proves much more useful in eliminating clover and oxalis than does 2,4-D. Similarly, 2,4,5-TP (silvex), the propionic form, does a better job against clover, chickweed, and other spring weeds. MCPP, although weaker against certain weeds, is less likely to burn sensitive grass cultivars. An ethyl sulfate salt, harmless itself, breaks down in contact with the soil to produce a temporarily lethal blanket against sprouting weed seeds. Dicamba (Banvel D) is quite effective against certain weeds rather immune to 2,4-D, such as sheep sorrel, and works as well in cool weather as warm.

The many excellent 2,4-D formulations make weed control so simple and inexpensive that it can be practiced regularly. Treatment may have to be repeated several times to catch all culprits, but as weeds are prevented from seeding, spraying becomes less necessary. There will always be some weed seeds left in the soil, and in areas where for one reason or another the turf has thinned, weed subjugation may be in order from time to time. Several companies have formulated 2,4-D herbicides with fertilizer, so that two jobs can be done at once. This proves excellent when weeding coincides with the need for feeding—

in autumn or late spring in northern states, and in spring or summer in the South.

CHEMICAL CONTROL OF WEEDY ANNUAL GRASSES. With grassy weeds, the problem becomes a little tougher; in separation of grass from grass, 2,4-D selectivity doesn't hold too well. Scientists have had to seek other selective chemicals, or have based the attack on killing annual grasses as they first sprout among the more resistant perennial species. Three major grass enemies of lawns—crabgrass, goosegrass, and foxtail—are annuals. Often they can be dealt a lethal blow as they first emerge. The following outline details methods of control.

Methods of Crabgrass Control

A. *Biologically:* "Outgrow" the crabgrass with perennial grasses.

B. *Chemically:*

    1. Pre-emergence: Treat soil before crabgrass seeds sprout (March in southern areas, to June). Familiar pre-emergence chemicals, most of them used about 10 lbs. a.i./A, are: Azak, the trade name (terbutol the common designation); Balan (benefin); Bandane; Betasan (bensulide); Dacthal (DCPA); Tupersan (siduron); Zytron (DMPA) formerly; and others.

    2. Post-emergence: Apply directly to the crabgrass plant (most effective in early growth stages). Particularly the methyl arsonates (DSMA, AMA, and CMA)—economical two-application materials; also useful on other annual grasses.

C. *Mechanically:* Physical removal of plants or seedheads by hand digging, raking, or special mowing devices (vertical cutters or special machines).

If this is too technical for the average homeowner who cannot distinguish grasses as they sprout, then chemicals selective in killing the unwanted grass while inflicting no permanent damage to the lawngrass will have to be relied upon. All of the before-sprouting or pre-emergence preventatives listed are effective in checking sprouting crabgrass without injuring established lawngrass, if used as directed; but only siduron (Tupersan) will not injure sprouting lawngrass seed. If a new bluegrass lawn seeding is to be made at the same time crabgrass prevention is undertaken, siduron should be selected. However, siduron is toxic to bermudagrass and should not be utilized with bermuda lawns.

Post-emergence elimination of annual grasses is a bit more confusing than broadleaf weed control. Arsonates (DSMA, AMA) are mostly used, reputable concerns selecting appropriate formulations and providing the instructions necessary for satisfactory results. Whether DSMA, AMA, or something else is used to shackle crabgrass makes little difference, but whether it is applied at the right rates, at the right season, the right number of times, makes a great difference. There is not quite the leeway here as with 2,4-D, and herbicide money may go down the drain unless the complete program recommended by the manufacturer is followed.

Spot killing of isolated weeds with a hand-pressure sprayer.

The pre-emergence herbicides must be used earlier in the season than types applied directly to vegetation. To achieve prevention, the chemical must be at the soil surface just before and as the weeds sprout. This means applying weed killer at exactly the right season when the time is ripe for pest-grass sprouting. Some of the chemicals remain effective a few weeks at most (depending on rain and weather conditions) and some build up relatively permanent concentrations in the soil. In either case, timing is the secret of successful use. The chemicals do little good after the weed grasses have started growth. And the impermanent sorts do little good if applied so early that they are dissipated before the weeds sprout.

Older pre-emergence weed killers for lawns are based upon high dosages of arsenicals. More recently, complex organic chemicals have found favor. Arsenicals (and chlordane when it was recommended for crabgrass control) deteriorate very little in the soil, and can even be applied the autumn before, to lie in wait for the crabgrass. Experience has indicated, however, that in climates of abundant rainfall, effectiveness is greater if used in spring, closer to crabgrass weather. As much as 25 pounds of arsenical for each 1,000 square feet of lawn area is recommended. Azak, Balan, Bandane, Betasan, Dacthal, and Tupersan are used at light rates, seldom over one pound of active ingredient per thousand square feet and often much less.

Comparison of Perennial and Annual Grass Growth Cycles

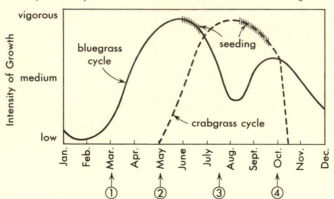

1. Good time to fertilize bluegrass, and mow higher to help shade and smother crabgrass.
2. Crabgrass seed sprouts; use pre-emergence chemical before this, selective herbicide after.
3. Main crabgrass growth period; it is most vulnerable to herbicides early in the season.
4. Crabgrass dead, carried over as seed; good season to fertilize bluegrass, reseed thin turf.

Crabgrass is an annual, and sprouts from seed when soil temperatures reach around 60° F. in late spring. In autumn it dies out by the time of heavy frosts. Seeds set during late summer over-winter in the soil. The raking of dead brown crabgrass out of the lawn in autumn is not only a waste of time, but also helps winnow and plant the ripe crabgrass seeds. On the graph, crabgrass is indicated by the dotted line, which could also represent other annual summer species such as goosegrass, foxtail, barnyardgrass, and switchgrass.

In contrast, the solid line represents the seasonal cycle of the permanent perennial lawngrasses in the North such as bluegrass. Pre-emergence herbicides in late spring should cause established bluegrass no harm while catching sprouting crabgrass. Note lawngrass' early growth; with feeding in autumn and early spring it can be encouraged to such thickness that the later sprouting crabgrass stands little chance of a foothold. Crabgrass won't grow in reduced light (never in the shade of trees, for example). A thick sod mowed tall is one of the best crabgrass controls.

Other agricultural chemicals can serve as pre-emergence weed killers too, but are riskier and may damage grass. Indeed, 2,4-D itself is effective at only a few pounds per acre if application coincides exactly with weed grass sprouting. Bromoxynil is not exactly a pre-emergence chemical, since it is sprayed on new lawn seedings soon after seed sprouting, to control most young and germinating annual broadleaf weeds without killing bluegrass, fescue, bentgrass and perennial ryegrass seedlings.

Pre-emergence chemicals are mostly applied before spring weather warms enough to trigger sprouting of annual grasses. The time for effective use can often be judged by noting the first weed grass seedlings in favorable locations, such as on exposed sunny slopes that warm ahead of the lawn. As soon as the first weeds are noted, spread the chemical uniformly over the entire surface at the rates recommended.

For lawns having weed grasses that can't be controlled by pre-emergence means, chemicals that destroy unwanted species but don't severely injure lawngrass must be sought. One of the earliest was sodium arsenite, inexpensive but not very selective. This was followed by potassium cyanate (KOCN), somewhat more selective but still prone to burn when used at effectively strong rates. Then came phenyl mercuries (PMA or PMAS, phenyl mercuric acetate) which do a nice job if used early enough in the season and with several repeat applications. Since about 1960, more selective compounds have been developed, although the perfect crabgrass herbicide, infallible in a single application, remains to be found.

Most satisfactory have been the methyl arsonates (DSMA, AMA, CMA). They have widespread effectiveness and usually require only two applications. Occasionally injury has been reported on desirable turf, but this is not permanent. Methyl arsonates and related compounds serve not only to control crabgrass but also other annual grasses such as goosegrass, dallisgrass, and foxtail, and even chickweed (usually in combination with 2,4-D) and nutsedge (repeated applications).

MECHANICAL CONTROL OF WEEDY ANNUAL GRASSES. Crabgrass and similar annuals can be controlled mechanically to a degree. If only a few show up, hand pulling is the obvious solution. But for very thick crabgrass, rakes (to kick up the grass ahead of the mower) and special vertical mowers (that cut down to about soil level), have been devised which tear out the trailing crabgrass stems. Upright grasses such as bluegrass and red fescue may become temporarily frayed, but they are not torn loose and revive from underground stems.

CONTROLLING UNWANTED PERENNIAL GRASSES. The undesirable coarse perennial grasses, such as quackgrass, tall fescue, timothy, nimblewill, and bermuda in northern lawns, are so similar to lawngrass in behavior and physiology that no really good means of selective elimination has been developed. As crabgrass becomes better controlled, these perennials loom increasingly important. Selective nimblewill control is possible with cleverly regulated use of liquid Zytron sprayed on the growing plant, but unfortunately Dow ceased making Zytron in the 1960's when it proved too costly to compete with other crabgrass preventers (its chief use).

Meanwhile, a variety of approaches may be taken with the general intent of crowding out unwanted grass with desirable turfgrass. Among them are correct timing of fertilization to spur the desirable grass at its season of greatest activity; mowing reasonably high to favor the turfgrass over the weeds; and perhaps direct attack, such as hand-pulling or spot treatment with herbicides that kill all vegetation (followed by reseeding with the desired grass). Some success has been obtained in freeing bluegrass turf from tall fescue, perhaps the most troublesome lawn weed now that crabgrass can be selectively controlled, by generous fertilization in autumn. The bluegrass is encouraged to greater competitiveness, and apparently the fescue made more vulnerable to winter-killing in climates where winter weather is fairly severe.

There are a number of chemicals that will put an end to all vegetation. This, coupled with some degree of persistence in the soil by many, makes them risky for use by the inexperienced. Be especially careful if spot killing is attempted with general herbicides such as amino triazole, cacodylic acid, dalapon, paraquat, simazine, vapam, or even cyanamid. Some of these are even being withdrawn from general use due to restrictions imposed on pesticides.

Use of non-selective herbicides, such as methyl bromide fumigation, is generally for lawns that contain little or no desirable turf, and where existing growth is to be completely eliminated before a new seeding is undertaken. General herbicides are not products for the careless; even a little left in the spraying equipment, or spilled where unwanted, can ruin desirable plantings and perhaps result in interim poisoning of the soil.

The Application of Chemical Weed Killers

CHOOSING THE TIME TO ATTACK. Weeds are more susceptible to herbicides when young and when growing actively than when mature. Plants grow actively when rainfall, temperature, and fertility are ample. Consequently, a herbicide should prove most effective a few days following a rain or watering, and when temperatures are warm enough to stimulate growth (of course, optimum temperature will differ for "winter" weeds as opposed to "summer" ones). Formulations containing 2,4-D often prove relatively ineffective during cold weather, but dicamba checks most broadleaf weeds even in winter.

Since weeds progressively develop more resistance as they mature, sometimes double the early rate may have to be used late in the season. There are specific differences among weeds too. Some of them (such as oxalis, knotweed and the spurges) are resistant to 2,4-D even in their early stages, but fortunately succumb more readily to 2,4-D when it is combined with silvex or dicamba.

Good weeding seasons for the broadleaf invaders in bluegrass lawns are autumn and warm days in spring. Pre-emergence treatment for crabgrass and similar warm-weather weeds is generally undertaken in spring. The more drastic selective removal of crabgrass might begin as early as April in the middle latitudes, and as late as June or July in the northern tier of states. Pre-emergence control for chickweed is well started in autumn.

In making plans for weed control, carefully evaluate the amount of lawn to be covered and the quantity of material needed. Have enough on hand for repeated applications if necessary, for a job half-done or allowed to slide because supplies run out is largely wasted effort. Also, be certain that proper equipment, in serviceable condition, is on hand. Nothing is more frustrating than having equipment clog or go wrong halfway through a weeding job, perhaps confusing the coverage pattern or upsetting the rate of application. Weed killing demands more precision than feeding or watering; a bit too much or too little can mean failure.

Most weed killers injure young seedlings, weed or grass. Consequently, weed control should not be undertaken at the same time as seeding, unless with products specifically known to be safe. By the same token, herbicide should be used with great care on young grass; in most instances it is wise to wait until the new lawn has had several mowings.

Herbicides are generally compatible with most other lawn materials. One exception is hydrated lime. The compounding of herbicide with fertilizer, and also with other herbicides, has proved feasible. Fertilizers combined with 2,4-D ordinarily spur grass to fill in voids as the weeds deteriorate. Fertilizer may be effectively combined with crabgrass preventers, but is less appropriate with post-emergence crabgrass killers, since midsummer is a slow period of growth for bluegrass (the fertilizer might nourish missed crabgrass more than lawngrass).

Many weeds behave as winter annuals, especially in middle and southern latitudes. Chickweed, henbit, and many of the cresses fall into this category. A warm day in mid-autumn is a good time to launch an attack here. With warm-weather grasses of the South (bermuda, st. augustine, zoysia, centipede, carpet, bahia), weed control and fertilization are appropriate at any time through the growing season, from early spring to late autumn in the deep South.

APPLYING THE WEED KILLER. There is no one preferred method of herbicide application. Choice depends upon personal inclination, size of lawn, and the availability of product or equipment. In general, sprays cover weeds more completely, with less chemical, than do dry applications. On the other hand, dry materials are generally used straight from the sack, and require little measuring, diluting, or dirtying of equipment that must be carefully cleaned afterward. A wax bar, impregnated with weed killer, for dragging over the lawn, perhaps behind the mower, has been offered, as have attachments for spraying weeds while mowing.

Cornell University Weed Control Recommendations
for Lawns, 1971 "Guide" (Bulletin 74).

Weeds	Pesticide and Utilization
Black medic	Silvex: do not use on bentgrass lawns.
Chickweed	Silvex or MCPP: do not use silvex on bentgrass lawns.
Clover	Silvex, MCPP: same precaution as above.
Coarse weedy grass	None.
Crabgrass:	
Post-emergence	Methyl arsonates (AMA or DMA).
Pre-emergence	Select any one of the following: Dacthal: most thoroughly tested of the newer chemicals; do not use before or after seeding. Bensulide (Betasan) or Azak: do not use before or after seeding. Siduron (Tupersan): can be used at any time. Benefin (Balan): least tested of all materials.
Dandelion	2,4-D.
Ground ivy	Silvex: spray more effective than granules.
Plantain (narrow- and broad-leaved)	2,4-D.
Wild onion	2,4-D: spray twice.
Veronica	Endothall: must be applied as a uniform fine spray.

The better wheeled spreaders drop dry granular herbicide with pin-point accuracy wherever the spreader is pushed. Cyclone or centrifugal seeder-spreaders, so convenient for quick coverage (as in feeding), may not be as precise for herbicide effectiveness as the drop-from-hopper types. They are, however, well suited for granular 2,4-D formulations where the granules are most effective if sifted onto foliage that remains as undisturbed as possible by the spreader.

Pressure sprayers can be purchased economically for spraying solutions. When using these it is hard to tell whether all of the lawn surface is uniformly treated, but three-gallon hand-pump models (the familiar "Hudson sprayer") are quite efficient for spot spraying and edging (chemical trimming). For those who have sizable lawns, or feel they can afford a more precise instrument, there are large knapsack sprayers that can be fitted with a "boom" of several nozzles to create a uniform pattern of known width. Whether built into a wheeled cart or carried on the back, such sprayers provide just the right amount of material, spread uniformly when adjusted for the normal walking pace of the operator. An inexpensive but effective liquid dispenser is the "Meter-Miser," which is pushed just like the spreaders for granular materials, and casts coarse droplets which don't drift beneath the solution tank (which resembles the hopper of spreaders used for granular materials).

The better suction devices, attached in place of the nozzle on the garden hose, are economical spray mechanisms. They are calibrated to eject an exact amount of spray concentrate into the water stream as the hose is played upon the lawn. When the finger is lifted from the gun, only water emerges, not chemical. Not quite so accurate as the spreader or a carefully calibrated pump, these proportioners nonetheless do a good weeding job. The operation is quick and the investment in apparatus is small.

Be especially careful with 2,4-D type herbicides. Even a little residue not washed out of spray equipment after use may injure tomatoes or roses. It is best to keep two separate sprayers, one for lawn weeding, the other for spraying garden flowers. Also, be wary of the ester forms of 2,4-D near susceptible plants such as redbud and roses. Volatile esters vaporize, then float sizable distances to affect susceptible plants. Low volatile esters and the amine forms are less hazardous in this respect, but are not always as effective herbicidally.

Vegetation damaged by 2,4-D characteristically twists and curls, a good identifying feature. Obviously, when there is a chance of damage, every precaution should be taken to use less volatile formulations. Apply them only on calm days, and keep the spray nozzle or hopper close to the ground. Lawsuits for damage to crops, ornamentals, and shade trees are not rare.

When a combination herbicide-fertilizer is employed, the chance of grass burn increases in hot weather. Major nutrients (such as ammonium or phosphorus of fertilizer) may enhance the effectiveness of 2,4-D, giving better weed kill. But trace elements such as boron, copper, iron, manganese, and zinc often reduce its effectiveness. Clay soils generally need heavier dosages of pre-emergent herbicide than do sands or loams. A number of these minor complications may influence weed killer performance and lead to slightly different results when comparing one day or place with another.

The Use of Soil Sterilants

The aims of soil sterilization are several: elimination of all competing vegetation, reduction of disease organisms and nematodes, and, above all, weed-seed destruction.

Besides being prolifically produced (see table below), most seeds are extremely durable, with the viable embryo surrounded by impenetrable, tough seed coats. Lotus and wheat seeds, entombed for thousands of years, still sprout; plantains, mustards, purslane, pigweeds, and other common lawn weeds show viability after more than forty years. Some, such as morning glory, can remain under water half a decade and still germinate, to say nothing of withstanding fire, or passage through an animal's digestive tract. Thus, a chemical that destroys weed seed in the seedbed merits respectful consideration.

Number of Seeds Produced by Single Weed Plants

Common name	Botanical name	Seeds per plant
annual bluegrass	Poa annua	2,100
barnyardgrass	Echinochloa crus-galli	7,200
chickweed	Stellaria media	15,000
dandelion	Taraxacum officinale	12,000
dock	Rumex crispus	29,500
green foxtail	Setaria viridis	34,000
knotweed	Polygonum aviculare	6,400
lambsquarters	Chenopodium album	72,500
plantain	Plantago major	36,000
shepherd's-purse	Capsella bursa-pastoris	38,500
veronica	Veronica peregrina	2,700

Methyl bromide is one of the most favored sterilants. When introduced under an ensheathing tarpaulin, it acts as a fumigant, the vapor produced by the liquid permeating the soil mass. Ten pounds of chemical for 1,000 square feet kills most weeds, seeds, fungi, and nematodes. It is most effective when soil temperatures are at least 60 degrees, and should not be used on cold soils. The treatment requires forty-eight hours; and after another forty-eight hours of airing, seed can be sown. Leak-proof tarpaulins and care to make a tight seal at the edges are imperative—requirements beyond the means of the usual lawnmaker, and ordinarily best delegated to a hired service.

Vapam, or VPM (sodium methyldithiocarbamate), is more easily used by homeowners, for it is applied with a watering can or hose proportioner as a soil drench. The chemical decomposes to a gas in the soil, and is "sealed in" by watering immediately after treatment. Residual toxicity may last several weeks.

Mylone (a dimethyltetrahydrothiadiazinethione) is much like vapam, but may be scattered dry over the loose soil or applied in water suspension. It should be followed with a water seal.

Paraquat (a dimethylbipyridiniumdichloride) is excellent for killing all green vegetation contacted. Although it is useful for a "chemical scorch" before renovation, it does not affect plant parts in the soil (such as rhizomes) which later send up new sprouts. The chemical is immediately inactivated by the soil, and seeding can follow within a day or two. Unfortunately, paraquat does not have label clearance for home use, only agriculture. Phytar or ansar (sodium cacodylate and methanearsenic acid salts) behave similarly, and are marketed chiefly for agricultural usage. As little as an ounce of paraquat with one-fourth ounce of wetting agent in a few gallons of water is sufficient for scorching back hundreds of square feet of unwanted vegetation. Scalping an old sod shortly before treatment will require less paraquat or phytar solution, since there will be less vegetation to be coated.

Dalapon (dichloropropionic acid) is effective in eliminating grassy weeds systemically when used as a spray at 0.2 lbs. to 1,000 square feet. It is translocated into underground parts, such as rhizomes, some distance from its point of treatment. Amitrol (aminotriazole) behaves similarly, but was withdrawn from food crop usage in 1971 because of the possibility of being a health hazard under certain circumstances. Calcium cyanamid kills many weeds when used at 50 or more pounds to 1,000 square feet; it breaks down to nitrogen and lime in the soil, and so has some fertility value. The other sterilants listed below are generally too tricky to be chanced by persons not familiar with their use.

Soil Sterilants

Chemical	Remarks
Amitrol	The spray blanches all foliage contacted, and is carried systemically to underground and distantly removed parts, such as expanding rhizomes.
Arsenites (sodium arsenite)	Employed as a drench, it "burns" back all vegetation and destroys seed and roots near the surface. May have lasting toxicity.

Chemical	Remarks
Borate-chlorate mixtures	For all weeds and grass; fair residual effect.
Chloropicrin	Tear gas; must be used with a sealed cover, vaporizing to effect fumigation; for professional handling only.
Cyanamid (calcium cyanamide)	Eventually breaks down in soil to calcium and nitrogen; short-lived, and not overly effective as sterilant.
Dalapon	More lasting than cyanamid, especially against grass weeds; needs at least a 4-week lag before seeding.
Methyl bromide	Volatile, and must be used with sealed cover; very effective when properly used; soil ready for replanting in few days.
Mylone (a thiodiazine-thione)	As drench, or mixed in soil, converts to toxic substance dissipating in a few weeks; take care not to injure trees and shrubs through roots.
Paraquat	A very effective contact herbicide at low concentration, scorching soft tissues contacted, but inactivated in the soil and harmless to woody stems.
Simazin (a chloro-amino-triazine)	Destroys most vegetation for perhaps several months; suited only for st. augustine, zoyzia and similar southern grass planting.
Substituted ureas (diuron, etc.)	Very effective and persistent, hence danger of residual effect.
Vapam (a dithiocarbamate)	Quite effective as a drench, but some danger from misapplication or residual toxicity.

The sterilization chemicals listed above by no means cover all possibilities. Many of the pre-emergents referred to earlier, or such general vegetation killers as TCA (sodium trichloroacetate) and PCP (pentachlorophenol), or even salt, kerosene and gasoline can be used in partial soil sterilization and as a contact vegetational herbicide. With some kinds such as the substituted ureas (fenuron, monuron, diuron), potency is so great that it might not be possible to plant grass for many months. With any chemical sterilant, observe rigidly the precautions and directions accompanying the product.

Alga and Moss Control

Perhaps it is stretching a point to include some of the lower plants, algae and mosses, as weeds. In lawns, they are more a result of mismanagement than a cause of trouble. They generally reproduce by spores, which may be ubiquitous and microscopic. Most algae and mosses prefer moist soils. Actually, neither algae nor mosses are directly harmful to the grass—merely unsightly.

Their incidence in a lawn is directly related to management—fertilization and soil care especially. When conditions are such as to restrict grass growth, mosses and algae may invade. This is especially true on compact soils that drain poorly.

Moss on a lawn is not necessarily an indicator of acid soils, as many believe. It is rather an indication of a poor soil, infertile and compact. The key to ridding a lawn of moss is to provide proper grass maintenance, as suggested in other chapters—especially generous fertilization and soil aeration.

Algae thrive on high fertility, but require constant, almost standing moisture. Providing better drainage will very likely eliminate conspicuous algal growth. Algae may also be checked by most fungicides, or by very dilute solutions of copper sulfate. Copper sulfate (or special chelated formulations such as cutrine) is often used in ponds to control algae, its concentration in the pond being brought to $\frac{1}{2}$–1 ppm (one-half to one part-per-million, or $\frac{1}{2}$–1 lb. of $CuSO_4$ in a million pounds of water). Liming also sometimes helps speed algal disappearance, perhaps partly due to its aggregating influence on the soil.

REGIONAL FOCUS

SOUTHEAST. Except for peninsular Florida, where it is possible to keep selected strains of *Zoysia matrella*, bermuda, and st. augustine grass growing almost the year around, the weed problem is intensified by short winters, ample rainfall, and the two-grass (summergrass-wintergrass) system.

All of the South has prolific "cool season" weeds. Washington, D.C., as typical of the upper South, boasts abundant wild strawberry *(Duchesnea indica)*, chickweed *(Stellaria media)*, henbit *(Lamium amplexicaule)*, wild onion *(Allium* sp.), wood sorrel *(Oxalis)*, the usual plantains, dandelions, and clover. 2,4-D (or combinations with other herbicides for oxalis and clover) might be used during an autumn warm spell, and again about March, especially where bluegrass is the permanent grass. On bermuda lawns planted late to winter rye, observe the precautions mentioned in using weed killers with new seedings. Where bermuda is a pest in bluegrass lawns the pre-emergent herbicide siduron, may be helpful in that it is toxic to bermuda (and, of course, should not be used as a crabgrass preventer on bermuda turf).

In many localities the most pernicious lawn weed is dallisgrass. Repeat treatments with methyl arsonates eliminate dallisgrass, although hand weeding is surer if there are not too many plants. Some folk smother out all grass with tar paper to get rid of dallisgrass, although spot treatment with one of the sterilants or kerosene might be quicker and less unsightly. Crabgrass is rampant in the upper South, from Tennessee to the Ohio Valley. Pre-emergents or the arsonates can help in the treatment of other troublesome annuals including goosegrass and foxtail.

Late spring and summer weeds in the Upper South are much the same as in the North, although starting earlier. Included are plantains, dandelions, dock, ground-ivy, sheep sorrel, speedwell, buttercup, and various cresses, followed by knotweed, spurge, lespedeza, bur clover, carpetweed, and mallow.

In the deep South, including Florida, variety among winter weeds is greater, and they are particularly objectionable amidst the brown of dormant bermudagrass or zoysia. Winter mowing, even though it is not needed for the grass, helps keep weeds under control.

Most of the weeds described in the previous chapter fall before 2,4-D on any warm day in late autumn or early winter. There is no certain herbicidal answer to tough weeds such as sedges (nutsedge and *Kyllinga*), sandbur, bullgrass, and volunteer bermuda. Silvex may help eliminate pennywort, fogfruit, beggarweed, oxalis, and others more or less resistant to 2,4-D. The familiar troublecausers of the North—dandelion, crabgrass, knotweed, chickweed, and plantains —are not serious in the deep South. Because of the diversity of weeds and the less concentrated growing season, pre-emergence treatment has less use here than in the North.

2,4-D may damage st. augustine and sometimes centipede in the deep South. Avoid its use and the use of methyl arsonates as well in warm weather. Methyl arsonate is best not used on bahia or st. augustine, at any season, and only with great care on centipede.

SOUTHWEST. Since most lawn weeds, as well as grasses, are not native, the majority of the southwestern weeds are the same as those of the Southeast. Aridity in the Southwest somewhat limits the diversity, with certain sorts (wild oats and puncture vine) assuming local importance. On dichondra lawns in southern California it is, of course, impossible to use 2,4-D, for it would kill this broadleaf plant. Weed control in dichondra is largely a matter of correct cultural practices to favor the dichondra, soil sterilization before planting, and careful (light-rate) chemical treatment, such as with dalapon. Otherwise, weed treatments generally follow the same practices and use the same products in the Southwest as elsewhere.

Repeated 2,4-D treatments for puncture vine and spurge (preferably when young) have been suggested. As would be expected, dandelions, plantains, and pennywort are rather readily eliminated. Oxalis and clover fall before silvex, and it may help with chickweeds and filaree, which are sometimes difficult to check with 2,4-D. Pre-emergent chemicals should help eliminate annual oats, annual bluegrass, sandbur, cresses, and various spring weeds.

Researchers have recommended methyl bromide fumigation to rid soils of nutsedge and volunteer bermuda. Vapam or other sterilants can be soaked into the soil for similar purposes, although nutsedge is fairly resistant here. As in the Southeast, to rid bermuda of carpetgrass and other weeds, strong applications of nitrogenous materials (urea, calcium cyanamide) burn back much unwanted vegetation, usually with a quick rebound of bermudagrass under the fertility impact.

Dalapon, light oils, and various chemicals mentioned under the crabgrass discussion find use in general nonselective weed control. This western country evokes good response from surface pre-emergence controls. Crabgrass usually sprouts in early March in the Los Angeles area, so pre-emergence treatment must be applied before then.

Weed killers seldom injure bermuda, zoysia, or bluegrass, but bentgrasses are more easily burned. If you are trying to keep bentgrass in the Southwest, hard enough as it is, use weed killers with discretion, exactly as recommended on the label.

Southern California has, more than any other area, adopted ground covers (ivy, trailing herbs, vines, and low shrubs) in place of grass. Often these are more temperamental and require more attention than grass. It goes without saying that herbicides must be used on them with extreme caution, since the broadleaf ground covers are more like the weeds than like lawngrass. With dichondra especially, an ounce of prevention taken in soil preparation saves much hand-weeding later. Dichondra is reasonably tolerant of methyl arsonate (post-emergence crabgrass control) and arsenates (pre-emergence, late winter). Dalapon, at light rates in spring and summer, eliminates weed grass in dichondra. Dichondra also tolerates low rates of substituted ureas (two pounds of monuron to the acre) that might eliminate oxalis and certain grasses.

NORTHERN SECTIONS. There is little reason for detailed discussion of weeds in the North, since weed problems there are no different from those considered in the general discussion, and weeds are by-and-large progressively less a problem as one proceeds northward. Often just fertilizing the grass is an effective weed control measure. When needed, 2,4-D and its combinations will keep plantains, dandelions, clover, and the like in check, and crabgrass is not as overwhelming as in the midcountry crabgrass belt.

Certain perennial weedgrasses, against which no adequate selective control has been developed, become serious in the North. Among these are nimblewill, quackgrass, and velvetgrass. Often they must be hand-pulled or an attempt made to outgrow and overwhelm them with desired turf. General herbicides or sterilants, spot-applied, can be of some help.

Mouse-ear chickweed is frequent in the North; it is harder to kill with 2,4-D than common chickweed, and 2,4,5-TP (silvex) or combinations of this with methyl arsonate is usually recommended. Pre-emergent treatment can be effective when timed to catch the concentrated rush of spring-sprouting annuals. Chickweed, knotweed, and *Poa annua* (annual bluegrass) can be checked to an extent with silvex, and frequently with pre-emergent crabgrass chemicals such as bensulide. Common chickweed is easily cleaned up with silvex. Two-4-D has been combined with dicamba effectively to turn back knotweed and spurge. Methyl arsenate alone foils foxtail and goosegrass. For sheep sorrel, dicamba is a ready answer, but it should not be used within the dripline of trees or shrubs for fear of damaging them through chemical pickup by the roots. Speedwell remains tough to eliminate unless conditions are favorable, although endothal has given good results with creeping speedwells.

Danger of burn to desirable grass is less in the cooler North. Ordinarily the lawnman need have no fear if herbicides are used at recommended rates. Bentgrass can take it better here than in hotter climates, and fine fescue is only a little less tolerant than bluegrass.

PLAINS STATES. These states afford an intermediate climate, with problems approaching those of the Southwest. Where irrigation is not possible, special drought-resistant grasses are sought (as buffalograss), and certain weeds appear (kochia, knapweed, leafy spurge). Where irrigation is used, the familiar weeds prosper with the familiar grasses. Weed problems are then much the same as for the northern section east of the Mississippi and the humid Pacific Northwest.

COMMON MISCONCEPTIONS

THE WEED MENACE TO LAWNS IS INCREASING. Actually, as the standards for lawns are raised, there are fewer weeds, although these may be noticed more. Never have there been so many efficient chemicals for aiding in weed control. A few weeds, such as nimblewill, do seem on the increase, but many, including crabgrass, that were once very difficult to control are now easily eliminated with herbicides.

HERBICIDES WHICH "BURN OUT" WEEDS MUST ALSO SET BACK GRASS. Once weed control was by direct destruction of the living plant. More recently a subtler method has been developed, whereby growth-regulating hormones are used to upset the internal balance of weeds. Fortunately, these cause many weeds to die, with little influence on the grass. At light rates they may even stimulate grass.

ANY WEED IS A MENACE. By definition a weed is a plant not wanted. Yet the same plant, in another location, may prove very attractive or useful. Moreover, weeds are better than bare soil for unplanted areas; weeds will help build up this soil and protect it from erosion.

MOST LAWN WEEDS ARE INTRODUCED WITH GRASS SEED. Almost every soil contains weed seeds, sometimes hundreds of them in each square foot. Weeds in the lawn almost invariably come from these seeds, or are tracked in from neighboring areas. Seed marketed through regular trade channels must be reasonably free of weeds in order to meet legal requirements. What few weeds are contained must be categorized on the box, and are seldom of sufficient frequency or kinds to be harmful to lawns.

IF THE WEEDS ARE KILLED, SO THEY DON'T SET SEED, THE WEED PROBLEM IS LICKED. Preventing seed formation is, of course, helpful. But nature has provided for her weeds as for her grasses; not all seeds will sprout in one year, so that additional sprouting may still occur even after many years of weed control. Weed seeds can lie dormant in the soil for decades, then sprout when brought to the surface, as with aerification.

DON'T FERTILIZE A WEEDY LAWN; IT WILL HELP THE WEEDS. This may be true temporarily, but the best weed control is vigorous grass, and grass needs fertilization to grow vigorously. Actually, fertilizer is one of the lawnman's best tools for weed control.

IT'S GOOD TO SCRATCH WEEDS OUT OF THE LAWN, AS WITH A TURF THINNER. Perhaps in some cases this will help restrict reseeding, or give certain types of weeds seasonal setback helpful when the grass recovers more quickly than the weed. But, just as often, you are helping to plant weed seeds already present, or thinning the grass enough to give weed seedlings greater opportunity. There is little point in raking dead annuals such as crabgrass or foxtail out of a lawn after frost; seeds have already been shed, and the agitation merely helps work them down into the soil into a position for sprouting next year. Generally, chemical weed control is more effective than mechanical removal, unless individual weed plants are hand-dug and discarded.

IF I COULD WATER MY LAWN, I'D HAVE FEWER WEEDS. This is doubtful, although the weeds would probably be different kinds. Intermittently dry lawns generally have fewer water-loving weeds such as crabgrass, *Poa annua*, rough bluegrass and sedges: but drought-ridden lawns may thin enough to give greater opportunity to knotweed, dandelion, and suchlike in summer.

CLIP LAWNS CLOSE TO RESTRAIN WEEDS. Scalping thins the grass, gives weeds greater opportunity: most lawns are mowed too close for the grass to compete well against weeds. Set the mowing height to suit the type of grass—low for most bentgrasses and bermudas, but higher for most bluegrasses, fescues, and southern species other than bermuda.

16

lawn insects

Insects are man's greatest competitors for the plant wealth of the land. Happily for homeowners, they seem less interested in lawngrass than in crops. At least in lawns their normal raids are kept inconspicuous by the continuous new foliage that good grass provides. In many years of tending lawns, I have not personally had to cope with any serious turf damage from insects—nothing more bothersome than ants and chiggers. However, insect depredations will loom large if it happens to be *your* lawn that is devastated. If yours is the st. augustine wiped out by Florida chinchbugs, the centipedegrass debilitated by Georgia ground pearls, the bermuda splotched by California webworms, or the New England sod laid loose by underground grub nibblings, major lawn repairs cloud your future.

Fortunately, the same insecticides are applicable whether the trouble is a grub below ground, a crawler above, or whether the attack comes in spring, summer, or autumn. In recent years, however, restriction on home use of certain insecticides, such as DDT or chlordane, has made it more difficult and expensive to stop certain types of lawn insects, especially those operative in the soil. Also, many insect species have built up populations resistant to traditional insecticide treatments, and can no longer be checked with certainty by available products.

The Troublemakers

There will always be some insects in the lawn. Indeed, balance in which one is pitted against another is Nature's way of holding populations in check. It is when we are not clever enough to maintain this natural balance that we call upon insecticides as emergency tools. Even where an application of insecticide has been made, some insects are little affected, and new leaf growth makes a fresh surface uncoated with insecticide so quickly that airborne invaders may miss contact with the poison.

An unusual abundance of insects in the lawn may be a warning signal. If trouble is suspected, a dousing with pyrethrum solution* should bring the insects hidden in grass crowns and debris to the surface where they can be identified. Their frequency can be estimated by thrusting an open-end tin can into the turf and filling it with pyrethrum solution (or even just water), then counting the insects that float to the surface. Chinchbugs can be estimated by shaking grass foliage suspected of attack over a stiff white paper or cardboard edged into the grass. Soil grubs, of course, can only be counted by lifting the sod and sifting the soil. Seldom is the lawnsman so alert, however, as to detect build-up before damage to the turf appears. Of course, the kind of damage will vary with the insect (see page 233).

Several insects are frequently troublesome, although not damaging the grass directly:

CICADA WASP. Large, buzzing, fearsome-looking wasps that sting cicadas and bury them in burrows for their young to feed on.

ANTS, CENTIPEDES, CRICKETS, MILLIPEDES, SCORPIONS, SPIDERS. Nuisances when lawn is in use; ant mounds disfigure the lawn, interfere with mowing.

CHIGGERS (nearly invisible mites), FLEAS, TICKS. All bite or embed themselves in the skin, causing itching and irritation.

EARWIGS. Large nocturnal scavengers, vicious-looking because of "pincers" at rear.

CLOVER MITES. Seldom attack grass where clover is present; chiefly a nuisance in the South where they enter homes in cooler months.

* One tablespoon of ½-1% pyrethrum extract to a gallon of water, used approximately one gallon per square yard.

Occasionally troublesome in lawns are: *grasshopper* (eats foliage), *fiery skipper* (similar to cutworm, feeds on leaves, especially bentgrass in California), *lucerne moth* (similar to sod webworm, feeds on foliage in California), *leaf bug* (consumes foliage), *cicada* (produces burrow openings), *false chinchbug* (sucks plant juices), *spittle bug* (produces white, unpleasant froth), *sowbug* and *pillbug* (may sometimes eat grass), *spider mites* (suck sap and may speckle leaves), and several other insects.

The more serious of the turfgrass insects listed above merit brief discussion.

GRUBS OF SEVERAL BEETLES AND CHAFERS. Adults are the familiar May or June beetles, Japanese beetles, and so forth, whose larval stages, embracing one to three years, are spent in the soil as soft white grubs. Abundant grubs sever grass roots, thinning and drying out sod in irregular patches, usually in sunny locations. Heavily infested sod simply lies on the lawn, its root anchorage broken; lifting it usually exposes the grubs. Developing from eggs laid in June, these are big enough by autumn to be visible, and a sample lifting of sod with a spade then or in spring will indicate the severity of infestation. Soil treatment when the ground is not frozen gradually eliminates grubs. Various kinds occur throughout the United States.

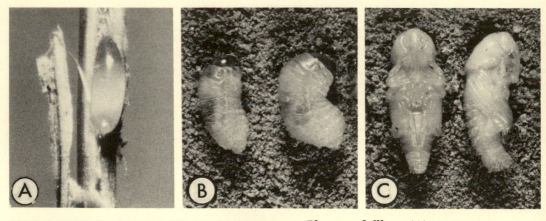

Bluegrass billbug: (A) egg on stem (disproportionately enlarged), (B) mature larvae, (C) pupae, (D) adults. (Photo courtesy of H. Tashiro, New York State Agricultural Experiment Station)

Major Lawn Insects and Type of Damage Inflicted

Symptoms	Cause
I. Damaging or consuming roots underground	
A. Dying, stunted sod that lifts like a carpet, usually exposing grubs.	a. Fleshy, crescent-shaped *Grubs*, the larvae of June, Japanese, and other beetles or chafers.
B. Centipede and bermuda weakened, resist drought poorly and fail to respond to care.	b. Small, round white *Ground Pearls*, an "underground scale."
C. Unthrifty grass, the roots bored into and consumed.	c. Elongated, horny *Wireworms*, the larvae of click beetles.
D. Burrows down to consume roots, the bulldozing activity uprooting seedlings and mounding soil, in South.	d. Large (1½") *Mole Crickets*, with short front legs for digging.
II. Sucking plant juices aboveground	
E. Grass dead in irregular patches, most prevalent in sunny, dry locations, especially troublesome on st. augustine in South.	e. Small red-and-black *Chinchbugs* hidden in foliage.
F. Grass gradually yellows, with waxy protrusions near crown, in South.	f. Stationary *Scale* insects which coat themselves with wax.
G. Blanched or whitened and dried-out foliage, especially on new turf.	g. Small jumping *Leaf-hoppers*, flattened vertically.
III. Consuming grass foliage	
H. Sometimes foliage chewed bare in circular areas or clean-cut winding trails.	h. Larvae (caterpillars) of moths, especially *Army-worm* and *Cutworm*.
I. Irregular brown patchiness of lawn, cut foliage, and silky webs near crown.	i. *Sod Webworm*, larvae of the lawn moth.
J. Burrows in midst of plants, some leaf consumption, grub-like larvae attacking roots, mostly in South.	j. Long-snouted weevil-like *Billbugs* and their larvae.

GROUND PEARLS. Nymphs of *Margarodes meridionalis* hatched from eggs secrete a hard, globular shell that looks like a pearl about ⅛ inch in diameter. Widespread debilitation of southern turfs, especially centipedegrass, is attributable to this and other scale insects; unfortunately, no very effective control has been found, so one nurses the turf along or replants it with more resistant grasses.

CHINCHBUGS. Several species of *Blissus* are agricultural and grass pests, but most lawn damage comes to st. augustine in the Gulf area where the bugs hibernate briefly if at all. Growing nymphs cause most of the damage as they pass through five molts, enlarging (on the juices sucked from grass) from half the size of a pinhead to more than ⅛ inch long. There may be two or three generations per year. Young nymphs are mostly red, becoming almost black with age. Swishing a stiff white cardboard deep into the grass about a foot outside the blemished area will generally expose a few culprits active in new grass. Damaged turf shows as irregular, enlarging brown splotches, new shoots dying back, usually during the drier intervals of summer and autumn. Insecticides should offer good control, especially if applied ahead of visible damage, but races of cinchbug resistant to familiar insecticides have developed.

SOD WEBWORM. Several species of the lawn moth, *Crambus*, are injurious in the larval stages when they are known as sod webworms. The slender buff moths (millers) are often seen late in the day fluttering over the lawn, depositing eggs and future trouble. There may be four generations in a year in California and at least three in the Midwest. The moths are first noted in April or May, but webworm damage is not serious until late summer. The black-spotted caterpillars, which

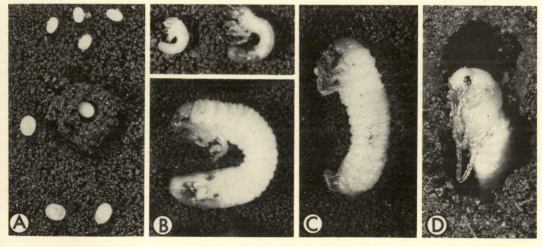

European chafer life history: (A) earthen egg cell and mature eggs, (B) larvae, (C) pre-pupae, (D) pupae, (E) adult. (Photo courtesy of H. Tashiro, New York State Agricultural Experiment Station).

One-season billbug damage to a New York lawn.

are about three-fourths of an inch long, feed at night on new green foliage. During the day they retire to silken tunnels or webs partly buried in the soil, which give rise to the common name. If infestation is heavy, large areas may be damaged in a short time, the cut foliage often being dragged into the burrows for food. Insecticidal treatment is quickly effective, but should be washed down well into the grass crowns.

Treating for Insects

Birds are often good indicators of as well as control for lawn insects. Flocks, particularly of grackles and starlings, can be noticed patrolling a lawn, pecking into the thatch (helping to loosen it) every few inches. These birds are great grub and caterpillar consumers. On my lawn in Ohio, I have noticed a greater incidence of lawn moths (adult webworms) since the grackles, red-wing blackbirds and starlings have been systematically poisoned and eliminated for agricultural reasons.

Years ago turfs were grub-proofed with lead arsenate, which has also been found effective since in repressing crabgrass. Heavy rates—10 to 30 pounds per 1,000 square feet—are needed, making the operation costly. With the development of DDT about the time of World War II, equally effective control became possible with one-fortieth as much chemical. DDT was gradually replaced by other chlorinated hydrocarbons such as chlordane, dieldrin, aldrin, toxaphene and heptachlor, which were found to have a long, effective life in the soil at even light rates. These chemicals kill by direct contact, through ingestion, or even through fumigant vapors, thus exhibiting a greater versatility than the old-time stomach poisons (Bordeaux), or contact poisons (nicotine sulfate). If applied during the heat of the day, the chemicals are most likely to volatilize, providing the fumigation effect referred to.

In most areas these chemicals are prohibited or difficult to procure, because of real or fancied ecological damage. There is no doubt that some of them can be detrimental if allowed to wash into streams and lakes, but substances such as chlordane and toxaphene applied to the lawn would seem to offer little hazard. Where chinchbugs, sod webworms, or other insect groups have built up resistance to commonly used insecticides (especially the chlorinated hydrocarbons), authorities suggest alternating insecticide types, or turning to others of a different chemical nature. Diazinon or Spectracide (a phosphorothioate); carbaryl or Sevin (a naphthylmethylcarbamate); malathion (a phosphatic mercaptosuccinate); methoxychlor (a methoxyphenyl trichloroethane); Dursban (a phosphorothioate); and Aspon (a dithiopyrophosphate) are a few suggested as suitable for home use.

Lawn insect-control measures largely rest with insecticides, although efforts have been made to trap adult Japanese beetles mechanically, and to introduce the spores of milky disease, which infect and kill grubs in the soil. The success of this method depends upon the spread of the disease from grub to grub, so treatment with chemical insecticides should not be made concurrently with efforts to inculcate milky spore disease. Chlordane has been the most frequently employed home lawn insecticide, but in recent years its usefulness has suffered somewhat from build-up of resistance by many lawn insects. It is effective both against soil pests and those aboveground, and retains toxicity in the soil for years, even when used at only a fraction of a pound to the thousand square feet. Both granular or dust formulations, and emulsifiable concentrates or wettable powders (to be diluted for spraying), are available. In some states chlordane can be applied only by licensed spraymen.

Listed below are the various chemicals and suggested rates of use for lawn insect control as recommended by the United States Department of Agriculture (in Home and Garden Bulletin No. 46, 1971), by Cornell University (in its 1972 Cornell Recommendations for Turfgrass), and by Ohio State University (in L-187-*Insecticide Recom-*

Billbug

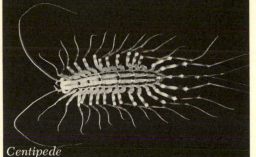

Centipede
Scutigera coleoptrata

Sod webworm (adult)

Millipede
Julius impressus

Sod webworm (larva)

White grub

White-lipped snail

Leafhopper

Adult Japanese
beetle

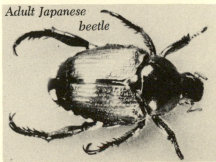

Mole cricket

Sowbug

mendations for Turf Pests, 1972). All are generally compatible and no harm results from applying them in combination with lawn fertilizers. Chlordane is rather slow-acting, and some weeks may pass before results are noticeable. Gradual availability is indicative of prolonged chemical effectiveness, and chlordane has a long residual life in the soil. Malathion, diazinon, Dursban, Aspon, and carbaryl are more easily biodegradable, and generally are recommended in place of chlorinated hydrocarbons where a "hard" pesticide may prove objectionable in the environment.

Recommended Insecticide Spray Formulations USDA, from Bulletin 46, 1971.

Insecticide	Formulation[1]	Amount of formulation to mix with 1 gallon of water
Carbaryl	50-percent WP	2 level tablespoons.
Chlordane	40-percent WP	1½ level tablespoons.
	or	
	45-percent EC	2 teaspoons.
Diazinon	25-percent EC	2 teaspoons.
Dicofol	18.5-percent WP	1 level tablespoon.
	or	
	18.5-percent EC	1 teaspoon.
Dimethoate	23.4-percent EC	1 teaspoon.
Endosulfan	50-percent WP	1 level tablespoon.
	or	
	2-pounds-per-gallon EC	2 teaspoons.
Malathion	57-percent EC	2 teaspoons.
Methoxychlor	50-percent WP	2 level tablespoons.
Naled	8-pounds-per-gallon EC	1 teaspoon.
Pyrethrum	Ready-prepared spray	([2]).
Rotenone	Derris or cube root powder (5-percent rotenone content)	4 level tablespoons.[3]
Sulfur	Wettable sulfur	3 level tablespoons.
Toxaphene	40-percent WP	3 level tablespoons.

[1] WP = wettable powder; EC = emulsifiable concentrate. If the available formulation contains more or less of the indicated active ingredient, mix proportionately more or less of the material with 1 gallon of water.

[2] Mix with water as directed on the container label.

[3] First, mix the powder with a small quantity of water; then add remaining water.

Cornell University Lawn Insect Control Recommendations**

All amounts given will treat 5,000 square feet. Apply emulsion, flowable, sprayable and wettable powder formulations in 50 to 150 gallons of water.

Pest	Recommendation	Comments
Grubs (Japanese beetle, oriental beetle, Asiatic garden beetle, susceptible European chafer)	*Chlordane (4 lb. AI/acre)—½ pint 72–75% E; 1¼ lbs. 40 W; 5 lbs. 10% dust or G; 10 lbs. 5% dust or G.	Treat with chlordane once every 4–5 years or when grubs appear in lawn again. Use primarily for prevention of infestation. When applied to mature grubs will reduce populations but not eliminate them. Applications can be made during spring, summer or fall.
Japanese beetle grubs (not effective against other grubs)	Milky disease powder—8 lbs./acre (apply 1 level teaspoon in spots at 5 foot intervals in rows 5 feet apart).	Do not use on areas treated with insecticides. Grubs must be present to spread and maintain disease. Useful on large, marginal, low value turf areas. To prevent damage to good turf, use insecticide.
European chafer grubs—chlorinated hydrocarbon-resistant in Rochester area (tentative recommendation)	Diazinon (6 lbs. AI/A.)—1½ pints 4 E; 1½ qts. 2 E; 1½ lbs. 50 W; 5 lbs. 14 G; 37½ lbs. 2 G; or Carbaryl (Sevin) (8 lb. AI/A.)—1 qt. 4F; 1¼ lbs. 80 S; 2 lbs. 50 W; 20 lbs. 5 G. Dursban (2 lbs. AI/A)—½ pint 4E; 1 pint 2 E; 50 lbs. 0.5 G.	Treat annually during August 1–31. Apply ½–1″ water immediately if directed only against the European chafer. Water 48–72 hours later if directed also against sod webworms. Diazinon (only) applied about July 1–10 for bluegrass billbug control effective also against susceptible and resistant European chafer grubs. Against European chafer grubs, carbaryl is less effective than Diazinon or Dursban but is less toxic. If birds graze area, water the insecticide in. Dursban should be watered in as soon as possible for maximum effectiveness.

Pest	Recommendation	Comments
Bluegrass billbug in Monroe County (tentative)	Diazinon (6 lbs. AI/A.)—1½ pints 4 E; 1½ qts. 2 E; 1½ lbs. 50 W; 5 lbs. 14 G; 37½ lbs. 2 G; or Carbaryl (8 lbs. AI/A.)—1 qt. 4F; 1¼ lbs. 80 S; 2 lbs. 50 W; 20 lbs. 5 G.	One application to newly mowed lawn during June 1–July 10 as soon as 5 billbugs can be collected in 5 min. on adjacent pavements. Apply spray applications with lower rates of water. Diazinon (only) applied during July should be effective against the susceptible and hydrocarbon-resistant European chafer grubs. Water Diazinon in if birds graze area.
Hyperodes weevil	Diazinon (4 lb. AI/A.) 1 pint 4 E; 1 qt. 2 E; 1 lb. 50 W; 3¼ lbs. 14 G; 25 lbs. 2 G; or Dursban (2 lb. AI/A.) ½ pint 4 E; 1 pint 2 E; 2½ lbs. 10 G.	Treat suspected problem areas in mid-April and again in mid-May.
Sod webworm and cutworms	carbaryl (8 lbs. AI/A.)—1 qt. 4 F; 1¼ lbs. 80 S; 2 lbs. 50 W; 20 lbs. 5 G; or Diazinon (6 lbs. AI/A.)—1½ pints 4 E; 1½ qts. 2 E; 1½ lbs. 50 W; 5 lbs. 14 G; 37½ lbs. 2 G; or Dursban (1 lb. AI/A)—7.5 fl. oz. 2 E; or 25 lbs. 0.5 G. *ethion—1⅔ to 2½ pints 4 E. *Akton—7.5–15 fl. oz. 2 E.	Evening treatments are preferred. Do not water in treatments after application. Apply spray applications with lower rates of water. Do not cut grass for 1–3 days after treatment. Avoid spraying before rain but if aimed also at resistant European chafers water in after 48–72 hours.
Hairy chinchbug (Long Island, Westchester, Rockland and southeastern-most counties primarily; some reported in upstate N.Y.)	carbaryl—1 qt. F; or 2 lbs. 50 W; or 10 lbs. 10% G; or Aspon—1¼ pints 6 E; or 17.5 lb. 5% G; or Diazinon—1 to 2 pints. 25 E; or 1½ lbs. 25 W; or 20 lbs. 5% G; or *Trithion—3½ pts. 2 E; or 18 lbs. 5 G; or *ethion—2 pts. 4 E; or 25 lbs. 5 G; or Dursban (1 lb. AI/A)—7.5 fl. oz. 2 E; or 25 lbs. 0.5 G. *Akton—7.5–15 fl. oz. 2 E.	Water lawn prior to treatment. Mix with 125–150 gal. of water to make application of spray. Water in granular materials after application. Carbaryl and Aspon are least hazardous. Diazinon is moderately toxic. Trithion and ethion are highly toxic phosphates. Soil treatments for grubs not effective against chinchbug infestation. Apply treatment in early June. A second application 2–3 weeks later may be necessary, except for Aspon.

Pest	Recommendation	Comments
Ants	Mirex	Follow directions on label.
Moles	Older type poison baits not effective. Traps continue to be effective when carefully set.	Moles feed on beetle grubs and earthworms. Grub-proofing often very effective in reducing mole damage. Mouse damage to turf in very early spring often attributed to moles.

E = emulsion; F = flowable; S = sprayable; W = wettable powder; G = granular.

* Purchase permits from the New York State Department of Environmental Conservation required for possession and application of Trithion and Akton, for ethion (higher concentrations) and for chlordane (except for formulations and package size not exceeding 20 lbs. 5 G., 5 lbs. 5% dust, and 8 oz. 45–50 E.

** From 1972 "Guide" CU-12 M.

Ohio State University Insecticide Recommendations, 1972.

Grubworm Control

Insecticide	Lbs. Active Ingredient/A	Formulation	Rate to Apply Per 1,000 sq. ft.	Per A	
Chlordane	5 lbs.	8 lb./gal. EC*	4 tbsp.	2½ qts.	
		5% granules	2½ lbs.	100 lbs.	
		40% WP*	5 oz.	12½ lbs.	
Heptachlor	2 lbs.	2 lbs./gal. EC	9 tbsp.	1 gal.	March—June or August— December
		2½% granules	2 lbs.	80 lbs.	
		25% WP	3 oz.	8 lbs.	
Aldrin	3 lbs.	4 lbs./gal. EC	5 tbsp.	3 qts.	Whenever ground is not frozen.
		20% granules	5½ oz.	15 lbs.	
		40% WP	3 oz.	7½ lbs.	
Dieldrin	2 lbs.	1.5 lbs./gal. EC	8 tbsp.	1⅓ gal.	
		10% granules	8½ oz.	20 lbs.	
		50% WP	1½ oz.	4 lbs.	
Milky spore disease		dust	2 tsp./5 ft. Broadcast	8 lbs. 20 lbs.	Spring or Fall

Insecticide	Lbs. Active Ingredient/A	Formulation	Rate to Apply		
			Per 1,000 sq. ft.	Per A	
Sod Webworm Control					
Sevin	9 lbs.	4 lbs./gal. EC	7 oz.	9 qts.	June 1—June 15
		5% granules	2¾ lbs.	120 lbs.	for first
		50% WP	7 oz.	18 lbs.	generation
		80% SP*	4 oz.	11¼ lbs.	and/or
Diazinon	5½ lbs.	4 lbs./gal. EC	4 oz.	5½ qts.	August 1—
		14% granules	15 oz.	40 lbs.	August 15
		50% WP	4 oz.	11 lbs.	for second
		25% EC	8 oz.	11 qts.	generation.
Dylox	8½ lbs.	80% SP	3 oz.	8½ lbs.	
Zectran	2 lbs.	2 lbs./gal. EC	3 oz.	8 pts.	
		25% WP	3 oz.	8 lbs.	
Baygon	5¾ lbs.	1.5 lbs./gal. EC	11 oz.	3¾ gal.	
		70% WP	2¾ oz.	7¼ lbs.	
Dursban	1 lb.	2 lbs./gal. EC	1½ oz.	2 qts.	
		4 lbs./gal. EC	¾ oz.	1 qt.	
		½% granules	5 lbs.	200 lbs.	
Ethion	8 lbs.	4 lbs./gal. EC	6 oz.	2 gal.	
		8 lbs./gal. EC	3 oz.	1 gal.	
		5% granules	4 lbs.	160 lbs.	
Akton	1½ lbs.	2 lbs./gal. EC	2¼ oz.	3 qts.	
Chinch Bug Control					
Sevin	9 lbs.	4 lbs./gal. EC	7 oz.	9 qts.	
		5% granules	2¾ lbs.	120 lbs.	
		50% WP	7 oz.	18 lbs.	
		80% SP	4 oz.	11¼ lbs.	
Diazinon	5½ lbs.	4 lbs./gal. EC	4 oz.	5½ qts.	June 1—June 10
		14% granules	15 oz.	40 lbs.	for first
		50% WP	4 oz.	11 lbs.	generation
		25% EC	8 oz.	11 qts.	and
					August 1—
Ethion	8 lbs.	4 lbs./gal. EC	6 oz.	2 gal.	August 10
		8 lbs./gal. EC	3 oz.	1 gal.	for second
		5% granules	4 lbs.	160 lbs.	generation.
Aspon	8½ lbs.	6 lbs./gal. EC	4 oz.	5¾ qts.	
		5% granules	4 lbs.	170 lbs.	

Insecticide	Lbs. Active Ingredient/A	Formulation	Rate to Apply Per 1,000 sq. ft.		Per A	
Akton	1½ lbs.	2 lbs./gal. EC	2¼ oz.		3	qts.
Dursban	1 lb.	2 lbs./gal. EC	1½ oz.		2	qts.
		4 lbs./gal. EC	¾ oz.		1	qt.
		½% granules	5 lbs.		200	lbs.

Bluegrass Billbug Control

Insecticide	Lbs. Active Ingredient/A	Formulation	Per 1,000 sq. ft.		Per A		
Sevin	4 lbs.	4 lbs./gal. EC	3 oz.		1	gal.	
		5% granules	2 lbs.		80	lbs.	
		50% WP	3 oz.		8	lbs.	
		80% SP	2 oz.		5	lbs.	Late June or
Diazinon	4 lbs.	4 lbs./gal. EC	3 oz.		1	gal.	very early July.
		14% granules	10 oz.		28	lbs.	
		50% WP	3 oz.		8	lbs.	
		25% EC	6 oz.		2	gal.	
Dursban	1 lb.	2 lbs./gal. EC	1½ oz.		2	qts.	(Not labeled for
		4 lbs./gal. EC	¾ oz.		1	qt.	billbug, but will
		½% granules	5 lbs.		200	lbs.	control it.)
Baygon	7½ lbs.	1.5 lbs./gal. EC	1 pt.		5	gal.	(Not labeled for
		70% WP	4 oz.		11	lbs.	billbug, but will control it.)

tsp. (teaspoonful), tbsp. (tablespoonful)
* EC (Emulsifiable Concentrate), WP (Wettable Powder), SP (Sprayable Powder)

Applying Insecticides

Insecticides come in many forms: liquid concentrates, emulsions, wettable powders for dissolving, ready-to-use dry granular and dust formulations. The same dusters, spreaders, sprinkling cans, and sprayers used generally for the lawn will suffice for insecticides. As a rule, sprays cover completely, adhering to the foliage better than dry materials and using less chemical. Five or six gallons of water containing the requisite amount of insecticide (say ¼ pound) is a suitable volume for drenching 1,000 square feet with a small sprayer or sprinkling can. Dry formulations are convenient, being ready to apply instantly with fertilizer and seed distributors.

Follow the instructions accompanying the product carefully, taking pains to dilute to proper concentration and distribute uniformly. Whatever the formulation, an insecticide should be applied beyond the area visibly affected, since the chances are that the insects are actively extending operations around the margins of the damaged turf. The heavier soils—clays and loams—may merit heavier application in treating for soil pests than sandy soils.

For quickest control of grubs and other soil insects, the insecticide is best flushed into the soil. Simply water the lawn briefly after the insecticide has been applied. Even for sod webworms and chinch bugs, which nestle in the foliage and hide deep in the crowns, it may be well to use a sufficient volume of spray or dust to cover exposed soil, sheaths, and culms thoroughly.

To control insects attacking foliage, however, don't wash the insecticide from the leaves; new, unprotected foliage will arise quickly enough. Repeated treatments may be necessary to control successive hatchings of such surface feeders. The generation cycle of sod webworms in warm weather is about a month from egg to adult lawn moth. Spraying about ten days after the moths have been noticed abundantly flitting over the lawn should catch most new caterpillars before they do much damage, but a repeat treatment may be needed anytime after moths appear in force to catch succeeding generations.

While no deadly chemicals would be licensed for home sale, all insecticides can be hazardous and should be handled with reasonable safety precautions. They should never be ingested nor inhaled, and their containers should be carefully disposed of. Used as directed, there is little chance of injury to vegetation, not so much as with herbicides or even fertilizers and fungicides. Bird life is felt to be the chief victim of persistent pesticides that become magnified in the food chain. With birds ranging as widely as they do, little harm is to be expected from insecticides applied only where some pest is a definite problem, rather than the blanket spraying that is sometimes undertaken from aircraft.

Nematodes

Nematodes are microscopic worms of the eelworm family, and are not true insects. These tiny worms are known to bore into roots of many crop plants, causing swellings or galls and a stunted root system. While seldom killing the plant, they reduce yields and growth.

Until recently, relatively little was known about nematodes in lawn grass. But some of the poorly defined, and otherwise inexplicable, lawn ailments are no doubt caused by nematodes. Symptoms might include stunting, uneven growth, leaf dieback or chlorosis (blanching). Certain root-knot nematodes (*Meloidogyne*) enter grass roots, and root-lesion types (*Pratylenchus, Rotylenchus*) or cyst nematodes

(*Heterodera*) attack turf. Several nematodes remain outside the root but are found associated with turfgrasses, such as the sting nematodes (*Belonolaimus*), ring nematodes (*Criconemoides*), awl nematodes (*Dolichodorus*), lance nematodes (*Hoplolaimus*), stubby-root nematodes (*Trichodorus*) and others. The sting nematodes are the most serious and widespread of the nematodes in Florida, where nematode problems are perhaps greater than in any other state.

In many instances, especially in Florida, soil treatment with nematicides has stimulated a vigorous grass response, although, in all truthfulness, most turfs languish again later, sometimes even more sorely beset than before treatment. Probably this is because natural controls have also been eliminated by the nematicide.

The interrelationships of the eelworms and their surroundings are imperfectly understood. Some nematodes prey upon others; certain types flourish under one set of soil conditions, others under another. It is not always certain that nematodes are harmful, for in cases they may be secondary to other damage or actually helpful in controlling more serious invaders. Blanket treatment may well eliminate the good with the bad, and the troublemakers, uninhibited by natural enemies, may then come back stronger than ever. When sting nematodes are controlled in Florida with dasanit, for example, lance nematodes then become a more serious problem.

For the present, nematode control is probably best left to the experts, although several of the chemicals listed in the tables as suitable for treating nematodes are available to the homeowner (DBCP, sarolex, and some of the older compounds). Soil sterilization, as discussed in Chapter 15, may prove an effective way of freeing a seedbed of nematode infestation.

Nematicides

Bay–68138 (an organophosphate)

Dasanit (a phosphorothioate)

DBCP (dibromochloropropane)

DD (dichloropropene-dichloropropane)

Ethylene dibromide

Methyl bromide

Mocap (an organophosphate)

Mylone (a thiadiazine-thione)

Nemagon (a dibromochloropropane)

Sarolex (a formulation of diazinon)

Vapam (a methyl-dithiocarbamate)

VC-13 (a chlorinated phosphorothioate)

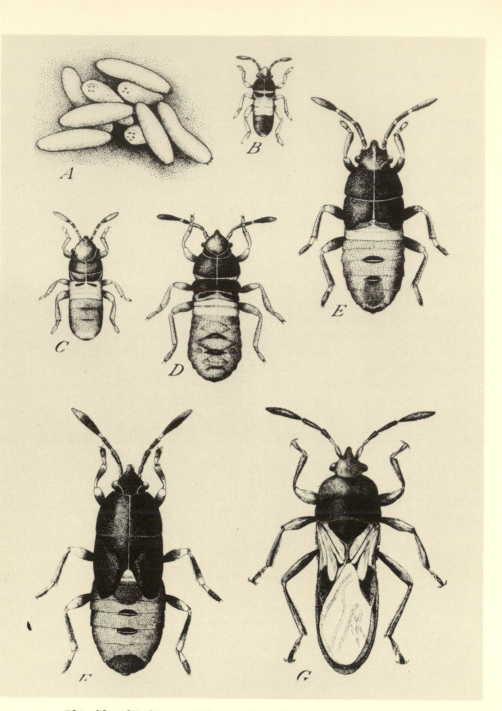

Chinchbug life history: (A) eggs, (B-F) the five immature stages, (G) winged adult. (Photo courtesy of U.S. Department of Agriculture)

Earthworms and Night Crawlers

Castings thrown on the surface by worms make small mounds, causing irregularities in closely clipped turfs. The aerating burrows and soil turnover may be helpful for improving the soil, but they are likely to be a nuisance in closely mowed turf (bentgrass, bermuda). Chlordane, arsenicals and similar chemicals will repress, but not entirely eliminate, earthworms. Evidently they are driven to deeper soil. In the average lawn, earthworms are seldom a problem.

Snails and Slugs

Like nematodes and earthworms, snails and slugs are not insects, but are frequent enough invaders of lawns to be a nuisance on occasion. Locally, they may be fairly common, as on the dichondra lawns in southern California. Unless voluminous, their consumption of vegetation will not be serious, but the creatures are unpleasant and leave a trail of slime behind.

It is difficult to control snails and slugs with sprays. Frequently, poison baits containing metaldehyde or zectran, available in garden stores, are quite helpful. Hand picking or crushing is also effective, but must be carried on with persistence since snails and slugs may migrate into a lawn area from considerable distances. Some have found that placing shallow pans of beer attracts the slugs, which then "drown" in the stale beer.

Moles

It may seem odd to discuss moles in a chapter devoted to insects and insecticides. Yet there is a direct relationship. The chief food of moles is soil insects; elimination of the insects usually encourages the moles to move elsewhere. The same is true to a lesser extent with skunks, which dig into lawns in search of grubs or similar succulent morsels.

For direct elimination of moles, poison baits dropped into the burrows, traps of several designs, or fumes introduced into the runs (as by a hose from an automobile exhaust) have all been advocated. Although they are sometimes successful, disappointments are frequent. The easiest way to eliminate moles is to spray an insecticide, paradoxical as this may sound.

Mole runs are not directly lethal to grass but they lift a ridge of sod which dries, separated as it is from the moist deeper soil, and which then becomes scalped in mowing. The tunnelings are unsightly and an inconvenience to operating equipment.

REGIONAL FOCUS

It is apparent from this rogue's gallery of lawn insects that insect troubles are not unique to any single area. If anything, the South suffers more seriously than the North from mites, scale, and billbugs generally, webworms in the Southwest, and chinch bugs, mole crickets, and ground pearls in the Southeast. Grubs are perhaps more plentiful in northern areas—especially the Japanese beetle zones of the Northeast—although the many types of beetles and chafers contributing to grub delinquency assure country-wide representation. Spittlebug, not serious in lawns, occurs mostly in the North Central and Northeastern states, and chiggers east of the Rockies from middle latitudes southward.

The vegetable weevil (*Listroderes*) has been detrimental to dichondra lawns in southern California. The small, green, legless larvae or grubs, only about three-eighths of an inch long, are active during winter and early spring. They hide in the soil during the day and feed on the foliage at night. Since the weevils cannot fly, infestations are localized, but may be severe if preventive action is not taken. Cutworms, too, do serious damage to dichondra in summer. Toxaphene generally gives good control where the "pyrethrum test" (page 231) shows more than two or three cutworms per square yard.

The various remedies listed in this chapter are widely effective. For insects in certain regions, such as chinch bug in Florida, stepped-up rates are suggested, and variations in insecticides should be used to help avoid a resistance build-up by the species. Much Florida chinch-bug control is by professional custom-spraying with parathion, far too hazardous for use by the homeowner. In localities having a history of persistent insect damage, precautionary insecticide applications just ahead of the usual time for insect appearance are worthwhile. The longevity of insecticides such as chlordane makes them ideal for one-shot preventive applications to the soil, but such "hard" pesticides are becoming increasingly difficult to obtain because of restrictions encouraged by environmentalists fearful of ecological damage.

COMMON MISCONCEPTIONS

MODERN INSECTICIDES MAKE INSECT PROBLEMS A THING OF THE PAST. Helpful as newer insecticides are, resistant strains of insects, once easily controlled, seem to develop. Or an insecticide may kill a species that, in turn, had held some other pest (such as mites) in check. Surest control in such instances is the alternate use of differing insecticides, or to use a mixture of different types, to provide broad-spectrum coverage. Biological controls (disease or predators) are, unfortunately, seldom available for most common insect pests.

APPROVED INSECTICIDES ARE COMPLETELY HARMLESS. Tests for new products are stringent for man and most household animals. But birds, fish, and other wildlife have been affected by heavy and widespread usage, especially if their food is primarily insects from treated areas. All pesticides should be used carefully according to label directions, the research for which was painstaking and costly—so take advantage of it!

MOLES, SKUNKS, AND ANIMALS DIGGING IN LAWNS MUST BE TRAPPED. Animals digging into the turf are usually searching for food, probably insects. Hence insect control makes such lawn digging unprofitable, and the animals search elsewhere.

WORMS AND "BUGS" ARE INSECTS. Eight and multiple-legged "critters" such as mites, ticks, and centipedes are not insects, although related. Earthworms and eelworms are not even closely related, and would not be expected to respond similarly to insecticides.

INSECTICIDES ARE DANGEROUS FOR PETS. With the possible exception of fish in outdoor pools, approved insecticides will be as safe for the usual pets (mammals) as for man, when used as recommended. Any precautions that need to be taken are mentioned as part of label directions.

17

lawn diseases

DIAGNOSING LAWN DISEASES with certainty is a problem difficult even for experts. Certain gross symptoms do become familiar, such as the purplish shot-holes of leafspot, or the round dead patches characteristic of dollarspot, but positive identification must usually come after the disease has been cultured and isolated in a laboratory.

Even when a disease organism has been authoritatively identified, there is still the question of whether this was the primary cause of the trouble, or whether it merely chanced to be present. Perhaps it took advantage only of vegetation already on the downgrade, or the advancing age of some leaves. The bluegrass seasonal cycle shows that an old leaf normally disintegrates as a new leaf arises, to maintain a fairly constant complement of foliage. Are these old, withering leaves to be considered diseased if they bear a few blemishes? They would yellow and die in any event.

Practical lawn-disease control is, therefore, still very much empirical, the offending pathogens invisible and guessed at, the affliction judged by vague symptoms (usually dying grass), the medicine some fungicide that has worked in a similar situation. With relatively few lawngrass diseases well identified, general-purpose fungicides are relied upon more than specific cures, especially by homeowners. General gardening fungicides such as might be kept for roses should benefit lawns too, but formulations designed specifically for the lawn are apt to be more economical and more easily applied.

When lawns are well managed they show remarkable recuperative powers. The important lawngrasses have withstood recurrent disease attacks through the ages with only temporary setbacks, and newer varieties have been bred and selected primarily for disease resistance. Most infections are mild, and probably pass unnoticed by the home-owner. Moreover, there are many natural limitations to diseases, such as change of weather and seasons. General preventive measures at seasons when disease can be expected are the most that average lawns need, and are more than most lawns ever get.

Cause of Disease

What is a lawngrass disease? There is no hard-and-fast rule. Grass is sometimes considered to have a deficiency disease when it is nutritionally unbalanced or lacking in trace elements. Tests have repeatedly shown that most diseases are more severe on grass heavily fertilized with nitrogen, or lacking sufficient potassium. Often nematode decline is classed with diseases. Waterlogged soil, polluted air (smog), and extremes in soil pH produce disease-like symptoms.

But in a strict sense disease can come only from a living plant *pathogen*, generally a fungus that causes symptoms recognized as a disease. Very few bacterial or virus fungi afflict grass. The most common disease causers are the filamentous fungi, a group that rivals insects in the magnitude of damage they inflict on crops (wheat rust, potato blight, and numerous smuts and rots). The troublesome types grow through the host tissues, absorbing nutriment and secreting wastes toxic to the grass plant. Other nonparasitic fungi live only on vegetation that is already dead, and are, then, not harmful but beneficial scavengers instead.

The mere presence of a disease-causing organism is no certain sign of trouble. As a matter of fact, the reproductive spores of fungi are everywhere, wafted tremendous distances in the air, abounding in the soil and about the lawngrasses. Although grass clippings may be a haven for resting spores and old fungus growth, parasites that attack living grass would seldom flourish on dead clippings. Since spores are probably around anyway, leaving clippings should not materially increase the chance of disease except as they may help to retain humidity, an essential to fungus growth.

For disease to appear there must be, in addition to the pathogen: (1) a susceptible host, or lawngrass which is vulnerable to that particular disease, (2) a host in susceptible condition (not too young nor too old, nor in a resistant physiological stage), (3) an environment suited to the specific fungus (proper humidity, temperature, and the like). Some diseases need cool weather, others warm. Almost all require humidity. A change to drier weather is one of the best natural checks of disease. Frequently the lawnsman can lessen the persistence of humidity by trimming shrubbery to allow more breeze (or even knock morning dew from the grass blades, as golf greenkeepers do with long, flexible poles).

Even when all conditions seem equal in comparing one year with another, disease attack is erratic. It may prove serious one year, yet scarcely appear the next. Disease "preferences," too, are often quite subtle. A laboratory test in Virginia showed that one of two very similar fescue varieties contracted a particular disease at a different season than the other—under differing light and environmental conditions! Much remains to be learned about plant pathology.

Recognizing Disease Symptoms

How does one recognize disease in a lawn? Gross symptoms are a weakening or thinning of the grass, or characteristic dying and dead patches of turf. One might first suspect the trouble to result from lack of water, infertility, dog urination, spilled chemical, or some such cause. But no response will be noticed to corrective measures for such ills. Next, insects might be suspected; finding none, disease would then appear a logical explanation, although nutritional imbalance or troubles hidden in the soil are still possibilities.

Many diseases leave calling cards on the grass for those experienced enough to read them. A black, spiderweb-like mycelium forming a halo around a dead or dying patch of grass is a telltale sign of brownpatch fungus; small silver-dollar-size dead spots with a faint white webbing in the morning are indicative of dollarspot; purplish oval lesions on the grass blades signify the leafspot stage of *Helminthosporium*, or "melting out." However, many of these symptoms look very much alike, and even experts cannot be certain until an organism has been cultured, isolated, and finally proved capable of reinfecting the same host.

The home lawnsman probably will not be sure what disease he finds. A more definite identification with specific control recommendations can usually be had from the plant pathology department of the state experiment station. A fresh turf sample must be sent for the identification. Meanwhile, there are but two practical control alternatives: (1) treat with a general fungicide, or (2) encourage natural control by modifying lawn maintenance if it currently favors disease. This might mean withholding watering or altering fertilization.

Treating for Disease

Although blights were recognized in Genesis, the true cause of disease awaited verification until little more than a century ago. Effective disease control is still a more recent accomplishment. Sulfur, lime-sulfur, copper sulfate mixed with lime (Bordeaux mixture), and similar inorganic compounds were among the first fungicides, found by trial and error to protect plants against disease with little damage to the plant. Some are still widely used, but in recent years they have been supplanted by cleaner, safer, and easier-to-apply compounds of mercury, copper, cadmium, chromium, and complex organic molecules with tongue-twisting names (see page 255). The mercurials, organic metallic salt mixtures, organic sulfur compounds, and certain antibiotics are the bases for most lawn-disease preventives on the market, although mercury compounds are fast becoming suspect as an environmental contaminant. The antibiotics seem to be absorbed by the grass as systemics, as are the newest and most hopeful class of chemical systemics typified by benomyl. Most others are little absorbed and act chiefly as protective coatings that kill germinating fungus spores on the foliage. All are reasonably effective against most familiar diseases. Where certain chemicals are superior for specific diseases, they are recommended in the descriptions that follow.

Application of fungicides is no different from that of herbicides and insecticides. Directions given with the product should be followed very carefully, the spraying or spreading accomplished so as to achieve complete and uniform coverage. This is usually best achieved by spreading half the application in one direction, the remaining half at right angles. As with other modern garden chemicals, surprisingly small quantities of the better fungicides are needed.

If disease can be anticipated, preventive treatment is more effective than attempting a cure. Since rainy periods foster disease, application of the fungicides might well precede and follow rains. Certain diseases are almost sure to crop up in certain seasons and regions, as leafspot in the Northeast in cool, damp springs. Waiting until the turf is seriously thinned, or until brown patches of dead grass are evident, is locking the barn door after the horse has been stolen.

Except with systemic treatments (which should last several weeks), more than a single treatment will ordinarily have to be made. This protects newly developing foliage against attack while disease conditions prevail. Applications ten to fourteen days apart during the season of attack usually prove adequate.

Cornell University Disease Control Recommendations*

Rates per 1,000 square feet

Leaf Spot and Crown Rot (*Helmintho-sporium vagans*)	Fore (mancozeb), 4 oz., or Daconil, 4 oz., or Dyrene (anilazine), 5 oz., or Kromad (cadmium sebecate), 3 oz., or Captan, 5 oz.	Apply at 5–10 day intervals in cool moist conditions especially April–June. Merion Kentucky bluegrass is resistant.
Dollar Spot (*Sclerotinia homeocarpa*)	Daconil, 4 oz., or Dyrene (analazine), 5 oz., or Kromad (cadmium sebecate), 4 oz., or Tersan 1991 (benomyl), 1 oz.	7–14 day intervals June–September, longer intervals possible with benomyl. Important to maintain proper nitrogen fertility.
Brown Patch (*Rhizoctonia solani*)	Daconil, 4 oz., or Dyrene (anilazine), 5 oz., or Fore (mancozeb), 4 oz., or Maneb, 4 oz., or Tersan 1991 (benomyl), 2 oz.	5–10 day intervals July–August, longer intervals possible with benomyl.
Rust (*Puccinia*)	Fore (mancozeb), 4 oz., or Actidione (cycloheximide), 4 oz., or Zineb, 4 oz.	Two or three applications 7–14 day intervals July–September. Maintain proper nitrogen fertility level.
Snow Mold (*Fusarium* & *Typhula*)	Dyrene (anilazine), 5 oz., or Cadminate (cadmium succinate), 2 oz.	Apply prior to first snow, at mid-winter and spring thaw.
Pythium Blight (*Pythium* sp.)	Zineb, 2–4 oz., or Dexon, 3 oz., or Koban, 4 oz.	7–14 day intervals especially during hot, wet weather of July and August.
Fusarium Blight (*Fusarium roseum*)	Tersan 1991 (benomyl), 4 oz.	Apply when symptoms appear and repeat as necessary.
Powdery Mildew (*Erysiphe graminis*)	Actidione (cycloheximide), 4 oz., or Karathane, 1/4 oz.	Apply when symptoms appear, July–September.
Stripe smut (*Ustilago striiformis*)	Tersan 1991 (benomyl), 6 oz.	Apply once in the fall or spring with 10 gal. of water per 1,000 sq. ft.

* From 1972 "Guide" CU-12 M.

Rates per 1,000 square feet

Fairy ring (toadstools and mushrooms) | Chemicals seldom helpful in control. Remove stumps or other dead organic matter from below soil surface, if localized. Otherwise, break up fruiting bodies and ignore. | The green rings more conspicuous on under-fertilized lawns and their presence can be masked somewhat by adequate fertilization.

Representative Fungicides for Control of Turfgrass Diseases

(Many trade products incorporate two or more chemicals and appear under generalized brand names.)

Type	Chemicals	Representative Trade Names
Mercury compounds	Mercury salts, especially chlorides; calomel; phenyl mercuric acetate.	Caloclor, Caloclure, Calogreen, Fungchex, etc.; Coromerc, Liquiphene, Phenmad, Phix, PMAS, Puratized, Scutl, Tag, Tat-C-Lect.
	Various methyl, ethyl and phenyl esters, including a mercuric dithiocarbamate and a hydroxy mercury chlorophenol.	Kromaclor, Memmi 8EC, Merbam, Merfusan; Panogen, Puraturf 10; Verdesan.
Other heavy metal complexes	Various cadmium salts, esters and combinations; calcium-zinc-copper-cadmium chromate mixture.	Caddy, Cadox, Cadminate, Puraturf 177; Kromad.
Antibiotics and systemics	Cycloheximide; benomyl; oxycarboxin; thiabendazole.	Acti-dione (various forms); Benlate (Tersan 1991); Plantvax; TBZ.
Other complex organics	Anilazine (a chlorinated triazine); captan (a thiophthalimide); daconil (a phthalonitrile); dexon (a benzenediazo sulfonate); folpet (a thiophthalimide); koban (a chlorinated thiadiazole); malachite green (a dye);	Dyrene; Captan, Orthocide; Daconil 2787; Dexon; Phaltan; Koban, Terrazole; Auragreen;

Type	Chemicals	Representative Trade Names
	mancozeb (a manganous and zinc dithiocarbamate);	Dithane-M 45, Fore, Manzate -200;
	maneb (manganese dithiocarbamate);	Dithane -M22, Manzate;
	PCNB (pentachloronitrobenzene);	Fungiclor, Terraclor;
	thiram (tetramethyl thiuram disulfide).	Panoram, Tersan, Thiuram 75, etc. (component in Cadtrete, Kromad, Mercuram, Scutl, Tersan OM, Thimer, etc.).

Lawn fungicides are more frequently formulated as sprays than as dry materials. To achieve good adherence and coverage of grass blades, the usual site of infection, some fungicides merit the addition of a spreader-sticker (used, for example, with antibiotics and captan). If special wetting agents are not available, a teaspoonful of household detergent to each gallon of spray may be used. Most fungicides can be applied with insecticides or mixed with fertilizer. They serve best, however, when timed specifically for disease attack; hence fungicides find less use in mixtures than do insecticides or soil-treatment chemicals.

Good sprayers or spreaders, discussed under insect control, apply fungicides efficiently. Pressure sprayers that produce a mist-like spray usually cover better, and more economically, than does syringing or low-pressure spraying. When a dust is used, application early or late in the day may result in better adherence of the powder to the grass because it is often damp at those times.

Fungicides are reasonably safe if used according to directions. Their tendency to damage the grass is perhaps a little greater than that of insecticides, but not as severe as that of herbicides and fertilizers. Seldom is there burn from recommended rates when temperatures are below 85° F. All fungicides are poisonous to a degree, and should be handled judiciously. Avoid appreciable contact or ingestion of any fungicide, especially the mercurials and metal-containing organics.

Major Lawn Diseases

Many of the more than one hundred diseases that have been reported for turfgrass are infrequent or cause minor damage. The lesser known ailments are omitted here. A few are characterized for quick identification in the key on page 257. Diseases discussed on the following pages are grouped according to their prevalence in northern and southern lawns.

Most diseases have been found on more than one kind of grass, but many are problems on only a single host. Thus treatment may depend upon both lawn and climate. While just a few similar insecticides suffice to serve all regions, there are a number of quite different fungicides from which to choose (see table, page 255). Hence disease prevention and control generally requires more careful diagnosis, timing, and choice of chemical than does insect control. But fungicides are, on the whole, less hazardous to higher forms of life (i.e., they are of less pressing environmental concern) than are either insecticides or herbicides.

Northern Lawn Diseases

All northern lawngrasses are subject to several diseases, with the disease organisms seldom completely specific. Bentgrasses are usually more severely attacked than other lawn species, possibly in part because of the heavier feeding and watering they are accorded, and because of their tendency toward dense (poorly ventilated) growth.

Quick Check for Some of the More Prevalent Diseases in Bluegrass Territory

(Select successively the appropriate alternatives in alphabetical order until the name of a disease is reached.)

A. Winter weather disease, important mainly in Canada and northerly states.. *Snowmold*

AA. Diseases of spring-summer-autumn

    B. grass affected in large circular rings or arcs, mushrooms often appearing seasonally in the affected bands...*Fairy Ring*

  BB. grass usually dying in patches or small circles, not in circular bands

      C. grayish ring ("smoke ring") around dying patch, visible especially with morning dew..*Brownpatch*

    CC. no "smoke ring"

        D. distinct spots, lesions or blemishes on leaf clearly evident.

          E. leaf spots with purplish border; especially in cool, moist weather
             Leafspot

          EE. leaf blemishes straw color with brown border; most active in hot weather; grass generally affected in small circular patches, although these may run together.............................*Dollarspot*

DD. general discoloration rather than distinct spots on the foliage.

F. Fungus growth coating easily noticed

G. coating white; generally in shade..................*Mildew*

GG. coating orange-red or black

H. coating orange-red; mostly autumn.................*Rust*

HH. coating black, in longitudinal lesions..........*Stripe smut*

FF. Fungal growth not obvious

I. dead grass straw-colored, in irregular patch, sometimes with green
center tuft of live grass; hot weather...........*Fusarium blight*

II. dead grass reddish-brown, with minute black spots on blemishes
Anthracnose

III. withered leaves flatten, turn sticky in circular "water-soaked"
patches often with a blackened "greasy" border.............
Pythium Greasespot

ANTHRACNOSE, *Colletotrichum spp.* Grass foliage yellows, darkens when dead, showing minute dark spots (spore bodies). Attacks all grasses in all areas, but is especially a problem in the Northeast. Use general preventive fungicidal treatment if disease becomes serious.

BROWNPATCH, *Pellicularia filamentosa* or *Rhizoctonia solani.* Another high-temperature, high-humidity disease, with water-soaked symptoms similar to greasespot. The damaged splotches usually have a "smoke ring," or dark halo of mycelium. The disease is especially severe where heavy feeding has been practiced, and on bentgrass during stagnant, humid spells in summer. Control with anilazine, benomyl, daconil, mancozeb, mercurials, PCNB, or thiram, and by reducing nitrogen and encouraging greater drying-out. Diseases passing for brownpatch are widespread over most of the nation, the pathogen often assumed rather than identified.

COPPERSPOT, *Gloeocercospora sorghi.* This seldom occurs on lawns, although it is not rare on creeping bentgrasses, especially near the coasts. Symptoms are similar to dollarspot, but the grass blades are covered by copper-colored spores. Control as for dollarspot.

DOLLARSPOT, *Sclerotinia homoeocarpa.* This is another cool-humid-season disease, especially prevalent on creeping bentgrass. Small

Summer damage, probably due to brownpatch.

silver-dollar-size circles of dead grass appear, often with a white mold, sometimes of sufficient frequency to nearly wipe out the turf. Almost all fungicides check this disease. Increased feeding lessens damage. Dollarspot is widely spread through northern areas and on northern grasses grown in the Southwest. Diseases in the South have also been attributed to dollarspot, but there is some doubt about the actual identity of the pathogen.

FAIRY RING, *Marasmius oreades* and other mushrooms. Fairy ring is not strictly a disease, but it is one of the most common fungus afflictions of lawns all over the United States. The fungus grows vigorously underground in an ever-widening circle. Occasionally spore-producing mushrooms appear aboveground, in a circle or arc corresponding to growth below the surface. Although the mushrooms may be unsightly in the turf, the chief objection comes from the damaged grass above sites of active mycelial growth. The fungus probably does not attack the grass directly, but desiccates, cements, and exhausts the soil so thoroughly that the ground becomes hard, impervious, and a drought zone for grass roots.

Immediately within the circle of active mycelia, nitrogenous materials released by the fungus stimulate the grass to make a circle of dark-green growth which is especially noticeable on underfertilized turf. The lawn surface becomes disfigured with circular markings, an outer zone with unthrifty grass adjacent to an inner zone of stimulated growth.

Control of fairy ring is difficult. Spiking the affected area helps loosen the soil, allowing water to penetrate. Fungicidal drenches, perhaps with a wetting agent added to facilitate penetration, may inhibit the fungus to a degree; but it is difficult to reach the active parts as much as two feet below ground without damaging the turf more than the fairy ring does.

A drastic remedy is to dig or trench the circle, then drench with some sterilant such as vapam. Of course, reseeding or resodding will have to be delayed until the sterilant has dissipated, or soil replacement can be made.

Perhaps the most practical answer is to live with fairy ring, spiking as suggested, and fertilizing and watering all of the turf sufficiently so that the stimulated grass does not stand out. Fairy rings come and go, for no evident reason, and are not too objectionable except on meticulously kept lawns.

FUSARIUM BLIGHT, *Fusarium roseum.* Especially an affliction of Merion bluegrass in the Northeast, but also attacking bentgrasses, fescues and ryegrasses. Causes roughly circular areas of dead grass in hot weather on exposed parts of the lawn, often with a patch of live

Fairy ring disease.

tures full of dark spores. Where the disease is epidemic, the best control is to introduce disease-resistant varieties into the lawn, although benomyl soaked into the sod seems an effective control.

Southern Lawn Diseases

Diseases of southern lawns have not been studied as extensively as northern lawns. Diseases called brownpatch and dollarspot in the South may not always be exactly equivalent to northern diseases bearing those names, but nevertheless, these are said to be the two most troublesome turf diseases in Florida, where they attack all species.

No serious diseases have been reported for centipede. Carpetgrass is seldom damaged, although several disease organisms have been found on it; bahia is attacked chiefly by *Helminthosporium*; st. augustine suffers mostly from gray leafspot brownpatch caused by *Rhizoctonia*, and SAD (st. augustine decline) virus in Texas–Louisiana; bermuda catches several leafspot diseases and a rust; zoysia suffers little from diseases, but leafspot, fading-out, brownpatch, and several other diseases have been known to attack it.

When northern species are used in the South, they suffer a wide array of diseases. Bentgrasses seem to catch everything in the book, while ryegrass, bluegrass, and fescue yield to leafspots, brownpatches, rusts and *Fusarium* rots.

BROWNPATCH OR "RHIZOC," *Rhizoctonia* or *Pellicularia*. Serious on st. augustine, ryegrass, tall fescue, and other northern grasses. Attacks any time temperatures rise above 70° F. PCNB has given excellent control on st. augustine, and is also used on dichondra; daconil, mancozeb, mercurials, and thiram are also recommended.

COTTONY SPOT, OR AERIAL BLIGHT, *Pythium ultimum, P. aphanidermatum*, and other species. Serious chiefly on overseeded ryegrass and bent in warm, damp weather, complete destruction of seedling turf often occurring within a few hours. Diseased foliage becomes "water-soaked," soft and slimy. A preventive spray program with dexon, koban, thiram, or zineb should provide control, and the new organics, demosan and thiophanate, have worked well in Florida.

GRAY LEAFSPOT, *Piricularia grisea*. The most prevalent spring disease of st. augustine. All fungicides apparently help in its control, with benomyl and thiram especially recommended.

The damage that disease can do to a lawn. This may be damage from Fusarium blight to east coast bluegrass.

green grass in the center (so-called "frog eye" appearance). Treat with benomyl or mancozeb (fore), and reduce nitrogen fertilization.

GREASESPOT, *Pythium* species. Greasespot, also known as firestreak, spotblight, cottony blight, and damping-off, causes roughly circular water-soaked areas of dead grass, usually with a blackened, greasy border. Leaf blades wither rapidly, tend to lie flat, and stick together. Blemishes develop under high temperature (90° F.) and humidity. Overwatering and excessive fertilization should be avoided, as should depressions with standing water. Dexon and koban fungicides are specifically recommended; thiram and zineb may help. Greasespot is widely distributed on many kinds of grass, especially bents, fescues, and ryegrass, in the South as well as the North.

Sometimes newly germinated seedlings suffer a wilting and "rotting" at soil level in spite of ample sprinkling. This is usually credited to *Pythium*. Once the disease is noted there is no really effective control, although letting the soil dry as much as possible will help check the disease. In theory, lawn seeds treated with protective fungicides (such as chloranil or thiram) before planting should have less chance of this damping-off; but in practice, the disease seems to arise "from the soil" even then. Damping-off is seldom such a problem that it justifies special treatment.

LEAFSPOT, *Helminthosporium vagans*, and *H. sorokinianum* (*H. sativum*). Helminth, going-out, melting-out, and zonate eyespot are other names for *Helminthosporium*. *H. vagans* is prone to attack bluegrass-fescue lawns in cool (55°–60° F.), damp weather; *H. sorokinianum* attacks during the heat of summer. Brownish specks, which gradually enlarge and turn purplish, appear on the grass. In severe attacks all but the newest leaves turn yellowish, and as the season progresses even the crown may rot, the whole culm turning watery brown and producing "footrot" or "Crownrot." The turf may become so thinned that weeds invade it readily. Most turfs will recover completely if warmer, drier weather comes during the leafspot phase. Anilazine, captan, cycloheximide, daconil, folpet, and mercurials are recommended for controlling leafspot. Grass that is soft from heavy nitrogen fertilization, is poorly drained, or mowed excessively low, seems most susceptible. The disease is most serious in the northeastern states and adjacent Canada. Merion bluegrass and other newer cultivars are less susceptible to *H. vagans* in the Northeast than is natural Kentucky bluegrass, but few varieties are entirely immune to *H. sorokinianum*, prevalent in the central states.

OPHIOBOLUS PATCH, *Ophiobolus spp.* This disease, resembling brownpatch, is especially a problem on bents in the Pacific Northwest. Control with mercurials and thiram is recommended.

PINK PATCH OR RED THREAD, *Corticium fuciforme.* This is a disease of cool, humid weather, the grass matting under pink mycelium; common in the Pacific Northwest and coastal New England where it attacks all grasses and fescue frequently. Control with Acti-dione-thiram, cadmium compounds, mercurials, and Tersan LSR.

POWDERY MILDEW, *Erisyphe sp.* Powdery mildew is a grayish-white coating, conspicuous on the grass blades of susceptible strains such as Merion bluegrass, especially during damp weather and where grass is growing in the shade. The disease is not serious, although it does weaken the grass to some extent; if very severe, the leaves may even shrivel. Dusts or sprays of Dinocap, sulfur, Mildex, Karathane, or acti-dione-thiram help to control powdery mildew, but a change to drier weather is usually all that is needed.

RUST, *Puccinia graminis, P. striiformis,* and other species. Strains of rust are prevalent on Merion bluegrass and ryegrass, often so completely covering foliage that it appears reddish-orange. Rust is less frequent on natural Kentucky bluegrass and most newer varieties,

and on fescues and bents. Close inspection of leaf blades sho dery pustules of orange-brown spores. Effective control is although oxycarboxin especially, antibiotics, and zineb m Heavy feeding and watering of Merion during summer will l leaf growth coming fast enough to minimize the unattracti ing. Rust usually attacks in summer and early autumn in and border states, and on ryegrass used for winter grass in 1

SNOWMOLD, *Fusarium nivale and Typhula spp.* Also ter or fusarium patch. Abetted by ample moisture and cool ter (40°–60° F.), snowmold often occurs where snow or ice bla turf for prolonged periods. Irregular bleached splotches, rounded by pinkish or grayish mold, show during winter thaws. Control may be had from anilazine, benomyl and applied ahead of winter freeze-up or during thaws. Sr common on bentgrass turfs in the northern tier of states a from coast to coast, but will attack bluegrasses, fescues, *Poa annua,* and even zoysia.

STRIPE SMUT, *Ustilago striiformis.* This is a relatively becoming epidemic on Merion, Windsor, and certain used bluegrasses as well as being found on some bentgra fescue, redtop, and ryegrass. Grass foliage develops long

Winter damage probably due to snowmold.

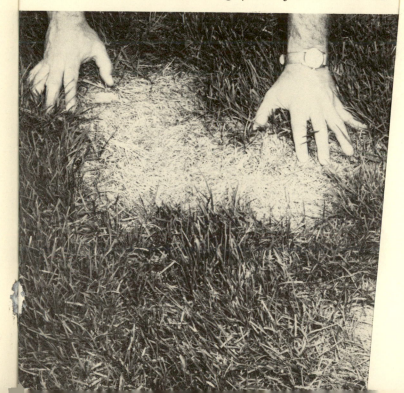

LEAFSPOT, EYE SPOT, MELTING-OUT, NET BLOTCH, CULM ROT, OR TURF-SPOT, *Helminthosporium* species. Several species of this fungus attack bahia, bermuda (where it is especially a problem), and zoysia; also ryegrass, tall fescue, and other northern grasses. General-purpose fungicides prove helpful, especially those mentioned for leafspot control with northern grasses. Captan and daconil sprays are suggested for zonate eyespot of bermuda, caused by *H. giganteum*, applied in July and August.

LOOSE SMUT, *Ustilago cynodontis*. Seedheads of bermuda become a mass of dark spores in warm weather as a result of this disease. Treat with mercurials and perhaps benomyl.

RUST, *Puccinia* species. Attacks bermuda (especially Sunturf) and northern grasses. No completely satisfactory control, although zineb, maneb, phygon, and antibiotics have given control when applied at seven- to ten-day intervals.

SPRING DEADSPOT, organism unidentified. A difficult disease of bermuda, especially in the border states. The grass dies in irregular patches that look like "winter kill," but which refuse to heal. Autumn treatment with a special fungicide called snapback has been encouraging, but where the disease is severe most custodians turn to other grasses.

REGIONAL FOCUS

Lawn diseases are ever present, although the causal fungi are usually inactive, checked by environmental conditions, or they are almost unnoticeable because a mild attack is obscured by normal grass vigor. However, when all conditions favor disease, inroads may be devastating. Since humidity is of paramount importance for promoting disease, it follows that the semiarid plains and western climates are less troubled. In such climates, even when watering is frequent, grass blades dry off quickly.

Diseases are difficult to diagnose, and knowledge of them is incomplete. Those listed have received attention largely because of golf-green importance in the Northeast. Many are of no greater consequence in lawns than numerous other leafspots, scalds, anthracnoses, rots, blights, rusts, smuts, and mildews might be. Insufficiently studied lawn diseases are especially troublesome in the humid South.

Disease may be confused with physiological disturbances, nutritional imbalance, spilled chemicals, dog damage, waterlogging, excessive wear, insect damage, and other minor calamities. The descriptions on previous pages indicate the familiar diseases of North and South and identifying symptoms.

Once disease is suspected, treatment involves adjusting management to stop their spread (humidity and high nitrogen fertility usually favor disease), and applying fungicides early enough to preserve the health of the turf. Products listed on page 255 will control most lawn pathogens if applied as recommended before the disease makes headway. Well-kept lawns of the East might profitably receive preventive fungicide application during the peak growing season of spring; northern bent turfs, midwestern bluegrass, and southern lawns, treatment during muggy weather in summer.

Fortunately, most lawns are strongly recuperative. Disease is likely to be temporary and to pass unnoticed by the average homeowner. Yet its control will add sparkle to well-kept lawns, and save lawns where epidemics threaten, usually in regions of frequent summer rainfall and high humidity. Best of all, the newer lawngrass cultivars are bred especially for disease-prevention.

COMMON MISCONCEPTIONS

FUNGI ARE HARMFUL. It is true that a few pathogens give trouble, but the great majority of fungi perform the vital service of decaying organic material, thus releasing for reuse the elements contained. Without fungi, life as we know it would not exist.

DISEASE ORGANISMS ARE RARE AND INFREQUENT. Fungi produce millions of microscopic spores more numerous than seeds in a pod, widely dispersed by the breeze. Fortunately, only an occasional one grows, on those rare occasions where host and environmental conditions are favorable. Spores are so easily introduced that keeping a lawn sterile is not feasible—nor is it necessary.

NEW DISEASE-RESISTANT VARIETIES END DISEASE PROBLEMS. No lawngrass variety can be bred resistant to all diseases; once the variety is widely planted, unsuspected "minor" afflictions may assume epidemic proportions, favored by the identical nature of a pedigreed grass population. New races of disease may also evolve which are able to attack the once-resistant variety, as happens perpetually with wheat.

MORE WATER IS THE CURE FOR BROWN GRASS. This is true only if dry soil is the cause. If grass is dying from disease, additional humidity may actually aggravate the ailing turf.

TREATED SEED IS ESSENTIAL FOR LAWNS. While fungicide-treated seed may lessen seed-borne disease (infrequent in lawn seed) and give greater sprouting assurance (more vital for crop seeds planted in rows), lawn-seed sowings are so voluminous that slightly less germination owing to disease is scarcely noticed and is over-shadowed by other happenings. Disease in the soil or disease attacking growing grass is not controlled by seed treatment.

HEAVILY FERTILIZED GRASS IS BETTER ABLE TO WITHSTAND DISEASE. As a rule, grass that has been heavily fertilized, especially with nitrogen, is "soft," and more susceptible to disease. Heavy fertilization in summer, when diseases are rampant, is an invitation for trouble in the bluegrass "twilight zone" from Kansas City through the Ohio Valley to Washington, D.C.

WELL-DEFINED PATCHES OF COMPLETELY DEAD GRASS ARE INDICATIVE OF DISEASE IN A LAWN. While this might be true on the bentgrass of golf greens, in a lawn such discrete areas more likely indicate that the trouble is not from disease. Check for chemical, fertilizer, gasoline burn; dry spots from buried debris; dog urination; or even grub damage. Most lawn diseases are diffuse and gradual, not in a spot-like pattern.

18

a turfgrass logbook

GRASS CHANGES day by day and, more noticeably, season by season. Consequently, experienced lawnsmen are reluctant to say that any one grass or method of management is superior to all others. It may seem so at a given moment, yet be a poor example a season later. And no two years offer identical conditions: weeds, rainfall, disease, and temperatures ebb and flow at the whim of nature.

The dynamic quality of lawn life is illustrated by the following excerpts from the recorded growth cycle of Kentucky bluegrass. The locale of the grass under observation is central Ohio. Comparable dates might vary by weeks from year to year, depending upon the arrival of spring and autumn, the rainfall and climatic patterns. On the average, spring is one day later, autumn one day earlier for each 13 miles northward, or the reverse for each 13 miles southward.

The same sort of record could be compiled for a southern lawn grass. One merely pulls up plants at intervals and notes their progress. With a southern species the overall growth cycle would be essentially the opposite of bluegrass.

Following any grass through its yearly cycle makes clear how much lawn response depends upon the contributions of individual plants. Major seasonal trends will be apparent, even if grass response varies tremendously with momentary drought, mowing height, fertilization, chemical treatments and, especially, the grass plant's location (whether tightly crowded in sod or free along a lawn edge; growing over hard subsoil or under a loose, protecting mulch).

Bluegrass is cognizant in autumn of declining day length. The leaves don't grow as long or stretch as far upward; instead they bend back and downward, making low, more compact growth. The grass needs much less mowing then than it needed in spring. Such growth continues, although at a declining pace, until about Christmas. In fact, deep down near the crown, rhizomes and new leaves will grow a little right through winter in any warm spell when the soil is not frozen. Through autumn and winter, bluegrass accumulates reserves for the burst of growth that spring will trigger.

Logbook of Kentucky Bluegrass in Central Ohio

JANUARY. On mild days, air temperatures sometimes rise well above 32° F. though the soil remains frozen. On such days, short green shoots emerge from under the brown cover of dead leaves. The newest leaf (No. 1) is sparkling green and has appeared since the last severe freeze; the next leaf (No. 2) is green along the lower two-thirds of its blade, but the tip is brown and wrinkled. The third leaf (No. 3) shows a little green at the base, but otherwise is brown. The oldest leaf (No. 4) is now dry and disappearing. Like No. 3, its tip was removed by a late autumn mowing. All new blades emerge close together, the internodes short in response to winter. Around the culm are withered leaf remnants. The whole bluegrass plant is barely two inches tall, its spread of leaves not over three inches.

Lawn companions behave similarly. Bentgrass responds to the warm air with a green end leaf and green tillers along the prostrate stolons. Two or three of the newer clover leaves are greenish. Rough bluegrass, a prolific tillerer, shows several green shoots at the base. Like Kentucky bluegrass, it generally has only three green leaves to the tiller at this season. As cold weather returns, the new growth is darkened by frost.

In the frozen soil there is almost no rhizome activity. Nor are tillers growing. Any that had started earlier, in autumn, have grown enough to be established. Most husky culms have about three tillers from their bases.

FEBRUARY. Though the ground is frozen, soil activity begins as an occasional short, white rhizome pokes through withered sheaths of the nubbin crown. Aboveground there is still some green, confined mostly to the short, new No. 1 leaf and the basal portion of No. 2 (January's No. 1) blade.

Older tillers are self-sustaining, the sheaths within which they arose having withered. Sometimes as many as six young tillers will be found around the base of an old culm. In February they do not yet have expanded blades, and are green only at the tips.

The old rhizomes are still evident, although many are turning brown. The plantlets created through their upturn are now ready for independent existence. Leaves Nos. 1, 2, 3 have appeared since the last cutting of autumn. Leaf No. 4, blotched and fading, is truncated from autumn mowing.

MARCH. Several mild days appear between snaps of bitter cold. Aboveground, bluegrass has not changed much, but belowground there is slow growth. The newer leaves (Nos. 1, 2, 3) are short, stiff, vigorous. No sign yet of leafspot. No. 4 leaf is till somewhat green, though obviously past its prime. In many instances leaves Nos. 3 and 4, products of autumn, have taller sheaths than Nos. 1 and 2, which protrude from the sides of the older sheaths. On the average, there are four green leaves to a culm, with at least Nos. 1 and 2 neither frost-burned nor cut. No. 3 frequently is tip-burned, indicating bitter winter experience.

APRIL. Some of the early spring leaves have had their tips scorched. But growth is apparent everywhere. Leaves are not as tightly folded as they were in March. Still, only Nos. 1, 2, 3 show much green as the month opens. Clover has a few new leaves toward the tip, and many new roots. Rough bluegrass is sprouting tillers.

As balmy weather arrives, the turf greens rapidly, before crocuses flower and trees leaf out. It is not yet necessary to mow, but the tillers are elongating. New blades stretch long and high before bending back. Leaves Nos. 1, 2, 3, 4 are green, although No. 4 is singed and mutilated. Sometimes leaf No. 5 is still green. Where leaf No. 6 remains, it is apt to be very discolored and withered.

The first mowing comes about the middle of the month as trees bud. Soils are drying and warming. New bluegrass leaves come so fast that the current No. 1 leaf always shows an intact tip, having pushed through since the latest mowing. No. 2 is decapitated, except occasionally where it bent downward opportunely ahead of mowing. No. 3 came early, before mowing started, having matured early in the month. Even when the leaf tips are cut off by mowing, the blade stubs still arch back to fill in the spaces between plants.

Merion bluegrass contrasts with natural Kentucky bluegrass at this season. The Merion is only about half as tall, the blades bent back 70 to 90 degrees as compared with the 45-degree bend of the natural bluegrass leaf.

Late in the month there is much growth of tillers. One rhizome may give rise to more than 20 shoots. Mowing is continuous enough to remove the tips from almost all leaves. The only momentary escapees are immature new leaves. Leafspot may show up on leaves Nos. 2 and 3.

Fat seedhead culms become prominent. They are about twice as husky, bluer, and more rigid than the tillers not intended for reproduction. Their newer "flag" leaves, beginning to form near their tip, are progressively shorter and wider.

The number of shoots per square inch is greatly increased by new tillers and may reach as many as 50 on thick sod. The newer leaves are now on more elongated sheaths, rising well above the older winter leaves.

Each culm destined to bear a seedhead will die, mowed or not. Nature so designed grass that a seedhead terminates the culm, and new growth to carry on the grass life cycle must arise from basal buds.

The strain of seed production begins to tell. Some of the sturdiest culms show dying companion tillers. By the end of the month, many of the basal ones have withered and completed their cycle.

MAY. Trees are leafing as the month opens. Lawns have had several mowings. Dandelions and cresses are reaching their peak, with plantains, knotweed, and the many other broadleafs on the increase. Bluegrass seed spikes emerge from the ensheathing "boot," producing tough shoots that are hard to mow. Rhizome growth slows while resources are marshaled for seed formation.

Almost all leaves now show the scars of mowing. Leaves Nos. 1–4 are green. The older leaves are still reasonably unblemished. Weaker tillers deteriorate as the seedheads form. An occasional rhizome turns up. By the time tulips are past and the oaks in flower, the early seed spikes show prominently. New leaves are tall, not much bent back. Mowing off the seed shoots probably husbands some of the resources that might go into seed. Even so, early summer is a time of thinning, yellowing, and the loss of many leaves and tillers. The lawn looks scraggly until the bluegrass can recoup from its seeding efforts—how well and how fast depends upon fertility, moisture, and temperature.

JUNE. Weather has become warm and the soil dry for the first time. Roses are at the peak of flowering. Clover is rampant. Some lawns are being watered.

Living tillers have three to five green leaves, the tips almost invariably decapitated from mowing. Rhizome activity is picking up, and new buds are forming.

Southward in the bluegrass belt, summers can be more telling. There will be some growth pickup before weather is really hot, but when the temperatures get up above 90°, food and vitality are sapped faster than they are renewed. Bluegrass should be treated understandingly in summer in those middle latitudes where temperature is high. It should be mowed tall to conserve all possible food-making foliage.

JULY. Redtop and clover are in flower, and there are still a few timothy seedheads. Chicory and summer weeds are abundant. Grass grows vigorously early in the month, with a fair amount of rhizoming evident. One unfettered clump showed 25 rhizomes, another 26 living tillers. Some young tillers form.

AUGUST. In years of ample rainfall there is little change from July. If the conditions are favorable, rhizomes are active, as many as four or five developing on the average plant.

During drought, leaves turn brown and wither, with only a few stunted examples green within the protection of old sheaths. This is a natural defense against exhausting the food reserves. There will seldom be permanent damage from drought, the crown sprouting again at the onset of moisture and coolness. But forcing growth at this time with heavy fertilization courts disaster. The grass may expire trying to grow when it is physiologically out of balance. Perhaps it dies of schizophrenia; more likely we blame disease for the demise, to which the grass, internally weakened, has become receptive.

SEPTEMBER. Buckeye fruits are mature, buckeye leaves browning. Roses still bloom profusely.

Sample bluegrass plants may have five or six green leaves, but sheaths are beginning to shorten and the new blades emerge more in a cluster. All but No. 1 show mowing mutilation. No appreciable tillering occurs this early, nor new rhizomes. If drought persists, only the basal portion of blades Nos. 1 and 2 remains green.

OCTOBER. As September fades into October, rain, cooler weather, and shorter days stimulate growth. Bluegrass shows some rhizoming, but more tillering. The turf tightens up. Leaves Nos. 1–5 are green, the newer leaves still emerging well above the sheaths of the old. The season is not far enough along in early October for the leaves to be short. Mowing must still be frequent.

During the month, frosts become increasingly frequent. Foxtail dies and is brown first, followed soon by crabgrass. Winter weeds begin, with asters in flower early in the month.

Indian summer finds bluegrass still growing vigorously. Leaves Nos. 1–4 are green, their tips all victims of the mower.

NOVEMBER. There now have been several severe frosts, and if the weather is dry, grass will be partly discolored by combined desiccation and cold. Clover is still green. About four bluegrass leaves to the culm are green, but the blades are now bending back, almost at right angles to the sheath. Total grass height is only about two inches, and mowing is finished for the year.

DECEMBER. Occasional snow and sequences of days below freezing occur. Grass begins to turn off-color. Most of the weeds are gone, frozen, and bluegrass is dominant in the lawn.

At the base of the culms there is a good bit of duff, a mixture of decomposing roots and leaves. On occasional warm days a rhizome may still turn up and a few new roots push out. Beneath the singed old leaves are several green ones, leaves Nos. 2, 3, usually with the tips lost, reminders of the mowing season. Leaf No. 1 is new but will not progress far; it will lose its tip through frost rather than mowing. The newer leaves are now on short sheaths, condensed and squat in the cluster of tillers.

Bentgrass looks poor in comparison with bluegrass, being greatly discolored. Any grass can be freshened in appearance by mowing away the singed leaf tips. Lawns well fertilized in autumn hold their color longer because of young growth.

In Résumé

If the foregoing logbook reflects grass' response to the seasons, what of the lawn custodian's response to the grass' response? Our concluding section of *A Perfect Lawn* is a review of what it takes to keep a typical bluegrass lawn going through the seasons, summarizing information from all of the subject areas that constitute chapters of this book.

The Lawnman's Year

The gardener's urge to get into action outdoors is never stronger than in the spring after a dreary winter indoors. We might as well face reality and begin on our lawn calendar with March, keeping in mind, however, that most of the things good to do in March are even better done in September—at least when it comes to seeding new lawns or improving thin sod. The Kentucky bluegrasses, fine fescues, and bentgrasses—the mainstay of fine lawn species for northern lawns —are at their best in autumn and spring. A head start in autumn gives them just that much extra jump on summer weeds and hot-weather problems.

March, April, May

SEEDING. Seed as early as possible in spring. When the soil is still cold, and the weather overcast, germination will be slow. But at least physiological stirrings begin in the seed, and it will root more quickly when warm weather does arrive. Under ideal conditions such as prevail in a germinator, with daytime temperatures around 80 degrees F. and nighttime ones in the low 60's, Kentucky bluegrass can sprout in as little as four days; fine fescues in perhaps three. It would take another week before you could see appreciable green from the first leaf popping out of the coleoptile. With an actual lawn the "man in a hurry" is very much at the mercy of the weather, and prevailing conditions far overshadow varietal differences. In most cases, the quick appearance of a nursegrass is due more to seedling vigor than to faster sprouting. A Kentucky bluegrass or Highland bentgrass seedling moves at a slower pace compared to an aggressive grass from a big seed such as annual ryegrass. Unfortunately, where an aggressive but short-lived nursegrass is used, it represses the good grasses, slowing them even more.

Fine fescues in lawn seed mixtures are a pretty good substitute for nursegrass. They sprout from an intermediate-sized seed about as quickly as ryegrass, but are not quite as aggressive in the seedling stage. Moreover, the fine fescues are perennial and attractive components of a lawn. On good soils and fertilized lawns, bluegrass will usually shoulder the fescue aside in time. But on sandy soils or under trees, fine fescues may be the best adapted species.

Experts may be aware of a particular variety's needs under prevailing conditions, and be able to provide for them. For example, straight Merion Kentucky bluegrass has become very popular and its requirement for heavy feeding well recognized. But where *Fusarium roseum,* or stripe smut, have struck, a homeowner may well wish he had other bluegrasses and fine fescues blended with the Merion. The suburbanite seldom has the skill to tend his lawn precisely, and is more likely to benefit from a blend of grasses, of which one or more will survive under varying kinds of treatment and lawn ecology. But the blend should include similar grasses, preferably all fine-textured; most seed packagers offer as their top mix combinations of Kentucky bluegrasses and fine fescues, sometimes with a small percentage of perennial ryegrass.

Spring seeding may be directed toward a new lawn or applied to bolstering (and upgrading) turf turned thin through winter. Sow about three pounds per thousand square feet of a fine-textured blend to a tilled seedbed for a start sufficiently thick to resist early weeds. A thin lawn can be "overseeded" at one-half or one-third this rate. It is suggested that scrawny sod be vertically "mowed" (you can rent power rakes for this) to remove duff and expose the soil. The new seed must reach mineral soil to have much of a chance. If you are spry enough to get this done while nights are still freezing, frost-pitting helps imbed the seed in the soil.

SOD AND SOIL. In early spring, before there is tender new grass to damage, it is not a bad idea to clip the lawn very close. Sun penetrates to the soil then, warming it, and off-color old leafage is out of the way. You might have a cheery green lawn a week before the neighbors. Removal of accumulated duff (good for the compost pile) is especially helpful to bolster seeding, as a thatch of old grass prevents new seed from reaching soil, and, in extreme cases, may hold fertilizer away from the root zone. Early spring is a good time to renovate with thatch-removal machines (or your own gusto at the end of a rake), because the scars from your effort will not show for long amidst reviving sod.

We can't detail all the steps for planting a new lawn. Common sense, in light of local conditions, must guide you. The objective is to stir up the soil, at least a couple of inches deep, when it is dry enough to work well. Soil crumbs as big as your thumbnail are not too large, and make a "pebbly" surface receptive to small seed. Fertilizer should be mixed into this seedbed, and it is an especially good time to get phosphorus into the root zone. A mulch is suggested to protect the new seeding and help hold the surface moist for quicker establishment.

FERTILIZATION. Fertilizer requirements vary with the soil and the grass. Merion Kentucky bluegrass needs generous feeding, fine fescues little, with the majority of other Kentucky bluegrasses somewhere in between. Sandy soils hold fertilizer poorly, and probably should be fertilized early in spring no matter what was done last autumn; but lawns on heavier clay soils, especially if well fertilized in autumn, may need little or no feeding until the main surge of spring growth passes (heavy feeding would only intensify the mowing requirements, and the lawn is for beauty, not yield.)

In any event, there are excellent high-analysis lawn fertilizers these days, so light that a twenty pound sack covers 5,000 square feet. Most will contain 20–30 per cent nitrogen, with about a third as much phosphorus and potassium. Distributed with a lawn spreader, they present very little danger of burning turf in spring, especially if the nitrogen source draws heavily upon ureaform. The better brands all do about an equivalent job at equivalent rates. Choose formulations that apply easily (fine particles may drift abnormally on a windy day). Follow the manufacturer's directions.

WEEDING. Systemic herbicides must be carefully applied (and never on a windy day), lest they drift to budding ornamentals. Even invisible "fumes" from volatile formulations of 2,4-D may wash downwind to disturb redbuds or tomato plants yards away.

Crabgrass preventers do not offer this problem. They are for established turf (only Siduron is totally harmless to new seedings), and should be spread early, before crabgrass sprouts (which begins when soil temperature warms toward 60° F.). Whether prevention is warranted depends upon how bad crabgrass customarily is. Crabgrass is never introduced in lawn seed, but sprouts from residual seed in the soil. Preventive chemicals such as azak, benefin, betasan, dacthal, and tupersan all control upwards of 90 per cent of the crabgrass if properly spread. Bluegrass is especially tolerant of herbicides.

Broadleaf weed controls perform better in warm mid and late spring, when weeds are growing vigorously. Good control of almost all weeds, except perennial grass types, is now available. 2,4-D has for many years been the inexpensive mainstay, suitable for ubiquitous lawn weeds such as dandelion and plantain. Silvex (2,4,5-TP) and related phenoxy compounds prove excellent for the few broadleaf weeds resistant to 2,4-D, including clover and certain chickweeds.

Dicamba, though of little use against plantain, handles clover and chickweed, and is about the best cure we have for knotweed, sheep sorrel, and creeping spurge. Keep it away from shrub and tree roots, though. Many products combine two of these herbicides.

An effective way of applying these herbicides is for them to be compounded with fertilizer—the familiar "weed-and-feed" products. A single application does double duty in late spring, removing weeds at their most susceptible stage, while improving the color and growth of the lawngrass.

June, July, August

MOWING. Not that you haven't been mowing at a furious pace all spring, but the practice is discussed here because in summer it becomes increasingly critical for the grass. All year long, mowing should be frequent enough so that the grass is never bereft of too much green leafage at one time—which could severely check its growth and even cause its death. Fairly frequent mowing at suitable clipping height yields the thickest, most vigorous lawn, and hence of itself is a weed control. Grass mowed unduly low is prone to weed invasion, shallow rooting (hence less resistance to drought), and other ills, including actual disease.

Don't cheat yourself with the lawn mower; a well-made implement, big enough to do your job comfortably without breakdown, is essential for pleasant mowing hours. Nothing dulls interest in the lawn more quickly than mowing frustrations, but few "duties" are more delightful than whipping through the week's mowing in a half hour or so with fine equipment. If you can afford it, try one of those versatile riding machines that makes mowing a frolic instead of a chore.

WATERING. Summer is normally a season of water deficit; plants lose more moisture than rainfall accumulates, thus lowering soil reserves. If you want a constantly green lawn during the longest, hottest days of the year, sprinkling becomes necessary whenever rain fails for long. Sandy soils need frequent, light watering, while heavier soils soak up several inches of water in a single application (and parcel it back to the grass for a longer time.) Bentgrasses particularly need frequent watering. Bluegrasses and fescues, once well established, can turn completely brown from drought, yet revive again when cooler weather and rains come. They are your candidates where summer watering restrictions prevail.

As a general rule, watering is best done infrequently but thoroughly. Drying of the surface soil between soakings is therapeutic in the sense that it helps control disease, and may cripple young weeds as they sprout. The objective in sprinkling the lawn is to achieve uniform dispersal at a rate adjusted to soil receptivity (the water should soak in, not run off). An inexpensive plastic set-up has been marketed by a prominent lawn firm, installable underground by the home-owner, without special tools or plumbing complications. A control box with electric time clock activates its wave-sprinklers (each covering a square up to forty feet across), which can be set to turn on the water at any time of day or night, for any sprinkling interval.

PEST CONTROL. There is no reason to cease spraying broadleaf weeds with 2,4-D if they present a continuing problem—as may well be the case in irrigated lawns. Crabgrass not controlled with a preventer may show too. The methyl arsonates (AMA, DSMA) do a good job of eliminating it; they are best used earlier in summer, rather than after the crabgrass is tough and starts setting seed. At least two sprays, about one week apart, are needed to lick the pest.

Insects are apt to be another summer bother. The second generation of sod webworms, larvae of the lawn moth, generally appears about July, often abundantly enough to be damaging. In dry, sunny spots, chinchbugs may brown the grass in irregular patches any time through summer. The larvae of Japanese and various other beetles sever the roots of grass underground, causing dying patches that can be lifted from the lawn like a toupee. Apply a good insecticide, of which (contrary to much publicity) there are many safe types. Sevin and diazinon are two that are well known in the garden, and that might be used for webworms and chinchbugs. The older, chlorinated hydrocarbons soaked into the soil do a good job on grubs. As a preventive for webworms, spray about ten days after noting late evening activity by the lawn moths, which will then be laying eggs. A treatment so timed catches young larvae before they have gorged themselves on your grass.

September, October

As mentioned earlier, autumn is properly not the end but the beginning. Having discussed all the things to do in spring, we can only advise again that most of them will be even more effective in autumn. In lieu of repeating this advice, these few notes will summarize them.

New lawns are relatively easy to establish in autumn. The dry, warm soil makes a seedbed easily, under pleasant circumstances. The top lawngrasses sprout quickly and fully in the weather then prevailing. With days growing shorter, sprinkling "lasts longer"; crabgrass and other weeds are at the end of their cycle and will be little trouble.

Lawngrasses grow short and low in autumn, rather than "reaching for the sky" as they do in spring. Mowing need not be frequent. And autumn is the time of year when sod thickens best, producing many tillers and food reserves when stimulated by fertilization. There is, therefore, no more efficient time of year to fertilize the lawn. A full-rate feeding is suggested for September—and again in October or November for bluegrass turfs.

This is also the season to renovate. Thatch removal or chemical knockdown should be undertaken early in autumn, while an excellent growing season still remains to thicken the turf and obliterate scars. Now weeds will be of little consequence. As with new-lawn seeding, bolster seeding in autumn has just that much more time to become self-reliant before the next summer's heat.

Nor is weed control inappropriate in autumn. Although not so prevalent as in spring, dandelions and other rosette weeds can start now. It is too late to do anything about crabgrass, but broadleaf weed treatment may have more profound effects than realized. Many spring weeds, such as chickweed, annual bluegrass and rosette "mustards" germinate, although their growth is mostly hidden; a 2,4-D spray on a warm day may eliminate future trouble from them. Many times, an all but forgotten 2,4-D spraying in autumn shows as a chickweed-free turf in spring, even though most homeowners probably don't credit the treatment.

With these chores done, let nature take over your lawn responsibilities until March. The bright, crisp days of autumn, even balmy interludes through winter, do more for the cool-season lawngrasses than all your summer attentions.

COMMON MISCONCEPTIONS

THE LAWN IS DORMANT IN WINTER. In appearance this is true. But there are intervals, even in the middle of winter, when grasses are growing appreciably. This is especially so belowground, where roots and rhizomes lengthen when the soil is not frozen. Even frozen soil has some "life," as evidenced by its ability to trap fertilizer applied in winter.

WAIT FOR SPRING TO "DO SOMETHING" ABOUT THE LAWN. Maybe this is so in the South (if winter grass is not planted), but definitely not in bluegrass lawnland! Northern grasses are best planted and most effectively encouraged in autumn, a great time of year for fertilizing the lawn (this stimulates tillering, thickening of the turf at a season when mowing will not need to be done more frequently). Also, weed-and-feed programs as late as October show fine results the next spring, without the hazards and turmoil of spring treatments.

glossary of technical terms

acidity—having a pH of less than 7 (an excess of hydrogen ions over hydroxyl ions); acid-like as opposed to neutral or alkaline.

adaptation (of grasses)—suitability for growth in a given area or under certain conditions; ability to perform well.

aerating machine—device for punching holes into the turf, removing soil cores and thus "cultivating" the living sod.

aerification—the process of cultivating turf by making perforations in it, usually with hollow-tined punches that remove a soil core.

aerobic—condition in which air (oxygen) circulates within the influencing environment, as opposed to anaerobic conditions where there is no ready access to oxygen.

alkali (soil)—an alkaline soil characteristic of arid climates having a high percentage of sodium.

alkalinity—characterized by a pH higher than 7 (excess of hydroxyl ions over hydrogen ions), characteristic of strong bases (lime-like materials) as opposed to acids.

anaerobic—characterized by absence of air (oxygen), such as putrefication where air does not circulate; contrast with aerobic.

analysis (of fertilizer)—the listing by percentage of nitrogen, phosphorus, and potassium (in that order) as indicative of fertilizer strength.

annual (grass)—a species which completes its growth cycle within one year and is typically perpetuated by seeding rather than by continued vegetative growth.

anoxious—the surrounding atmosphere devoid of oxygen.

apomictic—reproduction by seed but without fertilization of the egg by pollen; characteristic of Kentucky bluegrass and many other grasses; seed inheritance solely through the female parent.

Astroturf—synthetic, simulated grass; Monsanto's brand of artificial turf.

auricle—projections or "ears" at the collar of a grass leaf (where the sheath joins the spreading blade).

biennial—completion of the growth cycle over a span of two years.

biomass—total organic accumulation (all forms of life) in a given area.

blade (of grass leaf)—the typically flattened portion of the grass leaf, extending away from the stem at its juncture with the sheath (which normally invests the stem).

boreal—characterized by cool or cold conditions, as contrasted with tropical.

bunchgrasses—grasses that grow in individual, rooted clumps, as opposed to those which spread by rhizomes or stolons.

carbohydrate—organic compound consisting of carbon, hydrogen and oxygen in roughly a 1-2-1 ratio, including the simpler forms of food manufactured by plant photosynthesis.

castings (of earthworms)—mound-like accumulations of earthworm rejectamenta at the soil surface, often a nuisance in turf maintenance.

certified (seed)—seed of which the genetic identity is guaranteed through a scheme of inspection during its growing (usually by representatives of the state agricultural college).

chelates—mineral atoms (typically trace nutrients) held within and "protected" by an organic molecule that prevents their being immobilized by soil reactions; they thus remain relatively available for plant uptake.

chemical trimming—the use of contact herbicides to kill back or immobilize grass growth along borders, at the base of trees, etc.

chlorosis—a yellowing, usually caused by absence or imbalance of a minor nutrient (often iron), especially common on highly alkaline soils.

clay—a soil mineral of complex composition, characterized by very small particle size.

clippings—grass fragments resulting from mowing.

clones—plants originating vegetatively from a single source, hence genetically identical.

coleoptile—the cap-like covering over the emerging plantlet of a sprouting grass seed.

collar (of grass leaf)—the region where leaf sheath and leaf blade join.

colorant—dye sprayed on discolored turf to make it appear attractively green.

compaction (of soil)—soil made dense through elimination of most of its pore space, as by heavy traffic (especially when soil is wet).

complete fertilizer—plant food containing all major nutrients (nitrogen, phosphorus, potassium).

compost—partially decomposed organic materials, typically made by piling clippings, leaves, etc., in a dished mound and allowing them to decay.

crop (of seed label)—minor live seed inclusions that are not legally weeds, distinct from the named ingredients; agricultural species.

crown—the basal portion of a grass plant close to soil level, from which growth arises; the condensed basal stem of a grass plant.

crusting (of soil)—the dispersion and eventual hardening of surface soil particles; especially characteristic of soils having poor structure or being subject to heavy rain.

culm—the stem or "shoot" of a grass plant.

cultivar—a selection or horticultural variety (*culti*vated *vari*ety).

decomposition—decay or disintegration of organic materials.

deficiency (of nutrients)—growth afflictions (such as chlorosis) caused by insufficiency or non-availability of nutrients, minor ones particularly.

dethatcher—a machine for tearing loose thatch accumulations at the base of growing turf.

dicot (dicotyledon)—one of the two great groups of flowering plants, including most broadleaf weeds, characterized by the seed having two cotyledons; contrast with the monocots, which include the grass family.

dormancy—an interim respite from active growth, seasonally characteristic of grasses, or of seed before sprouting.

drift (of pesticides)—movement of small particles or vapors in air currents, from locale of spraying to adjacent surroundings.

duff—organic debris; mixture of decomposing roots and leaves.

ecological web—the interrelationships of organisms in the overall ecology.

ecology—study of the relationship of organisms to their environment.

embryo (of seed)—the live "germ" (as distinct from food storage portions) of seed that will become the new plant.

eutrophication—the "aging" of bodies of water due to the growth and accumulation of algae and other vegetation; the process is speeded by nutrient-rich runoff (i.e., pollution).

evapotranspiration—total water loss due to evaporation and transpiration ("breathing") by plants.

fertilizer—nutrients which stimulate plant growth; principally nitrogen, phosphorus, and potassium in lawn fertilizers.

flail (mower)—type of mower in which individual cutting heads hang loose from a rotating spindle, and are extended by centrifugal force.

French drain—a narrow, slit-like cut in ground, filled with porous material such as gravel. It serves to conduct soil water away from higher levels to a lower outlet.

fungicide—substance used for the control of fungi (plant diseases).

germination—the sprouting of a seed when environmental conditions are suitable.

gibberellin—plant-growth regulator derived from the *Gibberella* fungus.

grain (of turf)—the horizontal orientation of grass foliage in one direction.

green manuring—the plowing down of temporary cover (often a legume) for soil improvement.

ground cover—horticulturally, any low-growing vegetation that will carpet the ground; generally referring to broadleaf plants such as ivy rather than grass.

habitat—the environment or locale inhabited by living organisms.

"hard" pesticides—chemical products, primarily insecticides, which are very slow to disintegrate and disappear after use; poorly biodegradable.

hammerknife (mower)—the flail-type mowing machine.

herbicide—vegetation-killing compound; weed killer.

humus—the residual dark material left after decay of vegetation, mostly lignin.

hydraulic seeding—spraying of seed in a water slurry (often accompanied by fertilizer and mulch); "hydroseeding."

infiltration rate—measurement of water insoak into a soil.

inflorescence—the flower- and seed-bearing stalk of a plant; "seedhead."

inorganic (fertilizer)—composed of simple, generally soluble salts rather than of more complex organic molecules (those containing carbon).

insecticides—compounds used for the killing or control of insects.

internode—that portion of the stem between joints or nodes.

ion—electrically charged atom typical of dissociated salts in solution.

juvenile (growth)—early stages of a plant's growth cycle, characterized by rapid production of relatively "soft" (immature) tissues.

leaf mulcher—mechanical devices, even lawn mowers, which fragment fallen leaves and generally make raking unnecessary.

ligule—a protuberance (often nail-like, or a ring of hairs) on the collar of a grass leaf; a key identification feature with grasses.

lime—calcium compounds, principally calcium carbonate, used for "sweetening" acid soils.

loam—combination of clay, silt and sand components, to yield a soil of desirable texture and structure.

maintenance—procedures involved in keeping a lawn growing well.

mat (matting)—in one sense, the uppermost part of the thatch layer; the intertwining, mostly of living stems of grass toward the base of the sod.

minor elements—trace minerals needed only in small quantities compared to the major fertilizer nutrients.

monocots (monocotyledons)—large group of flowering plants (that includes the grass family), marked by a single-seed cotyledon; contrast with dicots.

monoculture—growing a crop of which the individual plants are all alike.

muck—"soil" developed in a swamp-like environment, consisting largely of organic remains (humus).

mulch—any protective covering for soil, especially straw, wood chips, sphagnum moss, etc.

mutation—a sudden genetic change resulting in an untypical plant or "sport."

nematode—small worms of the eelworm group, many of which attack plant roots.

node—the "joint" of a grass stem where the leaf sheath is attached.

nodule (on legume roots)—a growth on the roots of plants such as clover, containing symbiotic bacteria useful for trapping gaseous nitrogen and making this available to the legume.

nursegrass—a short-lived grass intended to be temporary until the slower-growing permanent grass develops.

nutrients (for fertilizer)—the various elements or minerals essential to plant growth.

organic (fertilizer)—a fertilizer derived from organic residues (as contrasted with simpler chemical sources).

organic matter—substance resulting from the growth of living organisms; cf. biomass, compost, humus.

panicle—a grass inflorescence (such as that found in Kentucky bluegrass) marked by a progressive branching pattern, the youngest portion of which is at the apex.

pathogen—a disease-causing organism.

percolation (soil water)—the ability of water to pass through soil.

perennial—having a prolonged and indefinite vegetative existence, as compared to an annual plant's yearly cycle.

pesticide—compound used for the killing or control of pests.

pH—an indicator of acidity-alkalinity, with 7 representing a neutral condition, and numbers lower than 7 indicating an acid condition: a mathematical representation of hydrogen ion concentration; specifically, its inverse logarithm.

phenoxy herbicide—systemic weed killers characterized by the phenoxy ring structure typical of 2,4-D.

pistil—the female reproductive apparatus in flowers.

plug—a fragment or biscuit of sod used for planting lawns vegetatively, especially in the South.

pollen—the male reproductive element in flowering plants, typically carried from the stamens to the pistil by wind or insects.

polymerize—the linkage of molecular units into a very large "molecule" or polymer.

porosity (of soil)—a reckoning of the pore space contained in soil, which in turn controls infiltration, percolation, and soil density.

post-emergence—placement of a treatment, such as a pesticide, after the crop has started growing.

pre-emergence—placement of a treatment, such as a pesticide, before the crop or planting has sprouted.

prill—spherical shot-like particles, especially of fertilizer.

purity (of seed)—the percentage of the whole, on a weight basis, of the particular component being identified; especially used on seed labels to characterize the prevalence of a particular grass distinct from all other seeds or inclusions.

ratio (of fertilizer)—the comparative abundance of the various nutrients; a fertilizer with a 20-10-10 analysis would have a 2-1-1 ratio.

reel mower—type of lawnmower in which a rotating reel cuts against a stationary bedknife with a scissors-like action.

rejuvenation—stimulation of fresh new growth; in lawns, usually by the removal of thatch and mature tissues.

renovation—the process of renewing or rejuvenating grass growth, usually involving overseeding.

rhizomes—spreading stems that grow underground, as with bluegrass and quackgrass.

rotary mower—lawn-cutting device in which clipping is accomplished through the impact of a rapidly rotating blade.

rotary tiller—a small, motorized cultivating implement in which vertically rotating tines churn the soil.

sand—coarse soil particles typically consisting of silica.

saturated (soil)—soil in which the pore space is filled with water; incapable of absorbing more water.

scald—the collapse and browning of turf under waterlogged conditions.

scalping—a very close mowing that removes most of the green leaf leaving only stubble.

scarification—the scratching of the soil surface to remove debris and make indentations of loose soil.

seedbed—a prepared soil readied for seeding.

seedhead—an inflorescence; with grasses usually a fruiting panicle or spike.

selective (weed control)—employment of a herbicide affecting certain species but not others.

sheath—the basal part of a grass leaf that invests or clasps the grass stem.

sicklebar (mower)—mowing device that cuts by the horizontal agitation of triangular blades operating between stationary teeth.

silt—soil particles of intermediate size.

slow-release (fertilizer)—fertilizer ingredients, primarily nitrogen, that are not immediately soluble (available), but which are slowly made available by the activity of soil microorganisms or weathering.

sod—sections of live grass with adhering soil, used for vegetative planting.

soil—accumulated rock fragments, organic matter, organisms, etc., of particular composition reflecting its history; anchoring medium for plant roots.

soilbed—soil readied for planting (same as seedbed if seed is planted).

soluble (fertilizer)—consisting of readily dissolved components that are immediately available; more conducive to lawn "burn" than slow-release fertilizers.

spiking—poking holes into turf with solid tine devices; making indentations into the soil.

spreader—a device for distributing seed, fertilizer and other lawn materials uniformly.

sprig—a stem fragment containing one or more nodes, used for propagating certain grasses vegetatively, especially in the South.

sterilization (of soil)—application of a chemical which kills weed seeds and other pests in a soilbed.

stolon—spreading stems that creep aboveground (as contrasted with rhizomes, which spread belowground).

stolonizing—the process of spreading stolon fragments on the surface, usually partially covered with topdressing, as a means of grass propagation.

structure (of soil)—the way the soil particles hold together, as distinct from their size.

stubble—the rigid, essentially leafless stems that remain after a very low mowing.

superphosphate—a phosphatic fertilizer ingredient derived by acid treatment of phosphate rock.

surfactant—an additive made to a spray which accentuates its emulsifying, spreading, and wetting properties.

syringing—a light watering, principally to maintain a moist seedbed, to keep turf from drying out, and to cool it during the heat of day.

systemics—pesticides carried in the sap stream to other parts of a plant no matter where applied; contrast with contact materials which affect only parts hit directly.

texture (of soil)—an evaluation of soil according to the size of its component particles.

texture (of grass)—the surface appearance of the lawn as reflected principally by the width of grass leaf blades (coarse texture is usually deemed less attractive; fine texture, more attractive).

thatch—the accumulation of partly decomposed organic debris at the base of sod, which often acts as a barrier between applied materials and soil, and if thick enough may adversely influence grass performance.

thinner—same as a "vertical mower," which thins turf by means of vertically-set toothed discs or tines that dig deep into the sod.

tillage (of soil)—soil cultivation, as in soilbed preparation.

tiller—see rotary tiller.

tillering—thickening of the turf by tiller production.

tillers—branch culms of grass formed aboveground.

topdressing—material spread over the surface of a lawn or seedbed, usually a soil (but sometimes referring to fertilization).

topsoil—the uppermost portion of native soil, usually several inches thick, typically of dark color; a general term for soil of good quality purchased for topdressing a lawn.

trace nutrients—minor fertility elements, absence of which may result in plant chlorosis or other imbalances.

transpiration—the "evaporation" of moisture through the plant leaf, especially through leaf "breathing pores" or stomata.

tropical—characteristic of warmer environments which prevail within 23 degrees north and south of the equator, as contrasted with boreal climates.

turfgrass—grass species accepted for fine (mowed) lawns and swards.

ureaform—a polymer of urea and formaldehyde, yielding a useful slow-release nitrogen fertilizer (viz. Nitroform).

variety—a particular type of plant distinguished in certain minor ways from other varieties of the same plant species; horticultural varieties are cultivars.

vegetative planting—non-sexual propagation of a plant by rooting pieces of the parent; with grass, sod, sprigs, plugs, etc., are vegetative.

vertical mower—a powered thinning machine for lawns, characteristically operating through the rotation of vertically set toothed discs or tines, much used for removal of thatch.

volatilization—formation of vapors from a solid material, usually under the influence of warmth.

waterlog—saturation of soil by water.

weed—a plant not wanted where it is growing; offensive plants invading the lawn, spoiling the appearance of the grass.

wetting agent—a spray additive which causes a solution to better contact and coat surfaces to which it is applied, overcoming the hygroscopic tendency of water.

winter grass—grass species planted into dormant southern turf in autumn; meant to provide green color through winter but disappear in spring as the permanent turf revives.

index